PHOTOSHOP 6
WEB MAGIC

By Jeff Foster

with contributions from Peter Bauer

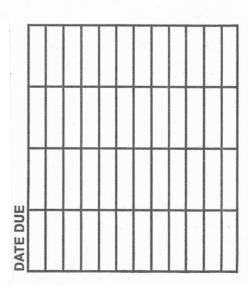

New Riders

201 West 103rd Street, Indianapolis, Indiana 46290

PHOTOSHOP 6 WEB MAGIC

Copyright © 2001 by New Riders Publishing

International Standard Book Number: 0-7357-1036-8

Library of Congress Catalog Card Number: 00-104523

Printed in the United States of America

First Printing: January 2001

05 04 03 02 01   7 6 5 4 3 2

Interpretation of the printing code: The rightmost double-digit number is the year of the book's printing; the rightmost single-digit number is the number of the book's printing. For example, the printing code 01-1 shows that the first printing of the book occurred in 2001.

Trademarks

Warning and Disclaimer

Publisher
David Dwyer

Associate Publisher
Al Valvano

Executive Editor
Steve Weiss

Product Marketing Manager
Kathy Malmloff

Managing Editor
Sarah Kearns

Acquisitions Editors
Linda Anne Bump
Theresa Gheen

Development Editor
John Rahm

Project Editor
Michael Thurston

Copy Editor
Amy Lepore

Technical Editors
Steve Gifford
Jeff Solenberg

Cover Designer / Project Opener Images
Aren Howell

Compositor
Wil Cruz

Proofreader
Marcia Deboy

Indexer
Lisa Stumpf

Software Development Specialist
Jay Payne

CONTENTS AT A GLANCE

ABOUT THE AUTHORS

Jeff Foster (**www.pixelpainter.com**) is an artist/musician of 27 years, and is the founder of Vicious Fishes Software in Fullerton, CA. His company has created graphic and audio content for Multimedia and Web developers. Jeff is currently serving as the Director of Research and Development at Narratus, Inc., a technology arts firm, specializing in a new method of mixed media corporate marketing called "Digital Storytelling." He also serves as the Director of Training for Narratus' internship and production mentoring programs.

He has been in the forefront of illustrative art and computer graphic design, creating images for clients such as Sanyo, McDonnell Douglas, FOX Television, Universal Studios, and Disney. Foster's production studio has been a beta site for such companies as Apple Computer, Adobe, Ultimatte, PIXAR, and MetaCreations—where he hosted the Multimedia and Web Animation chat in their AOL forum.

Foster has lectured and demonstrated his talent and ideas throughout Southern California, and has co-developed a multimedia program for the Department of Labor through the North Orange County Community College District. He has taught, lectured, and co-developed computer graphics and multimedia programs for NOCCD Continuing Education at the Fullerton College Wilshire campus, and California State Fullerton Continuing Education. He currently sits on the advisory boards of the Fullerton College Business School and California State Fullerton Extended Education.

Jeff has contributed to several magazine articles and books, including *Animation Magazine*, *Publish Magazine*, and *Photoshop Filter Finesse* (Bill Niffenegger, Random House). He has authored and co-authored *Special Edition: Using Photoshop* (Que, Macmillan), *Photoshop Web Magic 2* (Hayden Books), and *Photoshop 6 Web Magic* (New Riders).

You can learn more about Jeff's professional involvement with the following links:

Narratus, Inc.
www.narratus.com

Vicious Fishes Software
www.vicfish.com

Photoshop Web Magic Series
www.photoshopwebmagic.com

Peter J. Bauer (**http://PlanetPhotoshop.com**) is a computer graphics writer and efficiency consultant based in Columbus, Ohio. He is a Contributing Editor for *Mac Today* and a columnist for *Photoshop User*, as well as the lead columnist on the Photoshop Web portal PlanetPhotoshop.com. He has served as technical editor for *Sams Teach Yourself Adobe Photoshop 6 in 24 Hours* and *Sams Teach Yourself Illustrator 9 in 24 Hours*. He is a member of the Adjunct Faculty at Franklin University, and appears at Photoshop World as a speaker and panelist. Pete is married to Professor Mary Ellen O'Connell of the Ohio State University College of Law. They live in the historic German Village area of Columbus.

DEDICATION

This book is dedicated to the people who advance both art and technology, working together to enable the people of the world to tell their story. Everyone has a story worth sharing!

ACKNOWLEDGMENTS

I would first like to thank my wife, Cheryl, and my daughters, Jill, Britt, and Chelsea, for their love and support, as well as the many sacrifices they've made to allow me the freedom to take on this project. Thanks to Mom and Dad for their continued love and support. (And for not giving out my email address to everyone they meet!) I would also like to thank the rest of my extended family for their support and understanding of my absence as well. I owe you all an entire "make-up" summer!

Thanks to the great people at Narratus, Inc. for their continued support and vision (and for accepting my "self-inflicted narcolepsy" at the office). I promise I will give up the caffeine soon!

To Linda Bump, Theresa Gheen, John Rahm, and the rest of the New Riders development team. Thank you. I couldn't have done it without your supportive and encouraging words and help through the toughest development times.

To my contributory author, Peter Bauer, I thank you for your help and support—not to mention the occasional comic relief!

Thanks to the Adobe® Photoshop® Development team for listening to the suggestions (and begging?) from the beta group. I think you have an awesome product!

And to all of my friends and colleagues that I haven't had time for in the last six months…

I owe you:

A lunch

A dinner

A bottle of wine

A pint of beer

A cigar

A Web site

A T-shirt design

And a CD cover

—**Jeff Foster**

A MESSAGE FROM NEW RIDERS

As the reader of this book, you are our most important critic and commentator. We value your opinion and want to know what we're doing right, what we could do better, in what areas you'd like to see us publish, and any other words of wisdom you're willing to pass our way.

As Executive Editor at New Riders, I welcome your comments. You can fax, email, or write me directly to let me know what you did or didn't like about this book—as well as what we can do to make our books better. When you write, please be sure to include this book's title, ISBN, and author, as well as your name and phone or fax number. I will carefully review your comments and share them with the authors and editors who worked on the book.

Please note that I cannot help you with technical problems related to the topic of this book, and that due to the high volume of email I receive, I might not be able to reply to every message. If you run into a technical problem, it's best to contact our Customer Support department, as listed later in this section. Thanks.

Email: steve.weiss@newriders.com

Mail: Steve Weiss
        Executive Editor
        New Riders Publishing
        201 West 103rd Street
        Indianapolis, IN 46290 USA

Visit Our Web Site: www.newriders.com

On our Web site, you'll find information about our other books, the authors we partner with, book updates and file downloads, promotions, discussion boards for online interaction with other users and with technology experts, and a calendar of trade shows and other professional events with which we'll be involved. We hope to see you around.

Email Us from Our Web Site

Go to www.newriders.com and click on the Contact link if you

- Have comments or questions about this book.
- Want to report errors that you have found in this book.
- Have a book proposal or are interested in writing for New Riders.
- Would like us to send you one of our author kits.
- Are an expert in a computer topic or technology and are interested in being a reviewer or technical editor.
- Want to find a distributor for our titles in your area.
- Are an educator/instructor who wants to preview New Riders books for classroom use. In the body/comments area, include your name, school, department, address, phone number, office days/hours, text currently in use, and enrollment in your department, along with your request for either desk/examination copies or additional information.

Call Us or Fax Us

You can reach us toll-free at (800) 571-5840 + 9+ 3567 (ask for New Riders). If outside the U.S., please call 1-317-581-3500 and ask for New Riders. If you prefer, you can fax us at 1-317-581-4663, Attention: New Riders.

Technical Support and Customer Support for This Book Although we encourage entry-level users to get as much as they can out of our books, keep in mind that our books are written assuming a non-beginner level of user-knowledge of the technology. This assumption is reflected in the brevity and shorthand nature of some of the tutorials.

New Riders will continually work to create clearly written, thoroughly tested and reviewed technology books of the highest educational caliber and creative design. We value our customers more than anything—that's why we're in this business—but we cannot guarantee to each of the thousands of you who buy and use our books that we will be able to work individually with you through tutorials or content with which you may have questions. We urge readers who need help in working through exercises or other material in our books—and who need this assistance immediately—to use as many of the resources that our technology and technical communities can provide, especially the many online user groups and list servers available.

- If you have a physical problem with one of our books or accompanying CD-ROMs, please contact our Customer Support department.

- If you have questions about the content of the book—needing clarification about something as it is written or note of a possible error—please contact our Customer Support department.

- If you have comments of a general nature about this or other books by New Riders, please contact the Executive Editor.

To contact our Customer Support department, call 1-317-581-3833, from 10:00 a.m. to 3:00 p.m. U.S. EST (CST from April through October of each year—unlike the majority of the United States, Indiana doesn't change to Daylight Savings Time each April). You can also access our tech support Web site at http://www.mcp.com/support.

INTRODUCTION

INTRODUCTION

Photoshop 6 is probably the biggest advancement in the program since we first got layers! There are so many great tools and features that we've devoted this book to outlining their importance—and showing you how to get the most out of each one. Photoshop is no longer just a high-end imaging tool for the graphics professional; it's a user-friendly productivity tool for everyone who wants to build a better Web site!

WHO WE ARE

I am not a professional writer by trade; rather, I'm a working professional who relies on Adobe® Photoshop® daily. I've been using and teaching Photoshop for graphic design, illustration, and photo imaging since version 1.0. I've yet to find another imaging application that comes close to its full-feature functionality and consistent, production-savvy capabilities. Though there are several other applications that I use, it all comes back to Photoshop before it goes out the door. I have been involved with many design projects as well as software content creation— all involving Photoshop use in a big way.

This is my third Photoshop book, and I hope you find it to be a valuable resource for creating cool effects and animations for your Web designs.

For this book, I've requested a little help from Peter Bauer, a well-known and respected columnist for *Photoshop User* and *PlanetPhotoshop.com* and the author of several other books and publications. We can also thank Peter for the wonderful job he did on Appendix A at the back of this book. ☺

Who You Are

You should have a basic understanding of any previous version of Adobe Photoshop as well as basic Web page design. You should also have a computer … with a mouse … and a monitor … and, of course, Photoshop 6. Really, though, you don't have to be a master. You just need a good understanding of how the program generally works, how to open and save files, and so on ….

This is not a Web page design book. It will not teach you how to create the ultimate Web site. It will not teach you HTML authoring or Web page layout. Nor will it teach you how to give a cat a bath without being scratched. It will, however, familiarize you with the latest tools and features in Photoshop 6, teach you to create cool effects and design elements, and give you a creative edge in your design abilities. You should be able to work through the projects in this book and have a better understanding of how to use the tools and features in Photoshop 6. You will also get sequencing tips and tricks to create fun and exciting rollovers and animations that you may not get in other Photoshop 6 books on the market.

Although this book outlines different tools and features of Photoshop 6, it will not teach you everything about every item in the program. If you have a registered copy, you will already have a very good resource for that information in both your User Manual and the Online Help inside Photoshop 6. For reference, we've added a brief overview of Photoshop's tools in Appendix A at the back of this book.

It's also quite helpful if you already have a connection to the Internet because updated material, samples, and libraries will be made available to you at **www.photoshopwebmagic.com/members/**.

What's in This Book

Photoshop 6 is an entirely new application, and you're probably wondering where everything has moved, what's been added, and what's been changed. There are completely new features like Custom Layer Styles (which replace Layer Effects in a *big* way!), Custom Shapes, and virtually unlimited Custom Patterns and Brushes. There's also a new Liquify command and better integration with ImageReady 3.0. For an overview of the Photoshop 6 and ImageReady 3.0 tools, palettes, and features, refer to the illustrated Appendix A at the back of this book.

Although there are a lot of really nice preset Patterns, Layer Styles, Shapes, and Brushes built into Photoshop 6, an infinite amount of customization can be applied and saved into special libraries. These libraries are organized and sorted through the Preset Manager (see Appendix A). Furthermore, they can be saved differently for each project, so your choices for each palette can be limited only to the presets you'll need now—it's not necessary to load the entire collection. You'll be able to share your custom libraries with other users as well as download new libraries from professional sites.

We will teach you how to create and customize incredible effects that are *new* to Photoshop—with photorealistic imaging and effects. The ability to mix and match Patterns, Styles, Brushes, and Shapes to create effects will be covered in the projects of this book. We will also cover the use of the new Liquify command feature (Warp Mesh), which lets you smear, squish, bloat, and generally make a mess of whatever is on the image layer. It's lots of fun but even more, a powerful tool, with a little help we'll give you throughout this book.

Animation effects are king! Several of the projects in this book will result in some sort of animation whether it's an animated GIF or a rollover sequence. Making it move is where it's at!

All of the animation features for each effect will be outlined in ImageReady, and the process will be followed step-by-step for each occurrence. In addition, all of the projects will have completed examples on the book's Companion CD-ROM, which will run the animations in any Web browser.

You will notice that most of the projects are really too big in their pixel size to be useful as buttons or animations. We've done that intentionally to get you familiar with the process of using the tools and to make it easier to see what you're doing. Of course, you wouldn't want to just take a project out of the book and throw it up on your Web site. This is a learning process. Once you understand the principles we're teaching you in the projects, you will be able to apply the concepts to your own Web page designs.

I believe that the real "magic" in *Photoshop 6 Web Magic* is in you, the reader. How you apply what you learn in this book will help you tell your story—and will cause people to sit up and take notice.

THE CD-ROM

The accompanying CD-ROM is full of wonderful support materials for your *Photoshop 6 Web Magic* book. You will find working examples of the finished projects, animations, sample images, Photoshop 6 project files, and sample Web pages using the techniques of several projects. You will also be able to link directly to our online resource center (if you have an Internet connection), provided exclusively to you, our reader! Be sure to check for updates on Custom Styles, Patterns, and Brushes as well as tips and tricks for getting even more value out of your book.

For a more detailed description of the CD-ROM's contents, refer to Appendix C, "What's on the CD-ROM."

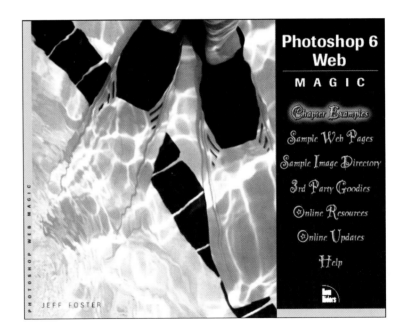

OUR ASSUMPTIONS AS WE WROTE THIS BOOK

You have at least taken a joy ride in Photoshop.

I'm not much of a manual reader. My wife always reminds me to maybe try the instructions—long after I've blown a fuse or assembled something completely backward because it "looked" like it should go together that way. "Joy riding" in a software application does work though because it's fairly harmless. You can open up a sample image and try just about every tool in the toolbox to see what it can do, and you can apply every filter you can find. It's a fun way to learn your way around the program, but it may not be very productive. The manual that comes with Photoshop 6 has been greatly improved, and so has the Online Help for searching for those "hidden" clues. It's necessary to understand the basics of the program, but we've also added a quick-reference guide in Appendix A at the back of this book.

You have some sense of basic design.

Face it. Unless you're just going to surf the Web and steal other people's buttons and animated graphics and try to "alter" them to meet your needs, you're going to be judged by your own design taste when people visit your site. We can show you how to do the projects, but we can't make you a better designer or teach you good taste.

If you're really lost in the "what to do/what not to do" design jungle out there, may I suggest that you regularly visit Vincent Flanders' **webpagesthatsuck.com**. Vincent will help you understand better Web page design by showing you what *not* to do. Beware, however, because he doesn't like too many animations and flashy stuff all on one page. Well, neither do we, but a little eye-catching fun here and there is a moral imperative!

You want to see what you're doing.

We've included finished examples of every project on the accompanying CD-ROM. All of the animations and rollovers can be viewed within the Web browser you open the CD-ROM menu with, so you can keep it open while you're working on your project. We've also included the Photoshop file for comparison or so you can "reverse-engineer" to see how it was originally done. In addition, we've included the finished Custom Layer Styles, Patterns, Shapes, and Brushes used throughout the book. So if you're in a hurry, you may skip that section and get busy!

You want results—now.

Even if you're not a top-notch designer, you will benefit from the projects in this book. If you can apply these techniques to the basic knowledge you already have of Web design, you will master many of the concepts that you otherwise would probably have to hire out to a freelance designer. Plus, you won't necessarily need a 3D program to get realistic animated text or buttons. Cool, huh?

One thing that has always bothered me about some computer design books is that they require you to buy something "extra" to complete the projects. Maybe it's my memory of the childhood disappointment of getting that car model home only to find out that I needed extra glue or paint to complete it. We believe that third-party plug-ins, applications, or utilities should never be required to complete a project in a book—even if demo versions are supplied on an accompanying CD-ROM.

CONVENTIONS USED IN THIS BOOK

Every computer book has its own style of presenting information. As you flip through the book, you'll notice we have an interesting layout going on here. Because we know most of you are really into graphics, the project openers contain way-cool eye candy. The real meat of the projects starts on the next page. Take a look…

In the left column, you'll find step-by-step instructions for completing the project as well as succinct but extremely valuable explanations. The text next to the number contains the action you must perform. In many cases, the action text is followed by a paragraph that contains contextual information. Note that, if you want to perform the steps quickly and without any background info, you need only read the text next to the step numbers.

In the corresponding columns to the right, you'll find screen captions (and/or code) illustrating the steps. You'll also find Notes and Tips, which will provide you with additional contextual information or customization techniques.

At the end of each project, you'll find unique customization information. Each *Magic* project is designed to be highly customizable; therefore, we provide many tips and examples of what you can do with the techniques you've learned so that you can apply them to your own work quickly and easily.

In addition, make sure to check out the enclosed CD-ROM. It's full of working examples, sample images, and project files that you can use as a template or as a comparison guide. If you should lose your CD-ROM, log on to **www.photoshopwebmagic.com/members/** and download any files you need.

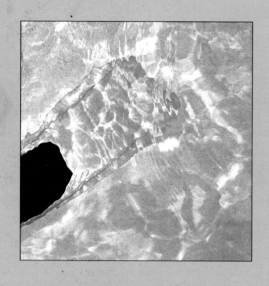

CREATING CUSTOM
LAYER STYLES

"Never eat more than you can lift."

—MISS PIGGY, FROM *THE MUPPET SHOW*

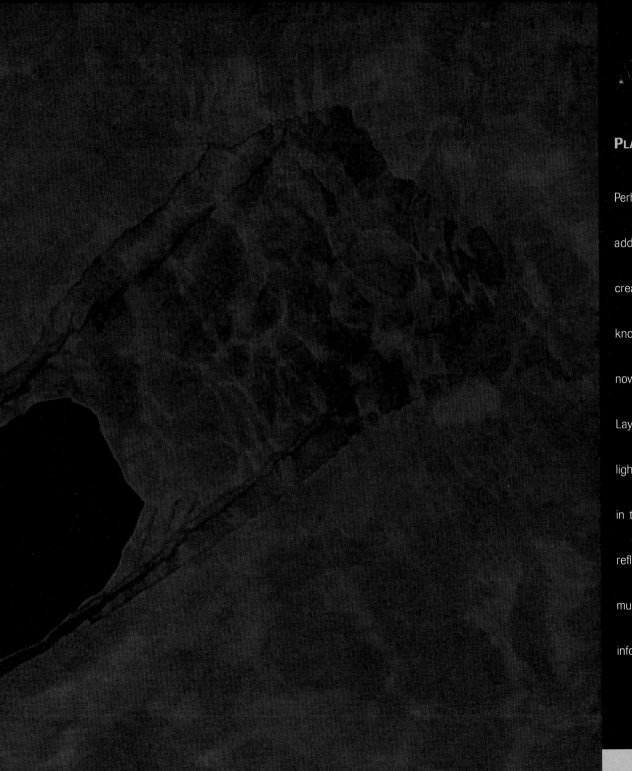

Play With Your Food!

Perhaps one of the most exciting new features

added to Photoshop 6 is the capability to

create and save custom layer styles. What was

known in Photoshop 5.5 as Layer Effects is

now a much more powerful tool set called

Layer Styles. It has more three-dimensional

lighting capabilities and many more choices

in texturing, contouring, shading and light

reflection, layer blending modes, and much,

much more. You can get more specific

information about Layer Styles in Appendix A.

Creating Custom Layer Styles

by Jeff Foster

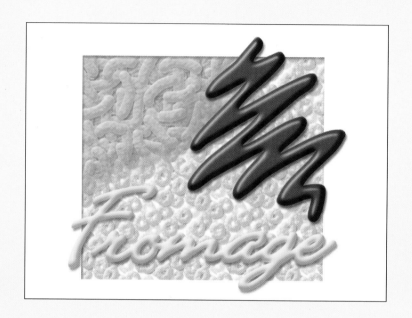

GETTING STARTED

In this section, you will explore how to create great Layer Styles, which will be used throughout the rest of the book. The final Styles and effects are also available on the CD-ROM. Though you can always load the Custom Styles included on the enclosed CD-ROM, there's just nothing like creating something incredibly realistic from scratch. Managing the Styles in saved libraries will ensure that you can access them for later use.

To load the saved Custom Brushes, Patterns, or Styles from your hard drive (or the included CD-ROM), you will need to use the Preset Manager. You can delete or load saved "libraries" for each Photoshop session or project if you want. If you have too many loaded at once, you will have to scroll through a lot of Styles to get to the one or two you might need for a single project.

1 Open the Preset Manager from the Edit menu.

2 Select Styles from the Preset Type pull-down menu.

In this window, you can delete and load saved Style libraries, and reorganize new sets—even rename existing libraries.

Select the Preset Manager from the Edit menu.

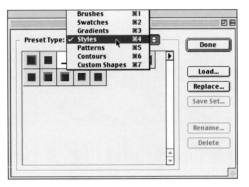

Select Styles from the Preset Type pull-down menu.

CREATE A TEST PREVIEW FILE

1 Create a new file that's small enough to easily test your new Style but that's close to the resolution of the projects you will be using it on.

Width: **300 pixels**

Height: **300 pixels**

Resolution: **72 pixels/inch**

Background color: **White**

Note: You will need something with which to preview your custom style as you're designing it. It's best to use something like text or a scribbled, painted line to see what the style's features will look like on both curved edges and straight lines.

2 Create a new layer called Layer 1 and, with the Paintbrush tool set to the Hard Round 19-pixel brush, draw a squiggly line that has transparency around it. Choose a color that contrasts with the white background.

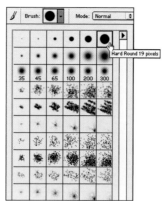

Select a paintbrush from the Brush palette.

3 On Layer 1, select Layer Style from the Layers palette.

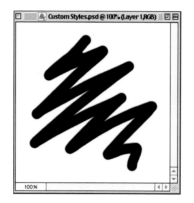

Draw a squiggle line with the paintbrush on a new layer.

Note: When you create a new custom Layer Style, you can try several variations and decide later what best suits your needs. You can also save the entire Style library for later retrieval.

CREATE A NEW CUSTOM STYLE—CHOCOLATE SYRUP

The coolest thing about the new Layer Styles effects is the capability to control the three-dimensional light source, reflection, contour, gloss, transparency, and much more. With just a few clicks, the effect will create the look of rich chocolate syrup when applied to the line drawn on Layer 1.

1 Select Color Overlay and then set the Blend Mode to Normal and the Opacity to 100%. Fill the squiggle with a deep chocolate brown color.

Note: Whenever possible in designing graphics for the Web, use only Web-safe colors. This will help keep the graphics smooth and cause less dithering when reducing the color palette down for animated GIFs.

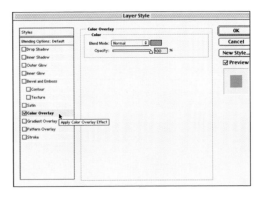

Select a color fill Overlay in the Layer Style window.

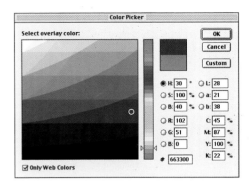

Choose a deep brown from the Color Picker palette.

2 Select Drop Shadow from the Layer Style window and apply the following settings:

Blend Mode: **Multiply**

Opacity: **50%**

Angle: **120°**

Use Global Light: **Checked**

Distance: **3 px**

Spread: **0%**

Size: **3 px**

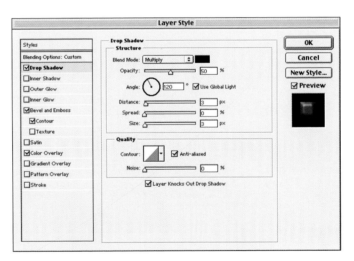

Select Drop Shadow from the Layer Style window.

3   Select Bevel and Emboss from the Layer Style
    window and apply the following settings:

    Style: **Inner Bevel**

    Technique: **Smooth**

    Depth: **150%**

    Direction: **Up**

    Size: **10 px**

    Soften: **2 px**

    Shading Angle: **120°**

    Use Global Light: **Checked**

    Altitude: **51°**

    Gloss Contour: **Linear**

    Anti-aliased: **Checked**

    Highlight Mode: **Screen**

    Opacity: **75%**

    Shadow Mode: **Multiply**

    Opacity: **50%**

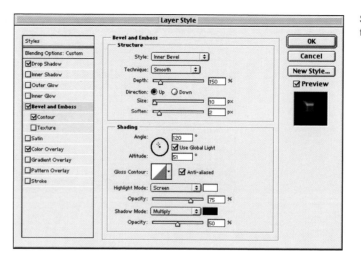

Select Bevel and Emboss
from the Layer Style window.

4   Set the contour of the bevel by selecting Contour
    under the Bevel and Emboss option.

    Contour: **Linear**

    Anti-aliased: **Checked**

    Range: **35%**

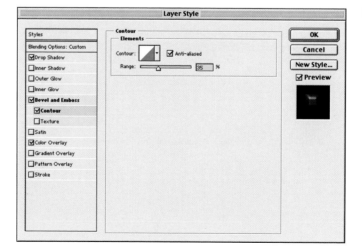

Set the Contour shape of the Style.

5　Select New Style to save your new custom Style and give it a descriptive name so you can recall it later from the Styles palette. This one has already been added to the Custom Styles library on the included CD-ROM, and it's called "Chocolate Syrup."

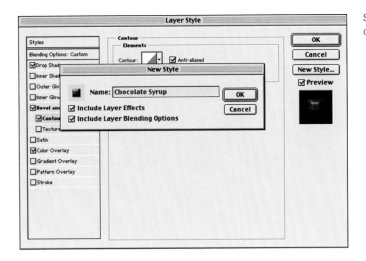

Save and name your new custom Style.

MODIFICATIONS

You can preview several Layer Styles on one layer image. These are included in the library found on the accompanying CD-ROM, along with their settings. (Is anyone else getting hungry here?)

This first Style variation is the effect of a liquid "Squeeze Cheese." This type of Style is fun to apply to a layer. Using a paintbrush, apply the cheesy goodness to the layer (crackers not included!). For this exercise, start with the Chocolate Syrup Layer Style on the layer you just ended with.

> **Note:** You can learn what makes a surface shiny, an effect transparent, or a contour round just by selecting a Style from a library, selecting the Layer Style window from the Layers palette, and studying the different settings. If you make any changes when this window is open, don't worry; it won't affect the saved Style.

1 Double-click the layer in the Layers palette to bring up the Layer Style editor. Choose Color Overlay with the color #FFCC33 to produce an orange cheese color. Make additional changes to the following Layer Style options:

Drop Shadow Settings

Blend Mode: **Multiply**

Opacity: **30%**

Angle: **120°**

Use Global Light: **Checked**

Distance: **3 px**

Spread: **0%**

Size: **3 px**

Bevel and Emboss Settings

Style: **Inner Bevel**

Technique: **Smooth**

Depth: **150%**

Direction: **Up**

Size: **10 px**

Soften: **5 px**

Shading Angle: **120°**

Use Global Light: **Checked**

Altitude: **56°**

Gloss Contour: **Gaussian**

Anti-aliased: **Checked**

Highlight Mode: **Hard Light**

Opacity: **70%**

Shadow Mode: **Multiply**

Color: **CC6600**

Opacity: **60%**

Contour: **Linear**

Anti-aliased: **Checked**

Range: **10%**

These changes should give a smooth and satiny sheen to the "Cheeze" texture.

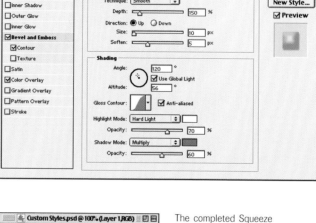

Set the Bevel and Emboss of the Style variation.

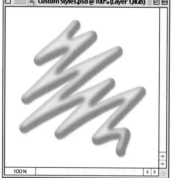

The completed Squeeze Cheeze Style.

The "Cheesy Poofs" Style uses a texture in addition to other Layer Settings to create another type of extruded effect. Because this Style is a solid rather than a liquid, it works best when created and stacked on several layers to create a completely covered texture.

1   Start with a new layer and select the Hard Round 19-pixel Paintbrush tool.

2   Using the Paintbrush tool, draw a few rough, short lines, making sure they don't touch each other.

3   Select the Layer Style option, set the Color Overlay to a "cheesy" orange color, and continue with the additional settings listed here:

Color Overlay: **#FFCC33**

Drop Shadow Settings

Blend Mode: **Multiply**

Color: **#996600**

Opacity: **35%**

Angle: **120°**

Use Global Light: **Checked**

Distance: **4 px**

Spread: **0%**

Size: **4 px**

Noise: **5%**

Bevel and Emboss Settings

Style: **Inner Bevel**

Technique: **Smooth**

Depth: **100%**

Direction: **Up**

Size: **10 px**

Soften: **3 px**

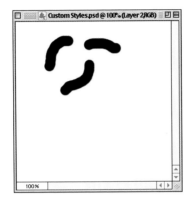

Draw squiggle lines with the Paintbrush tool.

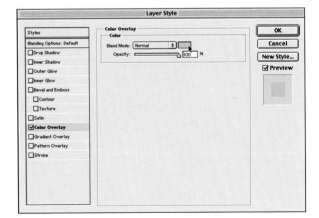

Set the Color Overlay to #FFCC33.

Shading Angle: **120°**

Use Global Light: **Checked**

Altitude: **56°**

Gloss Contour: **Half Round**

Anti-aliased: **Checked**

Highlight Mode: **Hard Light**

Opacity: **70%**

Shadow Mode: **Multiply**

Color: **CC6600**

Opacity: **50%**

Contour: **Half Round**

Anti-aliased: **Checked**

Range: **10%**

Texture Pattern: **Wrinkles**

Scale: **25%**

Depth: **+1000%**

Invert: **Checked**

Inner Glow Settings

Blend Mode: **Hard Light**

Opacity: **50%**

Noise: **5%**

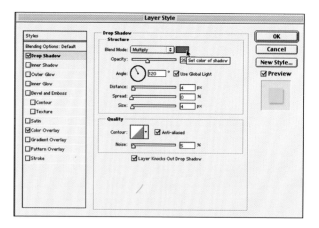

Select the Drop Shadow color and settings.

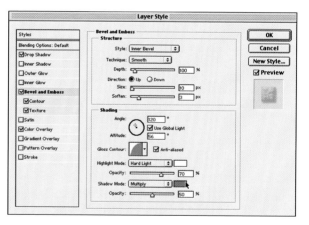

Create a 3D effect with the Bevel and Contour settings.

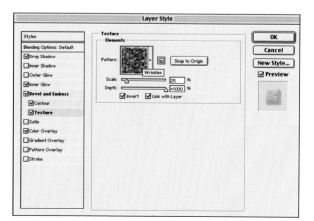

Give the effect some Texture.

4   Continue "painting" the Cheezy Poofs randomly around the project window, using the Paintbrush tool.

5   To create the layered "pile of Cheezy Poofs" effect, keep creating new layers and painting to fill in the gaps. Cmd (Ctrl)+click the layer, choose Copy Layer Style, and then paste it into the new layers.

6   Continue with the layers until you've reached the desired "depth" effect.

7   To create the illusion of a bottomless pile of Cheezy Poofs, create a new layer and fill it with a solid foreground color. Apply the Cheezy Poofs texture to the filled layer and place it underneath the other layers in the Layer palette.

Adjusting the Opacity of the layers will help enhance the effect of depth in the "pile."

8   You can now flatten this image.

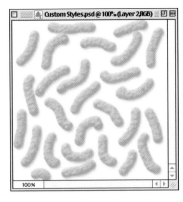

Create a random pattern with the Styled Paintbrush.

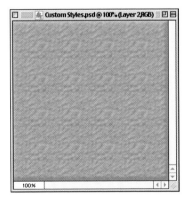

Fill in with more of the Cheezy Poofs on separate layers.

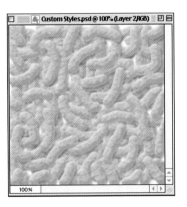

Continue adding new layers until you reach the desired depth.

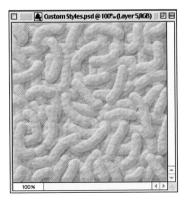

Create a new layer and fill it with the texture.

The completed pile of Cheezy Poofs.

EDITING BUILT-IN LAYER STYLES FOR REALISM

"Get your facts first, and then you can

distort them as much as you please."

—MARK TWAIN

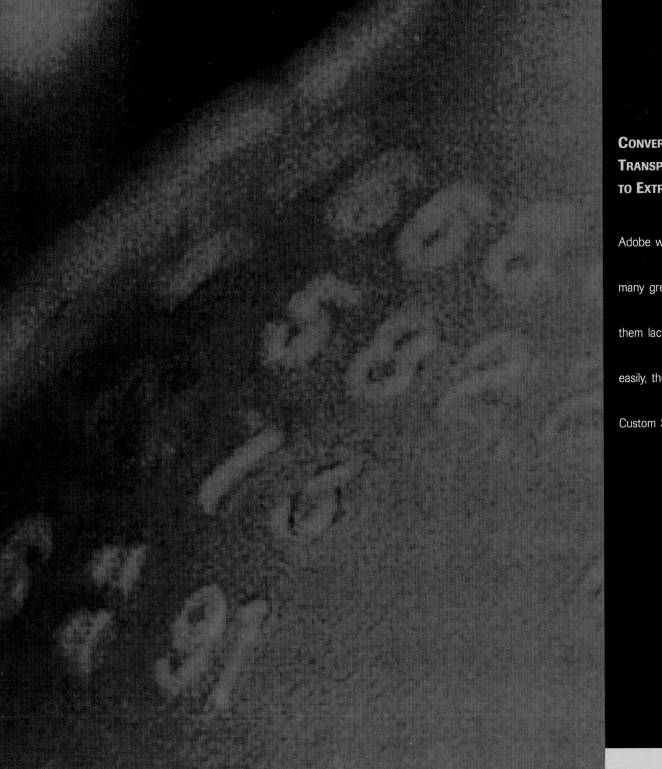

CONVERT "COLORED GLASS" TO TRANSPARENT GLASS TUBES EMBOSSED TO EXTRUDED LOGO SHAPE ANIMATION

Adobe was really generous in giving us so

many great Styles to start with, but many of

them lack realism. These can be edited

easily, though, and resaved as your own

Custom Styles.

Project 2

Editing Built-In Layer Styles for Realism

by Jeff Foster

GETTING STARTED

The purpose of this project is to familiarize you with some of the Layer Styles editing options and how to manipulate the built-in Styles to achieve a more realistic and believable result in your images. This project is actually two in one, as it also covers using ImageReady to create an animation using a built-in Style simply by modifying it over several frames.

Though a whole book could be written on this subject alone, I'm only going to concentrate on two major areas: Using color, light, shading, and transparency to create realism, and getting the most out of animation by simply editing a basic Style.

FROM CARNIVAL GLASS TO TIFFANY'S—
EDITING THE BUILT-IN GLASS STYLES

Starting with realism, let's take a look at the "glass" presets with which Adobe
has provided us. They're hardly what I'd call glass, unless they're supposed to
represent a chip off a plate at Denny's. Using proper characteristics of how glass
is really affected by its environment, you can edit the existing glass Styles and
create your own set with vibrant color, transparency, highlights, glow, and even
a slight shadow. In addition to these features, you might want to experiment
with reflection maps. Unfortunately, a method of creating refraction or
displacement automatically within the Style is not yet available, but I'm sure
that, in time, they'll find a way to make it a reality.

1   Start with a small file, **300×300** pixels and **72**
    pixels/inch.

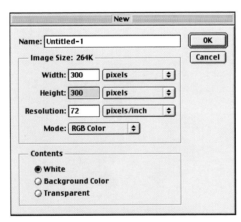

Create a small file to work in.

2   Fill the background with a tight, even pattern with
    which you can judge the transparency of the Style.

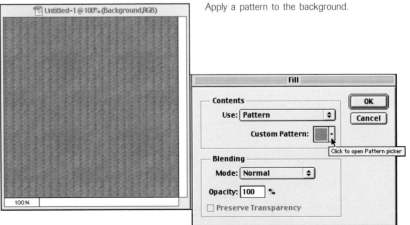

Apply a pattern to the background.

3   Create some large text, shapes, and brushstrokes to apply to the Style. Make sure to rasterize the text and shapes' layers and merge them to only one layer above the Background layer.

Create text, shapes, and brushstrokes to apply to the Style.

4   Apply the Style "Orange Glass" from the built-in Photoshop Styles palette.

Note: If the Orange Glass Style does not appear in your Styles palette, open the Preset Manager and load the Glass Buttons Style from the Photoshop Presets Styles folder.

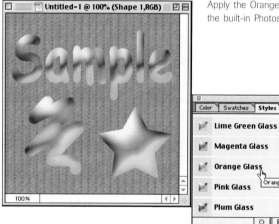

Apply the Orange Glass Style from the built-in Photoshop palette.

5 Set the Blending Options as follows:

Opacity: **75%**

Fill Opacity: **0%**

Gradient Overlay: **Unchecked**

Note: Don't worry about changes you make; they are not overwriting the original Style. Your changes can be saved as a new Custom Style when you are finished.

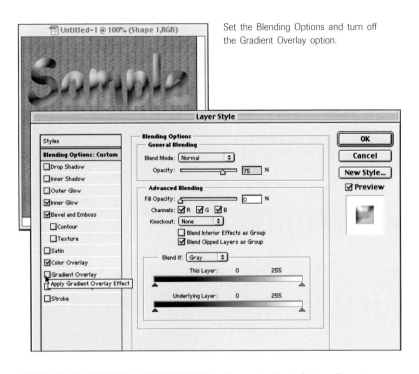

Set the Blending Options and turn off the Gradient Overlay option.

6 Select the Bevel Contour Elements and change the following:

Contour: **Gaussian**

Anti-aliased: **Checked**

Range: **100%**

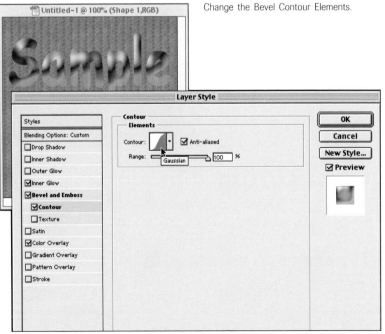

Change the Bevel Contour Elements.

7 Select the Bevel and Emboss option and make the
following changes:

> Depth: **500%**
>
> Size: **15 px**
>
> Soften: **3 px**
>
> Angle: **120°**
>
> Use Global Light: **Checked**
>
> Altitude: **39°**
>
> Highlight Mode: **Screen**
>
> Color: **White**
>
> Opacity: **100%**
>
> Shadow Mode: **Screen**
>
> Color: **#FF9933**
>
> Opacity: **80%**

Be sure to change the shadow color and its mode
because this is what helps give the glass its glow.

8 Select Inner Glow and change the Opacity to 60%.
Then reset the color gradient to the color #FFCC00,
Foreground to Transparent.

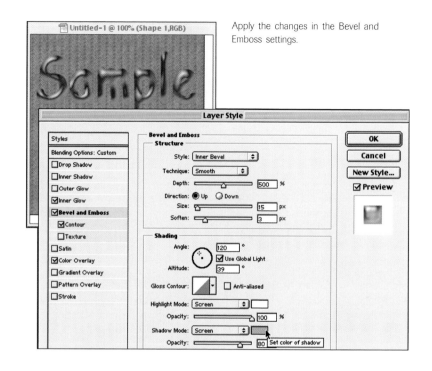

Apply the changes in the Bevel and
Emboss settings.

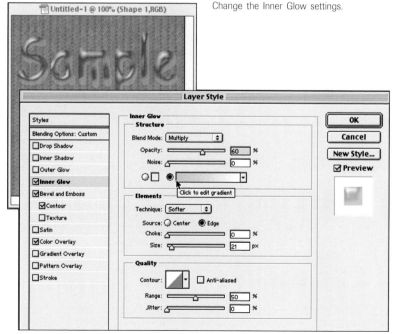

Change the Inner Glow settings.

9   Change the Color Overlay Color, Blend Mode, and Opacity settings as listed here:

Blend Mode: **Multiply**

Color: **#FF9900**

Opacity: **50%** (approx.)

Since Opacity is where most of the color of the glass comes from, you can choose to adjust it to make it richer in color or more transparent.

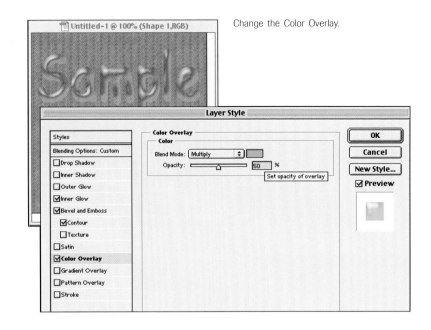

Change the Color Overlay.

10 Select the Drop Shadow option, changing the Color, Opacity, and Size settings.

Blend Mode: **Multiply**

Color: **#993300**

Opacity: **30%**

Distance: **7 px**

Size: **3 px**

Note: Colors can be easily edited using the Photoshop Color Picker and Web-safe colors. You can change the glass color to almost any other color imaginable—just remember to change shadow and shading colors as well as fills and glows.

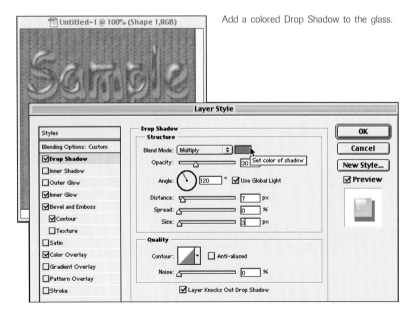

Add a colored Drop Shadow to the glass.

11 Save your completed Style and rename it as your own. Experiment with the Layer Opacity settings and try other textures or patterns on the background.

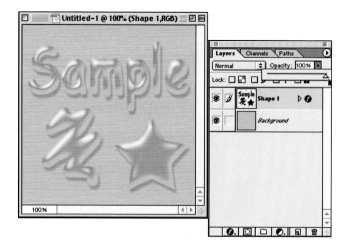

Experiment with Layer Opacity levels and test with different background textures.

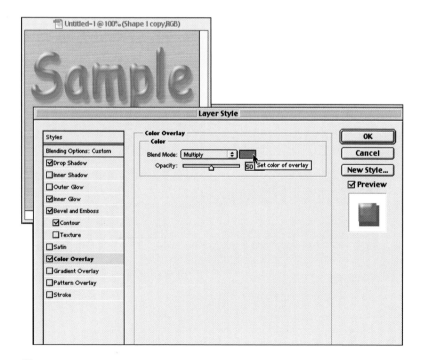

Changing the color of the glass is easy; this can be modified on all levels.

EDITING STYLES IN IMAGEREADY TO CREATE A SMOOTH "EMBOSSED" ANIMATION

Using some built-in Patterns, Shapes, and Styles, an embossed "logo" animation can be created quickly and smoothly with minor editing of a Style in ImageReady. The file is first created in Photoshop, and then you jump to ImageReady for the animation.

1   Start with a small file size, **300×200** pixels. Create a new layer filled with the foreground color and apply the built-in Photoshop Style "Painted Wallboard" to the entire layer.

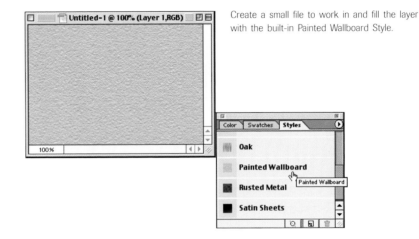

Create a small file to work in and fill the layer with the built-in Painted Wallboard Style.

2   Use the Shape tool to create a shape in the middle of your image. Use the Hand shape for this project. Select Rasterize Layer after you have sized and placed the shape.

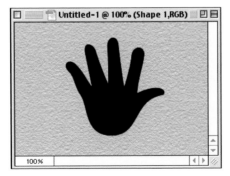

Add a shape to the image and rasterize the layer.

3　With the shape layer selected, apply the built-in Style "Clear Embossed-Inner Bevel," making no changes or adjustments at this point.

4　Select File, Jump to, Adobe ImageReady 3.0.

Frame 1 is automatically added to the Animation bar as soon as ImageReady is opened.

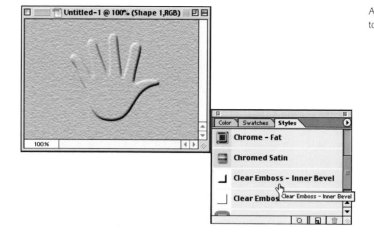

Apply the built-in Clear Embossed Style to the shape layer.

5　Click on the arrow on the Shape 1 layer. Double-click the Bevel and Emboss effect and change the Emboss mode from Inner Bevel to Emboss.

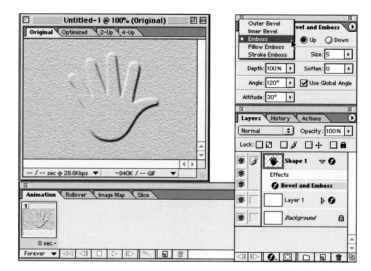

Set the Emboss mode on the Shape Layer Style.

6 Set the Bevel Size to **50**.

The shape will now appear as if it's pressing from the other side of the texture.

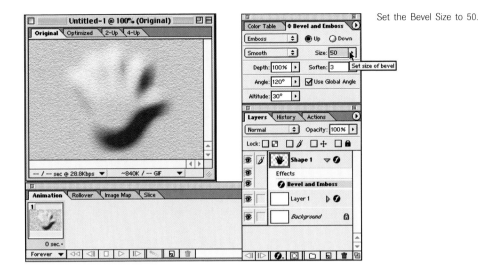

Set the Bevel Size to 50.

7 Set the Depth of the Emboss to 1%.

Since you are already on Frame 1, the animation will start with a nearly blank texture.

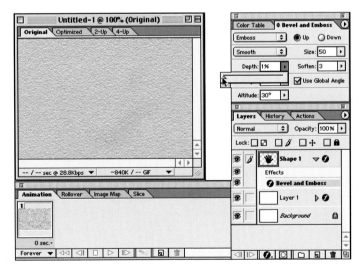

Set the Depth of the Emboss to 1% for the first frame of animation.

8   Click the Duplicate Frame icon at the bottom-right of Animation bar.

This will duplicate the currently selected frame with all of its settings, so you only have to make minor adjustments for that current frame.

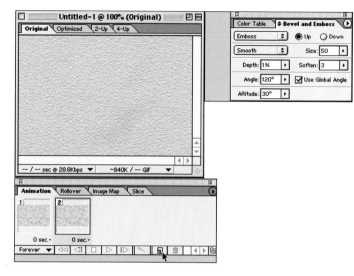

Duplicate the current frame to make minor changes.

9   Change the Depth of the Emboss to **15%**. Repeat this process several times, at 15% increments, until you reach the desired maximum effect. (We used 195% for this example.)

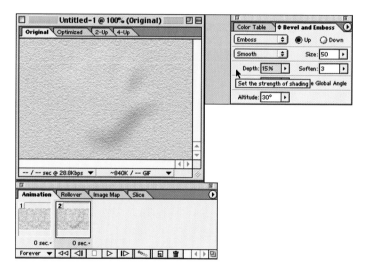

Make changes in the Depth of the Emboss to create the animation.

10 Define the shape and lower its level. Set the Size of the Bevel to **48** and duplicate the frame again.

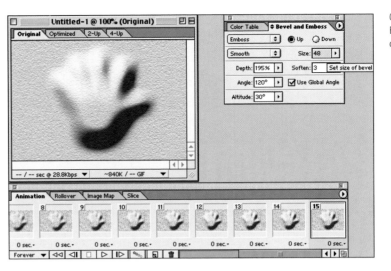

Change the Size of the Bevel for the second part of the animation.

11 Repeat this process of lowering the Size in increments of 2 until you reach a level of **10**.

This will end your animation sequence, so set the timing of this frame to at least 1 second.

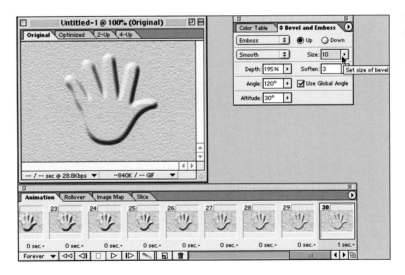

End the animation sequence by setting the timing of the last frame to a minimum of 1 second.

12 Click the Preview in Browser button to see what your animation looks like in your favorite browser. You can choose to reset the timing of the frames or to add/delete frames for a smoother animation.

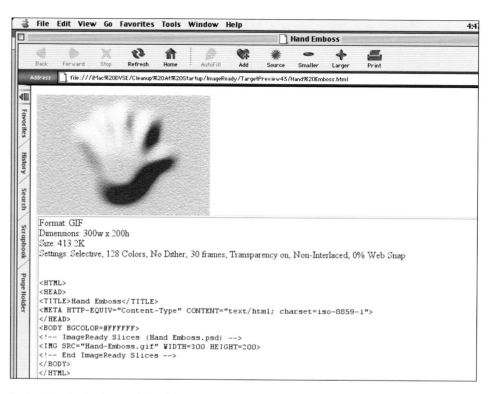

Preview the animation in your choice of browsers.

MODIFICATION

Several Styles can be modified with a transparent effect to give photographs a unique look. Designers use this technique of layering photographic elements to enhance the subject matter or message they are attempting to convey. In this case, I've created an effect of a colored vinegar over the image of the bottled vinegars to enhance the liquid "feel" of the composition.

To create this design, I started by opening the file **Bottles.psd** found in the Adobe Photoshop 6.0 Samples folder. I then created a new layer and used the Paintbrush tool to create the liquidy shape. Applying the modified orange colored glass Style created earlier in this project, I then duplicated the liquid layer to concentrate the effect. This gave it the appearance of a colored, transparent liquid that enhances the colors in the photo.

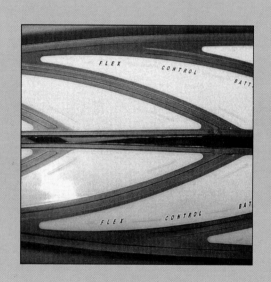

CREATING CUSTOM
PATTERNS FROM NOTHING

"If you want to make an apple pie from

scratch, you must first create the universe."

—CARL SAGAN

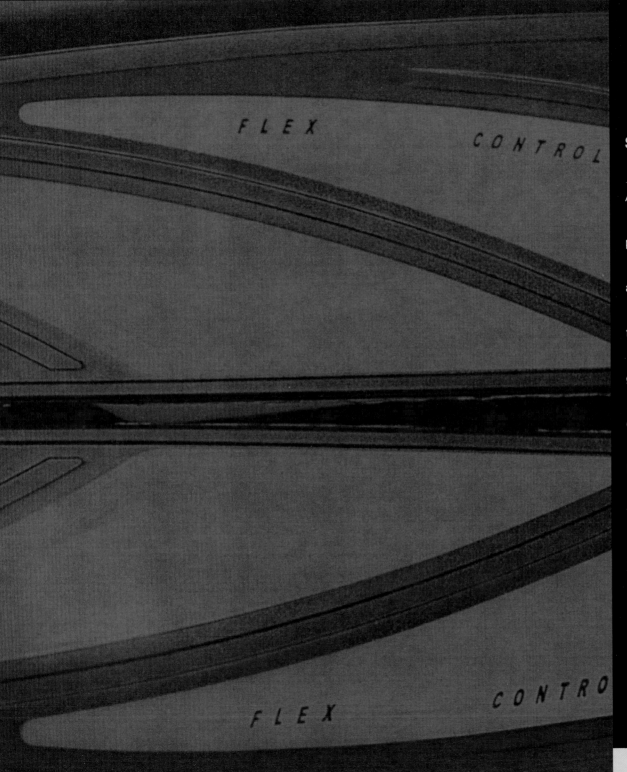

SOMETHING FROM NOTHING

Although Photoshop 6 ships with myriad

patterns and textures, there's bound to come

a time when you won't be able to find the one

that suits your particular needs. This project will

give you the tools to create many of your own

organic tiles from nothing more than a few

built-in Photoshop filters and a little trickery.

You can save these textures for future use by

saving them in the Custom Patterns library.

Project 3

Creating Custom
Patterns from Nothing

by Jeff Foster

GETTING STARTED

By using Photoshop's built-in filters and a few tricks, you can create seamless tileable textures that can be saved as styles or patterns for later use. In this project, you'll use the Noise and Offset filters to create basic textures from an empty file. You can then build off the textures to create additional looks such as dirt and wood grain.

CREATING A BASE TEXTURE

In this section, you'll set up a simple, seamlessly tiling, buff parchment pattern with the help of the Noise and Offset filters to create the basic texture. From that, several additional textures or patterns can be made in just a few steps.

1 Start with a **200×200**-pixel file with the background set to White.

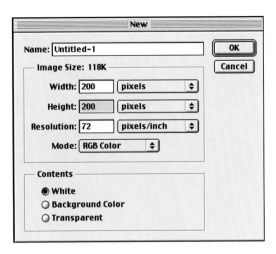

Create a new 200×200-pixel file to build the textures in.

2 Choose the Add Noise filter. Set the Amount to 15%, the Distribution to Gaussian, and select the Monochromatic option.

Noise is added to the image because, to build your texture, you need to begin with some type of image data placed on your background.

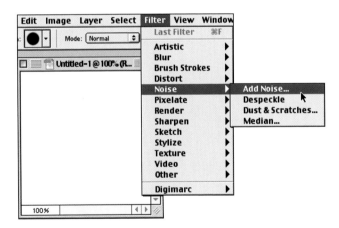

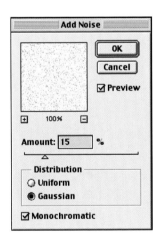

Setting the Add Noise filter amounts.

3   Choose the Gaussian Blur filter and set the Radius
    to 2 pixels.

    This softens the noise to create a smoother, yet still
    lumpy, texture.

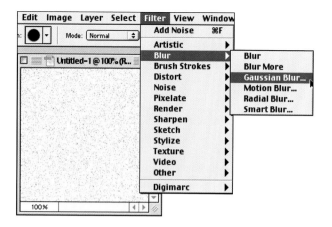

Set the Gaussian Blur Radius to 2 pixels.

4   Choose Image, Adjust, Hue/Saturation and set the
    following options:

    Colorize: **Checked**

    Hue: **40**

    Saturation: **40**

    Lightness: **−5**

    Color will be added without painting or filling
    anything on the image; instead the image data itself
    will be used to generate the color.

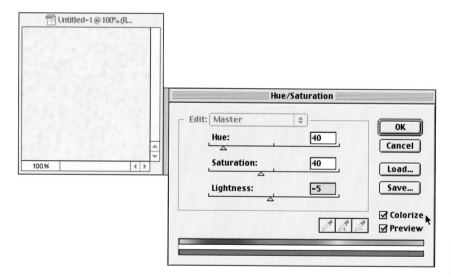

Create color without
painting or using
color fills.

5 Apply the Offset filter. Set the Horizontal option to **100** pixels right and the Vertical option to **100** pixels down. Turn on Wrap Around.

To make this texture tile seamlessly, it has to be modified at the edges so that it will "wrap" continuously. These settings bring the outside edges into the middle of the image (halfway in both directions), creating a "cross" pattern. Notice the hard lines that now run through the middle of the image.

6 Clean up the edges of the tile by using the Clone tool on the outside edges and any intersecting lines. Take care not to clone off the edge of the image area, or you will create even more work for yourself when you Offset the image back!

Remember that the goal is for the texture to wrap seamlessly so that the pattern appears to be random. If you miss any of the edges or lines, when your pattern is tiled, it will be obvious that you used a tile.

Note: Modifying and cleaning up the edges of the tile can be done several ways. When there is a smooth organic pattern like this one, the Clone tool is the best option. Other cases might call for the use of the Paintbrush tool to paint evenly colored areas or the Smudge tool to blend them across the hard-edged lines.

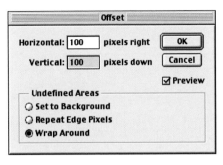

Setting the Offset filter to prepare for edge modifications.

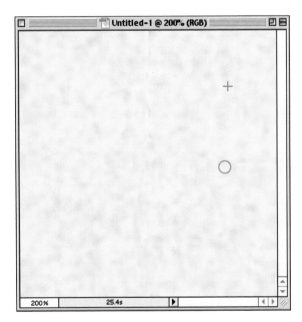

Using the Clone tool to clean up the image edges.

7 Select the Offset filter once more and check for hard lines down the middle.

You can also choose Filter, Offset (Last Filter).

8 When you're satisfied with your work, save it to the Patterns library by selecting Edit, Define Pattern.

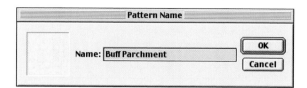

Save the Parchment texture into the Patterns library.

9 To test your new pattern for seamlessness, create a new file that is **600×600** pixels.

Your test file needs to be much larger than the tiled texture so that you can fill it and check for potential problems or obnoxious repeating patterns.

10 Select Edit, Fill, Pattern and choose your newly created pattern from the Custom Pattern Picker.

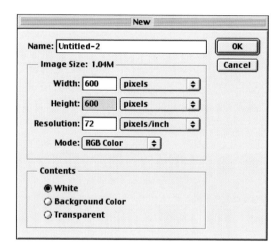

Create a new file to test the seamless pattern in.

If you did a clean job with your texture, it should look like one large random pattern in the entire image area of the window. If you see any hard lines, cracks, or obnoxious repeating patterns, simply return to Step 8, repair the problematic areas, and repeat the test process.

The final test image should be clean and randomly filled.

Note: Take care not to create too many versions of a Pattern saved to the Patterns library. You might be confused later on as to which one is the "clean" one. It is recommended that you purge the incorrect patterns using the Preset Manager outlined in Appendix A.

MODIFYING THE BASIC PATTERN TO CREATE NEW PATTERNS

Using the Parchment texture you just created to design more textures is a great practice for modifying built-in Patterns and making your own new textures as well. From the original texture, you will be able to create granular textures with depth, such as the dirt shown here, using simple Filters, Image Adjustment commands.

1   Open the parchment texture you created in the preceding section. Add a new layer to it, filled with white.

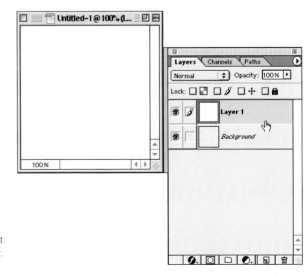

Open the original Parchment Pattern file and add a new layer.

2 Choose the Add Noise filter. Set the Amount to 100%, the Distribution to Gaussian, and select the Monochromatic option.

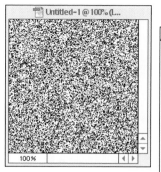

Add Noise to the new layer to begin building the next texture.

3 Set the noise layer's Blending Mode to Multiply.

The original Parchment texture now shows through the white space. This will eventually be the "shaded" side of the granular texture.

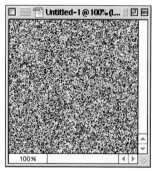

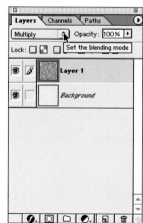

Set the layer's Blending Mode to Multiply to allow the background texture to show through.

4 Duplicate the noise layer and set the new layer's Blending Mode to Screen.

Although it looks just like the original noise layer, it will soon become the "highlighted" portion of the granular texture.

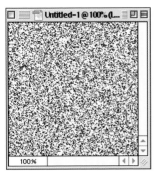

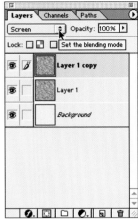

Duplicate the noise layer and set the layer's Blending Mode to Screen.

5 Select the Offset filter again, only this time, set the Horizontal and Vertical settings to **−3**. Make sure Wrap Around is turned on.

This will place the highlight in the upper-left direction from the shaded granules.

6 With the top noise layer selected, choose Image, Adjust, Invert.

This will create tiny white highlights on the layer.

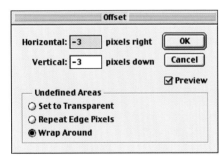

Offset the highlighted noise layer in the upper-left direction.

7 Apply a Gaussian Blur filter with a Radius of 1 pixel to soften the amount of noise slightly.

Apply Gaussian Blur to the highlight noise layer.

8 Select the shaded noise layer and apply Gaussian Blur to it but just slightly more at 1.5 pixels.

Add noise to the shaded noise layer.

9 Select the Background layer and apply Hue/Saturation adjustment to colorize it:

Colorize   **Checked**

Hue: **20**

Saturation: **40**

Lightness: **−40**

The granules are more predominant, and the background is now a gritty dirt-brown color.

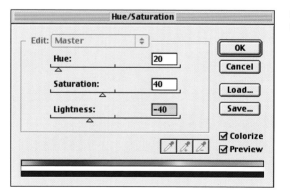

Colorize the background layer to make the noise layers more predominant.

By simply making a few adjustments to both the highlight layer and shaded layers, you can create several different textures. Change the background color in Hue/Saturation for a completely new look … the possibilities are endless from this point. Even if you're not sure where you're going with a texture at any time you're making adjustments, if it looks cool, grab a "snapshot" of it by saving it as a Pattern. You can always reload that Pattern later and go from there with further manipulations.

Note: It's a good idea to save your master Photoshop file with its layers before making major adjustments to the layers or flattening the image, just in case you need to revert to a point where you won't have to start all over.

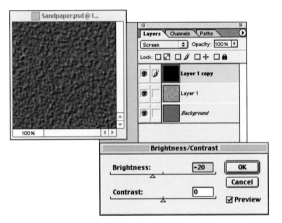

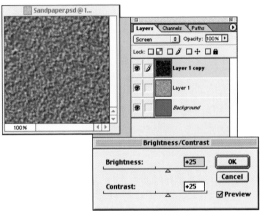

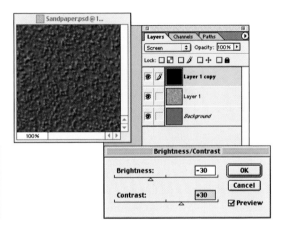

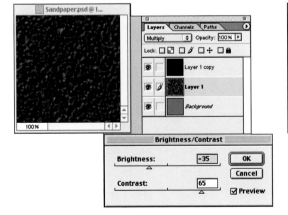

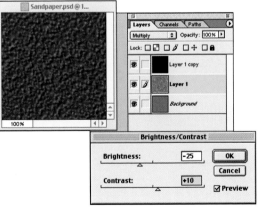

Make adjustments to both noise layers to create several different textures.

10 Flatten the image before going on to the other modifications.

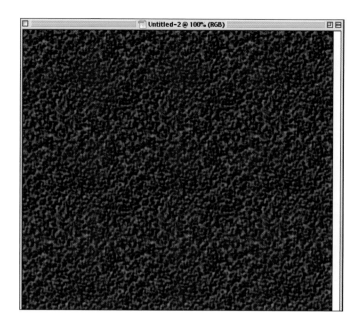

Fill the larger test file with the saved patterns to check for overall organic flow.

CREATE EVEN MORE TEXTURES

In this section, you'll take the dirt texture, which was created from the parchment texture, and modify it to resemble tree bark. If wood isn't your thing, be sure to pay particular attention to the sidebar Note, which will show you how to create brushed aluminum instead.

1 Open the dirt texture from the preceding section. Select the Motion Blur filter, setting the Angle to 90° and the Distance to 25 pixels.

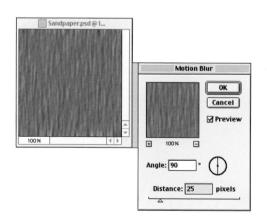

Apply Motion Blur to the flattened dirt texture.

2 Apply the Offset filter to check the edges of the blurred texture. Set the Horizontal and Vertical values each to **100** pixels and turn on Wrap Around.

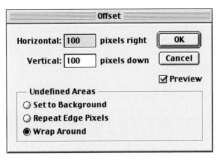

Apply the Offset filter to prepare for cleanup.

3 Use the Clone tool and a small brush to blend in the hard edges that appear in the middle of the image.

Make sure to follow the grain with your brushstrokes.

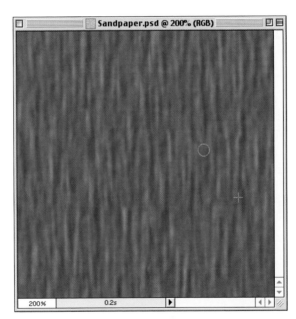

Use the Clone tool and a small brush size to clean up the image.

4   Save the finished coarse grain pattern for future
     retrieval for modifications.

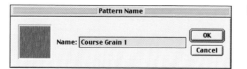

Save the cleaned-up pattern for later retrieval.

Note: If you want to create a quick brushed aluminum
texture instead of tree bark, apply Hue/Saturation as
follows:

Colorize: **Checked**

Hue: **272**

Saturation: **10**

Lightness: **+30**

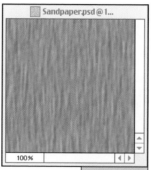

Modifying the pattern to create a
brushed aluminum texture.

5 Copy the background to a new layer and apply the Ocean Ripple filter to it. Set the Ripple Size to 15 and the Ripple Magnitude to 4.

6 Set the layer's Blending Mode to Darken, keeping the Opacity at 100%.

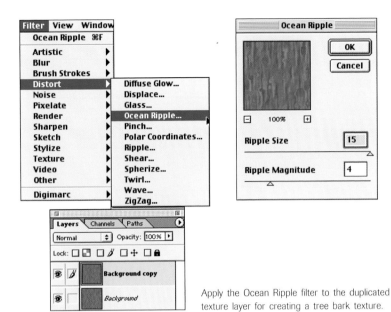

Set the Ocean Ripple filter settings to distort the vertical grain.

Apply the Ocean Ripple filter to the duplicated texture layer for creating a tree bark texture.

7 Duplicate the layer and set the new layer's Blending Mode to Multiply.

This creates a deeper color and brings out the texture of the tree bark.

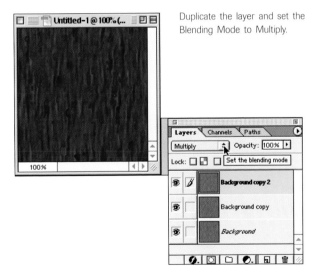

Duplicate the layer and set the Blending Mode to Multiply.

8 Flatten the image, apply the Offset filter, and clean up any necessary edges. Save the Pattern for future use.

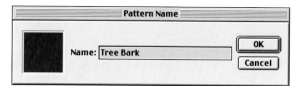

Flatten the image, check for seamless edges with the Offset filter, and clean as necessary. Save the Pattern when complete.

MODIFICATION

As I mentioned earlier in this project, you can keep digging deeper with these patterns, creating more and more interesting textures. This last effect takes the Dirt Pattern created earlier in this chapter and evolves it into a beautiful hardwood texture.

1 Create a new **200×200**-pixel file, **72** pixels/inch. Fill it with the saved Dirt Pattern.

2 Colorize the texture using Hue/Saturation:

Colorize: **Checked**

Hue: **30**

Saturation: **50**

Lightness: **30**

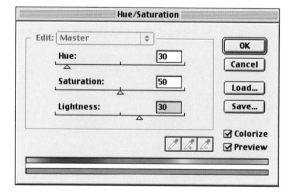

Colorize the texture using Hue/Saturation.

3   Adjust the Brightness to 10 and the Contrast to 25 to lighten up the image.

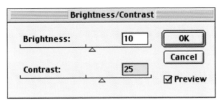

Apply Brightness/Contrast to lighten the image.

Note: Remember to take "snapshots" of the textures as you're working through the steps in each effect by selecting Define Pattern. Maybe I'm just hungry, but this looks like a delicious coconut/macadamia nut brittle that I had in Hawaii...so I'm saving it for you on the enclosed CD in the Sample Images folder!

4   Apply Motion Blur to the texture at an Angle of 45° and a Distance of 20 pixels. Then apply the Distort, Ripple filter with the Amount set to 125% and the Size set to Large.

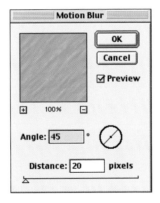

Apply the Motion Blur filter at an angle to the image.

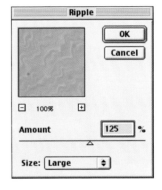

The Ripple Distortion filter adds the wavy hardwood texture.

5 Use the Offset filter to see the edges of the texture. You will definitely need to clean this texture up but not with the Clone tool this time. For this type of pattern that is wavy and asymmetrical, it is best to use the Smudge tool and a small brush to "push" across the line edges.

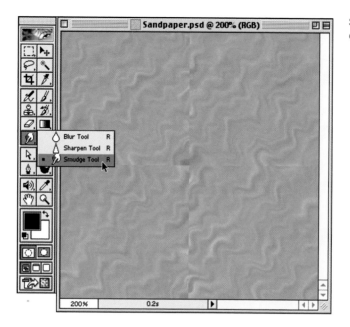

Select the Smudge tool to begin cleanup of the tile image.

6 Select a small brush and set the Pressure to around 80%. Carefully "smudge" the colors across the hard lines until they blend in with the adjoining colors. This may require some practice to get it to look "untouched."

Smudge tool settings:

Paintbrush: **Hard Round 3 pixels**

Mode: **Normal**

Pressure: **80%**

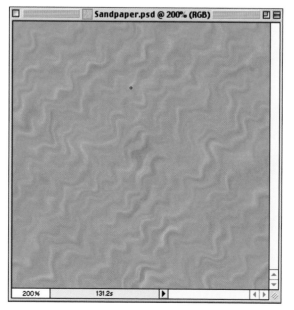

Clean up the texture using the Smudge tool to smooth out the hard edges.

7 Save the Pattern when you've finished and check it for seamlessness in the larger test file. Make any corrections as necessary. The finished result should look like a fine piece of furniture or paneling in a five-star hotel. Try using this pattern within a Custom Style for a varnished, glossy look.

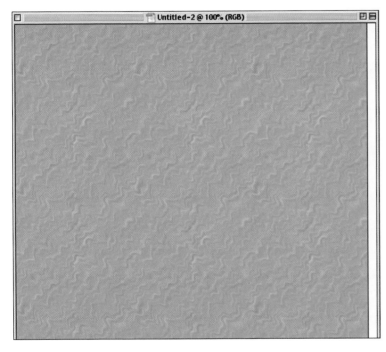

Testing the finished Pattern in a larger file.

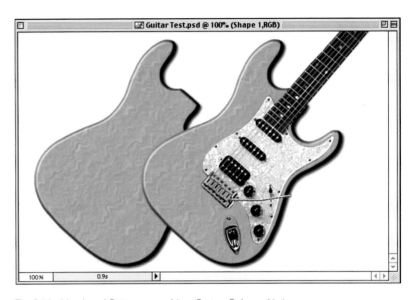

The finished hardwood Pattern as used in a Custom Style on this image.

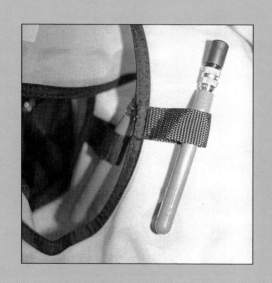

VERTICAL MICRO-TILES

"Too many pieces of music finish

too long after the end."

—IGOR STRAVINSKY

BACKGROUNDS IN UNDER 1KB

Now that everyone is hooked up with cable modems, DSL, and T1 lines, who needs to worry about graphic file sizes? Okay, so we're a ways from *that* being a reality, but where has the design sense gone in favor of the tiny, quick-loading blocks of solid color and volumes of text on a blank background? Enter the 1-pixel micro-tile. You can have a tiled background pattern, sidebar, or table filler that's less than 1KB in size!

Project 4

Vertical Micro-Tiles

by Jeff Foster

GETTING STARTED

The trick to making a good background tile is to create an interesting pattern without being too busy or distracting. By working with smooth color pixel transitions across the width of the tile, the result will be long, smooth streaks of color that will actually look like a never-ending pattern. It may take several attempts before you get the exact look you're trying to achieve; just remember to keep the colors you choose light and subtle.

THE BASIC MICRO-TILE

In this project, we will be making tiles that are only 1 pixel high and 2,000 pixels wide. (You can choose to make your tiles a bit narrower for design's sake or if you just want to "squeeze" your effect down.)

1 Create a new file using the following settings:

Width: **2,000 pixels**

Height: **1 pixel**

Resolution: **72 pixels/inch**

Mode: **RGB**

Note: Most people run their monitors at 1,200 pixels wide or less and their browser windows at less than that. It's always a good idea, however, to make vertical tiles wider than people will stretch their browser windows.

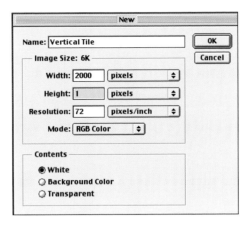

Create a new file that is 2,000×1 pixels in size.

2 Set the Units and Rulers preferences to Pixels, select View Rulers, and drag out a guide from the left side of the project window to approximately 200 pixels.

To create a vertically running "sidebar" along the left side of the page, you need to determine how wide it should be. It needs to be wide enough for your navigational graphics or text links. (Approximately 200 pixels is a good start.)

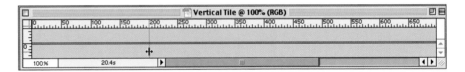

Set the guide at 200 pixels.

3 Select a Hard Round Paintbrush at 100% Opacity. Using any color, paint the area from the guide all the way to the left side of the image area.

Even though the image is only 1 pixel in height, you don't want a fuzzy edge on the sidebar if you want a three-dimensional look.

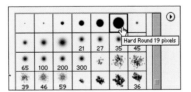

Select a Hard Round Paintbrush tool to apply the sidebar color.

Apply the sidebar color with the Paintbrush tool.

4 Select a Soft Round Airbrush tool and set to 15%
Pressure. Set the foreground color to Black and apply
the Airbrush tool to the intersection of the guide and
the image area. Click once or twice to get the desired
amount.

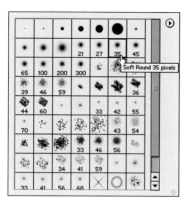

Select a Soft Round Airbrush tool.

5 When creating the rounded edge and drop shadow
off the right side of the sidebar, don't hold down the
tool too long; otherwise, the edge will get covered by
a fuzzy, black blob.

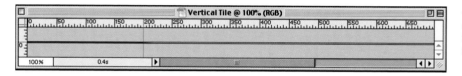

Apply the
Airbrush tool
to create the
shadows.

6 Define the pattern and save it.

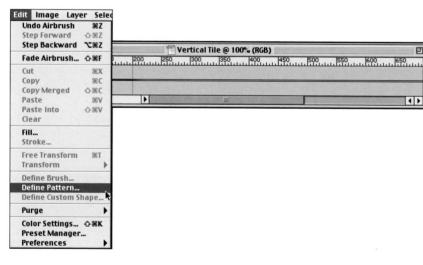

Define the pattern
of the tile image to
test it in another
file.

7 Create a file large enough to test the tile pattern you just saved. Select Edit, Fill, and choose Pattern. Select the tile pattern.

Amazingly, the tiny tile pattern fills up the image window and looks like a solid image! What could easily be several hundred kilobytes in size is less than ½KB in file size. That means the tile image would load before the other graphics on the page, extremely fast—even on a slow modem connection!

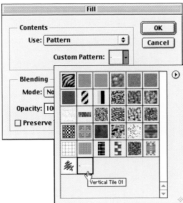

Select the tile pattern and fill a new, larger file to test it.

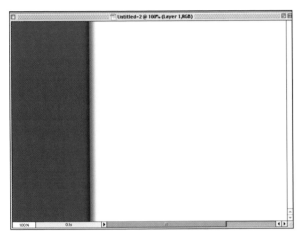

Test the tile to make sure the color and contour are what you expected.

CREATE DUAL "STEEL BARS"

You might not want a solid sidebar, so experiment with different variations on the theme. This exercise will show you how simple it is to make a metallic look with a couple of brushes.

1 On your 2,000×1 pixel file, create a new layer and fill with white.

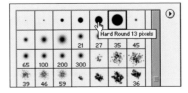

Select a Paintbrush from the Brush palette.

55

2 Select a Hard Round 13-pixel Paintbrush with the Pressure set to 100%. Set the foreground color to Black. Use the Paintbrush tool to place "bars" at the far left side of the image and at the intersection of the guide and the image.

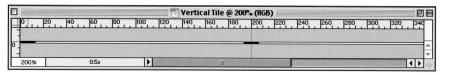

Paint the "bars" base with the Paintbrush tool.

3 Select a small Soft Round Airbrush tool with the Pressure set to 15%. Set the foreground color to White. Carefully apply the highlights with a few quick clicks of the Airbrush tool toward the center of the black areas.

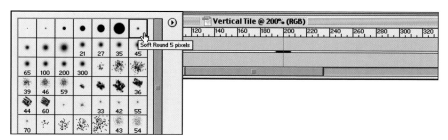

Select a small Soft Round Airbrush tool to paint the highlights.

4 Define the pattern and Fill with the saved pattern in a new layer on your test file.

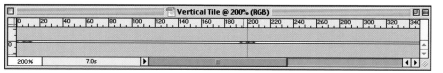

Apply the highlights using the Airbrush tool.

5 Notice how the "metal bars" run smoothly down the image. Try several variations of this technique, including color and placement of the "bars."

6 Examine the differences in the Save For Web dialog boxes. The GIF image, set at 32 selective colors and No Dithering, is only 212 bytes. The JPEG image, set to Medium compression, is 533 bytes—approximately ½KB in size!

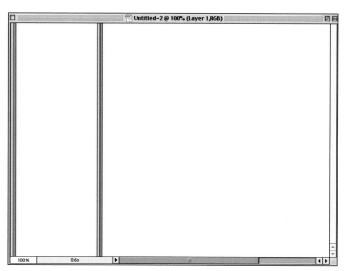

Fill the test file with the saved pattern to test the Metal Bars tile.

TEXTURES FROM MICRO-TILES

Now that you understand how a single row of pixels can create a "streaked" effect that runs down the entire width of your Web page, let's take a look at how to create a texture from the same 2,000×1 pixel file.

1   Create a new **2,000×1** pixel file with the background set at White.

2   Select Filter, Noise, Add Noise. Set Amount to 3.00, Gaussian, and Monochromatic.

This will put a random pattern of darker pixels across the width of the image.

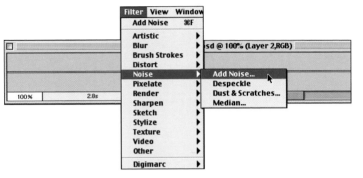

Create a new 2,000×1 pixel file and select the Add Noise filter.

Note: You can add more noise; if desired, select Filter, Add Noise (or click Cmd+F [Ctrl+F]). You can lessen the amount of Noise applied by selecting Edit, Fade Add Noise (or by clicking Shift+Cmd+F [Shift+Ctrl+F]).

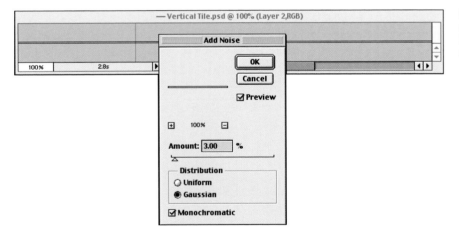

Set the amount of Gaussian Noise to 3.00, Monochromatic.

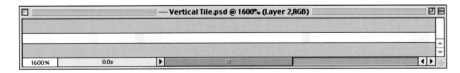

Observe the amount of noise added by zooming to 1600%.

3 Define the image as a pattern and open your master test file. Select the saved pattern and fill.

After applying the pattern, you can see that the noise has created a streaking effect. Though it's only grayscale, it almost appears as if there's a slight coloration to the design. This makes a great subtle background texture for just about any kind of Web site design.

Check out the "Modifications" section for ideas in colorizing and creating other textures with this noise pattern.

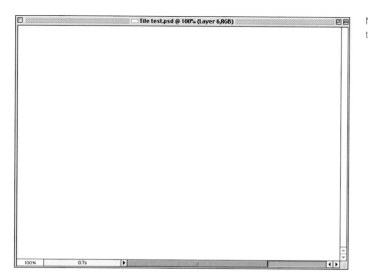

Notice the "streaking" effect that the noise pattern gives the tile.

MODIFICATIONS

With only a few quick steps, you can create several textures from the noise micro-tile. By adding colorizing layers and saturating the noise itself, you can imitate wood, brushed aluminum, and more.

1 Create a new layer in your previous 2,000×1 pixel file. In the Tools palette, select the Gradient tool. Click on the Gradient presets and select the Spectrum gradient. Drag the Gradient tool across the width of your image to apply the gradient.

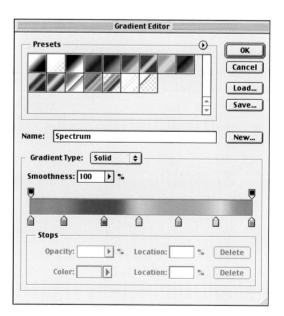

Create a new layer and fill with the Gradient tool.

2   On the Layers palette, select the Color mode for the
new gradient layer.

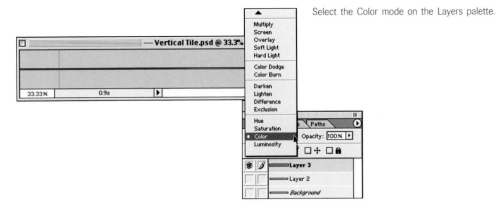

Select the Color mode on the Layers palette.

3   Make sure the noise layer is visible beneath the
gradient color layer and then select Define Pattern
from the Edit menu.

Open the test master file and fill a new layer with
the saved pattern to observe the effect that the color
gradient had on the noise.

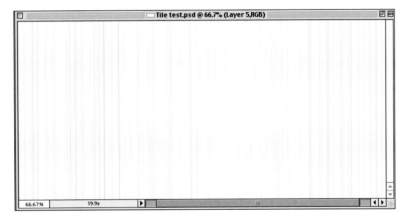

Observe in the test file the
effect that the colorizing
gradient layer had on the
noise tile.

4 To create a "wood grain" texture, first duplicate the noise layer and then select Image, Adjust, Hue/Saturation and colorize the layer.

Colorize: **Selected**

Hue: **25**

Saturation: **50**

Lightness: **-30**

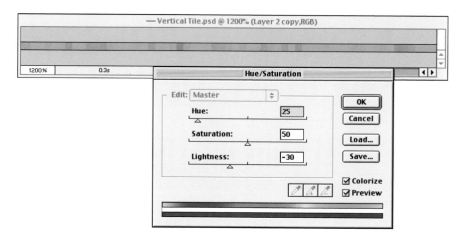

Colorize a duplicate noise layer to create a wood grain effect.

5 Define the pattern and open the test file. Fill a new layer with the newly saved pattern and observe the wood grain effect this tiny tile has made!

Experiment with the Hue/Saturation technique in Step 4. You can also experiment with all the layers, overlapping the transparency, Multiply mode, Colorize mode, and so on…. You can create amazing effects like these with just a few minor adjustments—all under 1KB in size!

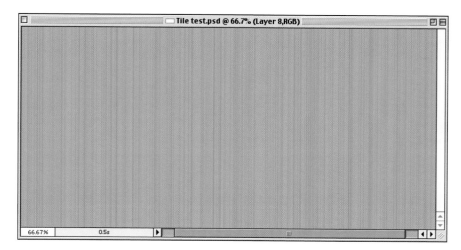

Observe in the test file how the tiny tile creates a wood grain effect.

This technique doesn't just work for vertically tiling horizontal tiles. Try experimenting with tiles that are 1 pixel in width and 800 pixels in height—it might be just what you're looking for.

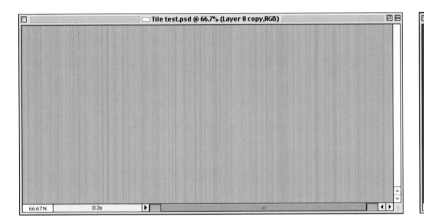

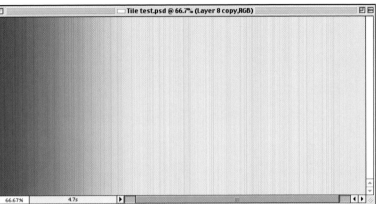

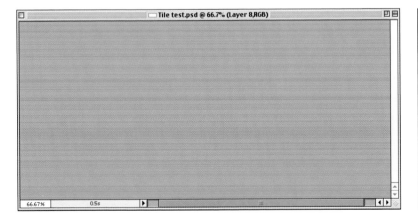

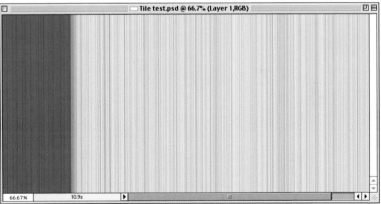

Making subtle changes in the Hue/Saturation and Layer modes will enable you to create amazing effects!

SEAMLESS PHOTO TILES
AND CUSTOM PATTERNS

"Once all struggle is grasped,

miracles are possible."

—MAO TSE-TUNG

CREATING BACKGROUNDS USING TILES AND PATTERNS

It's important to understand how to create

seamless photo tiles for use as Patterns,

image maps, and backgrounds for Web pages.

If you browse through the built-in Patterns

selection in Photoshop 6, you'll notice there

aren't many photographically generated images.

Virtually any photograph can be chopped and

cropped for use as a tile—though some might

require a great deal more editing to make

them seamless.

Project 5

Seamless Photo Tiles and Custom Patterns

by Jeff Foster

GETTING STARTED

There are several reasons why you might need a seamless photo tile, whether it's for a Custom Pattern you can use to fill backgrounds, fill text, or for use as a bump map in the Custom Layer Styles. With the aid of a digital camera, you might just find textures around your home or office that you can take and tile on the spot. Once you understand the technique of creating seamless photo tiles, you'll look at the world in a whole new way!

PREPARING THE IMAGE

Even the seemingly simplest tileable images might require some work in adjusting the skew, angle, or perspective prior to tiling. This project begins with a usable image, but shadows and imperfections in the photo keep it from being easily tiled. Some minor preparations are necessary to get the image ready for tiling.

1 Open the file **BrickWall.jpg** from the Sample
Images folder on the accompanying CD-ROM.

Open the image Brick Wall.jpg in the
Images for Tiling folder on the CD-ROM.

2 Select Show Rulers and drag out some horizontal
guides toward both ends of the image and one near
the center. Align the guides near the closest cracks in
the bricks.

3 Duplicate the Background layer and select Edit,
Transform, Perpective to adjust the image.

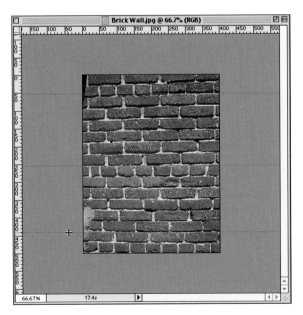

Select Show Rulers and drag out guides
to line up the cracks in the bricks.

4   Grab the upper-left handle of the Transform box and pull it straight up, just enough to align the middle guide with a crack in the bricks. Some minor adjustments and skewing might need to be done to get the cracks to align perfectly.

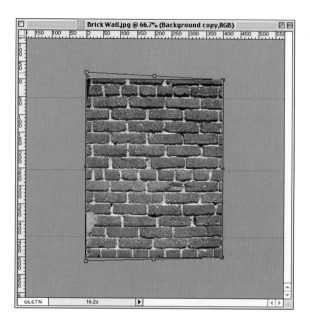

Drag out the Transform box to skew the image to match the guides.

5   Select the Crop tool and drag out a selection that would evenly tile the brick shapes. Be sure to align the edges and ends of bricks.

Note: Keep in mind, while you select the crop area, that you will need to consider the amount of "mortar" you will need between the bricks and how the bricks will line up when tiled. Be sure, if you use a mortar line between the bricks, that you split it in half. This way, when it tiles, the mortar lines won't be too thick or too thin.

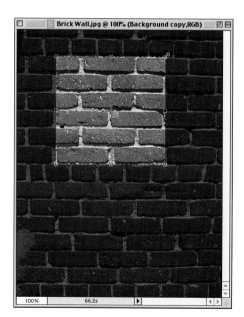

Carefully select a tileable area with the Crop tool.

MAKING THE TILE SEAMLESS

Very seldom can you get away with simply cropping an image and ending up with a seamless tile. It's important to clean up all the edges so they cannot be seen when tiled continuously in a background, on the surface of an object, or on text. This is a suggestive process involving the Clone and Smudge tools and may require some practice (and patience!).

1 Continuing with the cropped image file, select the Offset filter.

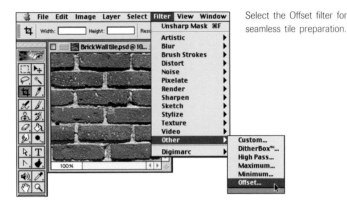

Select the Offset filter for seamless tile preparation.

2 Set the Horizontal and Vertical offset to approximately ½ the width and height of the image dimensions and select Wrap Around.

   Notice how the color changes in the bricks down the middle and the black line running horizontally across the middle.

3 Select the Clone tool and choose the Soft Round 13-pixel brush. You will need to use several different brush sizes to effectively match the cloned areas throughout this process.

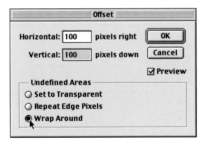

Set the Horizontal and Vertical offset to ½ the image dimensions.

4   Using the Clone tool, carefully select from areas that have a clean, unmarked surface from brick to brick. Eliminate the hard lines down the middle of the bricks. Be sure to check the mortar in between the bricks for any hard, cut-off lines or misaligned edges.

Apply the Clone tool to the hard, mismatched lines and hard edges.

5   Select the Offset filter again to make sure that editing the tile didn't inadvertently create any additional hard edges and that the look is seamless. Repeat Step 4 to do any further editing on the tile if necessary.

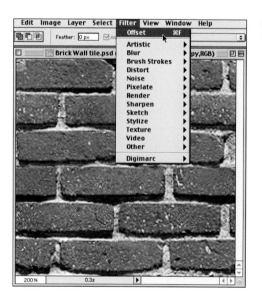

Select the Offset filter to check the final editing.

6 When you're satisfied with the tile, select Define Pattern from the Edit menu and save the tile to your Custom Pattern library.

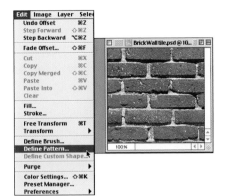

Select Define Pattern to save the new Custom Pattern tile.

7 Create a new file that's **500×500** pixels to test the new Custom Pattern tile. Select Pattern Fill from the Edit menu and select the new Custom Pattern. Check to make sure the tile has no visible hard edges or major color shifts between the bricks. The result should be an even brick wall pattern.

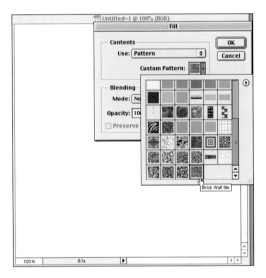

Create a new 500×500-pixel file and fill it with the brick pattern.

The result should be an even brick wall pattern.

If you want to use the brick pattern as a simple background image, you can choose to convert it to a Sepia
tone with the Hue/Saturation, Colorize option. You could
also simply fill a layer over a white background and lower
the Opacity to soften the image to make overlaying text
more legible.

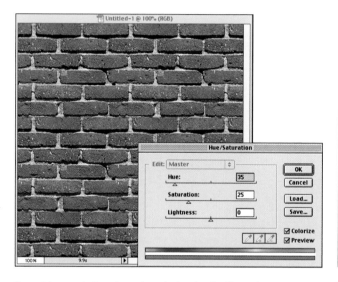

Convert to a sepia tone image by selecting the Hue/Saturation,
Colorize option.

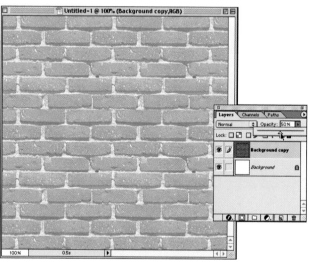

Lighten the effect by setting the opacity down over a white background.

MODIFICATION

You can have a lot of fun animating small tiles in the background of a Web
page, or you can fill a sidebar frame to enhance a site's design. In this part of
the project, you will be cutting and pasting part of the tile image onto itself
and modifying it so that the clouds appear to be floating over the background.
This example is quite exaggerated for demonstration purposes, so you would
naturally want to choose an effect that's much subtler in a Web design.

1   Open the file **Clouds.jpg** from the Sample Images
    folder on the accompanying CD-ROM.

Open the Clouds.jpg file from
the Images for Tiling folder on
the enclosed CD-ROM.

2   Use the Crop tool to select an area as shown. You
    want enough contrast to easily see the clouds move
    over the background in the final animation.

Crop an area with high
contrast in the image.

3   Follow the previous steps to offset the image to reveal the hard edges in the center. Using the Clone tool, carefully reconstruct clouds over the hard-lined edges. Use of the Smudge tool may help, but use caution not to make the image appear too soft.

Use the Clone and Smudge tools to reconstruct clouds over the center hard lines.

4   After you apply the Offset filter and verify that the tile is seamless, select Define Pattern. Test the pattern in a test file as you did previously in Step 7.

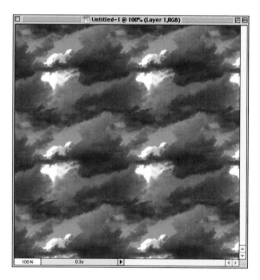

Once the tile is completed, select Define Pattern and fill a larger test file.

5 Position the image so that there is one prominent area of cloud you could extract using the Offset filter. In this example, a Horizontal offset is all that is needed.

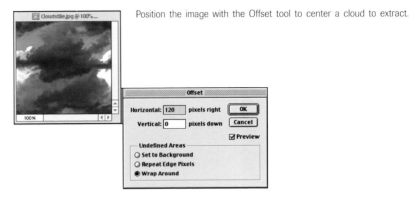

Position the image with the Offset tool to center a cloud to extract.

6 Using the Lasso tool, select an area around the cloud you want to use as the moving foreground and copy/paste it to a new layer.

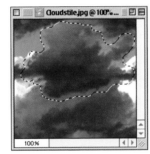

Select a cloud with the Lasso tool and copy/paste it to a new layer.

7 Hide the pasted cloud layer and "remove" it from the background layer using the Paintbrush, Clone, and Smudge tools. Offset the image to check for inadvertent hard edges created while editing.

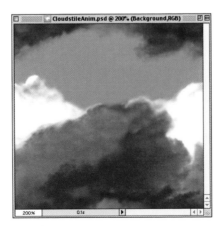

Edit out the cloud on the background layer using the Paintbrush, Clone, and Smudge tools.

8 Make the cloud layer active and remove any
   unwanted material around the edges with the Eraser
   tool and a Soft Edged Paintbrush. Complete a soft,
   semitransparent edge around the cloud with the
   Airbrush Eraser tool at low-pressure settings.

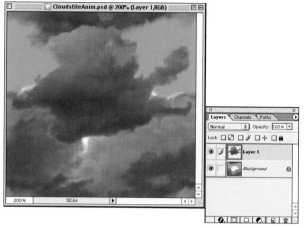

Activate the cloud layer and remove excess material
around it with the Paintbrush and Airbrush Eraser tools.

CREATING THE ANIMATION

Now it's time to add some motion to the tiled image. We will start by manually
moving the floating cloud step by step and saving each sequence as a new layer.
The entire project will then be animated in ImageReady.

1 Duplicate the cloud layer and hide the original layer.
   Offset the new cloud layer Horizontally **15** pixels.
   Repeat the layer duplication and offset process until
   the cloud has come full circle to the position you
   started in. Using the Last Filter command will repeat
   the offset where you last set it and will speed up your
   process.

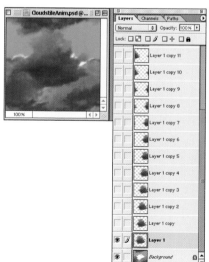

Duplicate the cloud layer and offset Horizontally 15 pixels.
Repeat the process for the remaining layers.

2　Jump to ImageReady and set up the animation
sequence, matching each frame to a visible layer in
the file. Test the animation sequence by clicking the
Play button on the Animation bar.

3　Preview in Netscape Communicator or Internet
Explorer. The number of frames in your animation
will determine the speed and smoothness of the
playback. Select Save Optimized As and place in
the background of an HTML document to test.

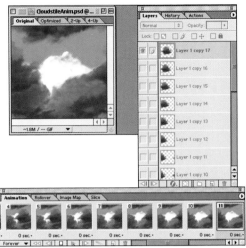

Jump to ImageReady and match the animation frames to the layers in the file. Play the animation to test it.

Once you master this great technique, imagine how
even a very subtle animation could really captivate your
Web site visitors!

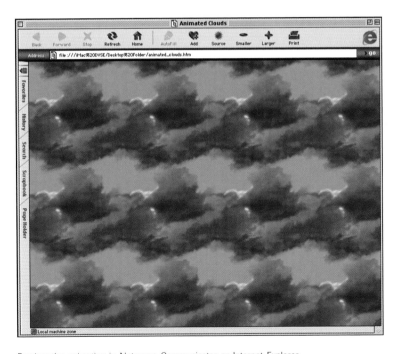

Preview the animation in Netscape Communicator or Internet Explorer.

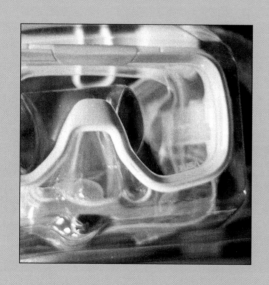

CREATING AND EDITING CUSTOM SHAPES

"Try not to have a good time…

this is supposed to be educational."

—CHARLES SCHULTZ

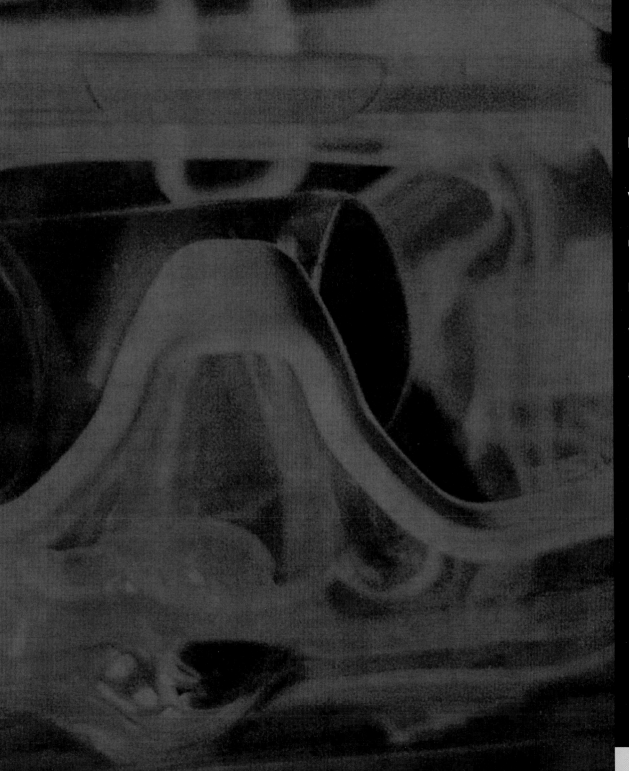

NEW CUSTOM SHAPES

Vector Shapes in Photoshop at last! You can now select Custom Shapes from a built-in library or create your own from layers or paths. Vector Shapes are scalable and are editable with Path tools. If you apply a Custom Layer Style to a shape, the Style will scale with the shape.

Project 6

Creating and Editing Custom Shapes

by Jeff Foster

GETTING STARTED

The new Custom Shapes tool palette in Photoshop 6 already has quite a selection
of basic shapes, but you can apply subtle edits and changes to these shapes to create
your own new custom library of shapes. What's even more impressive is the ability to
create new Custom Shapes from any Path or to create a Custom Brush from several
variable-size shapes!

EDITING AN EXISTING SHAPE TO CREATE A NEW ONE

This part of the project will show you how to edit an existing shape with the Path tools
and then save it as a new Custom Shape in your library.

1 Start by creating a new file that's **300×300** pixels.

2 Select the 5 Point Star shape in the Custom Shape
   palette pop-up library.

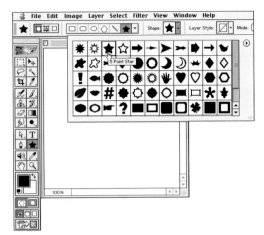

Select the 5 Point Star Custom Shape.

3 Draw out a large star shape in the center of the image
   window, holding down the Shift key to make sure
   it's an even shape with constrained proportions.

4 Select the Convert Point Tool from the Pen Tool
   pull-down on the Toolbar.

   To edit the points of this shape, they have to first be
   converted to anchor points with handles to create
   Bezier curves.

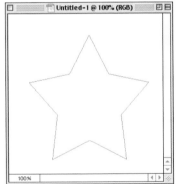

Draw out a perfect star in the center of
the image area.

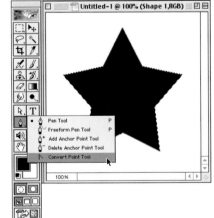

Select the Convert Point Tool from the Toolbar.

5 Begin the transformation with the inner anchor points. Click on one point and drag it out to the side so that an equidistant handle is perpendicular to the curve as shown.

Be sure to keep both sides of the anchor point handles equidistant from the curve to keep the curve as even as possible.

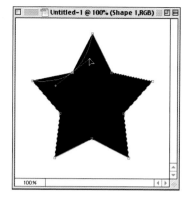

Click and drag out the anchor point to create an even curve.

6 Repeat this process all around the inside anchor points of the star. Make sure you drag out an even distance for each anchor point; otherwise, the end result will be uneven.

Note: If you see that your anchor-point edits are uneven, you can readjust the handles individually using the Direct Selection Tool from the Toolbar.

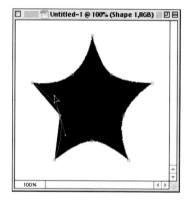

Repeat the anchor-point modification all around the inside points of the star.

7 Select the Direct Selection Tool from the Toolbar.

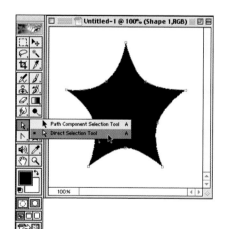

Select the Direct Selection Tool from the Toolbar.

8   Pull the inner anchor points out from the center
    of the star until the handles from the anchor points
    just touch the edge of the star as shown. Repeat all
    around the inner anchor points of the star.

    It's important that your initial edits be as similar as
    possible before attempting this step. If you need to
    tweak the original edits first, do so before continuing
    with this step.

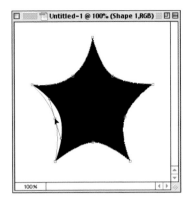

Pull the inner anchor points out
from the center of the star.

9   Re-select the Convert Point tool, click on one of the
    outer points on the star, and drag out the handles an
    equal distance. Only the tips of the star should start
    to take on a rounded shape, so don't pull them out
    too far.

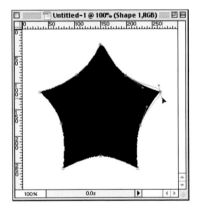

Click and drag out the outer anchor
points to create rounded tips on the star.

10 Once you're satisfied with the shape edits, save the
    shape for future use or distribution. Select Define
    Custom Shape from the Edit pull-down menu. Give
    the shape a unique name so that it's easily identifiable
    from the Custom Shapes palette.

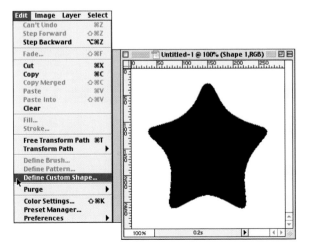

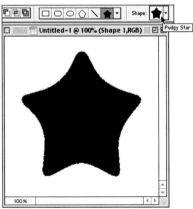

Save the edited star shape as a
new Custom Shape in the library.

CREATING A CUSTOM BRUSH FROM THE NEW CUSTOM SHAPE

Continuing with the new Custom Shape that was created, we will walk through the steps of creating a Custom Brush from this shape. Virtually anything that is visible on the image area of the file can be made into a Custom Brush. You'll learn more about creating Custom Brushes in Project 7.

1   Hide the original Shape layer and create a new layer. Select the new Custom Shape from the Shape Options palette. Draw out a small shape about the size of the Custom Brush you want to create, holding down the Shift key to keep the shape even.

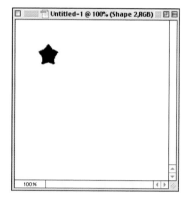

Draw out a small shape on a new layer; make it about the size of the Custom Brush you want to create.

2   Rasterize the new Shape layer in the Layer palette.

3   Select the Define Brush option from the Edit pull-down menu.

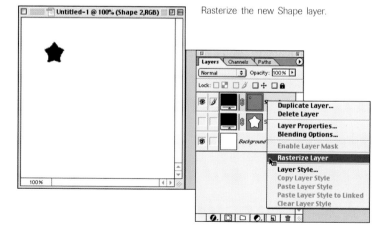

Rasterize the new Shape layer.

4 Set the spacing of the Custom Brush to 125%.

   This will dictate how often the brush will draw on
   the screen, associated to its pixel dimension.

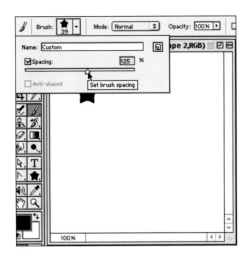

Set the spacing of the Custom Brush to 125%.

5 Hide or delete the new Shape layer and create a
   new layer. Select the Paintbrush tool with your new
   Custom Brush selected and draw out a line on the
   image area of the file.

   Notice how the brush only draws at equidistant
   spacing, as if it were on a string.

Draw out a squiggle line with the new Custom Paintbrush.

6 Apply a Custom Style to the layer to see the effect in
   3D. The Red Balloon Animals Style applied here can
   be found on the enclosed CD-ROM.

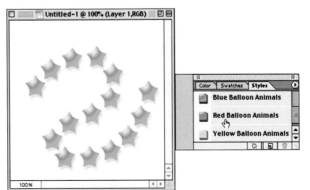

Apply a Custom Layer Style to the
layer to achieve a 3D effect.

7 To get a feel for the real usefulness of this technique, start with a new layer and apply the Blue Balloon Animals Custom Style to the empty layer.

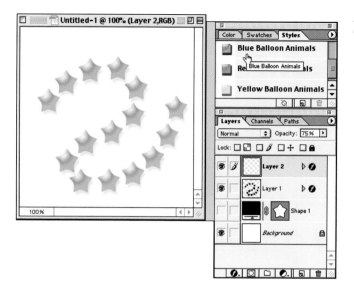

Apply the Blue Balloon Animals Custom Style to a new layer.

8 Use the same Custom Paintbrush to draw around on the layer and watch the 3D balloons appear on the screen as if you were dumping them out of a bag! Notice the transparency of the Custom Style over the lower layer with the red balloons on it.

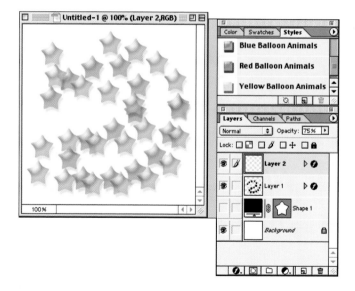

Draw out a string of balloons with the Custom Paintbrush.

9 Experiment with different-size Custom Brushes and shapes. Keep different Styles on different layers to create a cluster of balloons as shown.

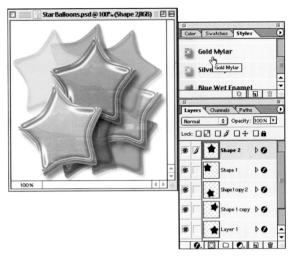

Create a cluster of balloons on separate layers with larger shapes.

CREATING A NEW CUSTOM SHAPE FROM A RASTERIZED LAYER IMAGE

Now it's time to come full circle from an outline-based shape to a rasterized Custom Brush and back to creating an outline-based shape. Just as you can make any shape on a layer a Custom Brush, you can take any rasterized image layer and create a Custom Shape from it. In this example, we'll simply paint a squiggle line on a layer and convert it to a scaleable outline Custom Shape.

1 Create a new layer on your test file (or start over with a new file of the same dimensions). Create a new layer and paint a squiggle line with the Paintbrush tool and a large, hard-edged brush. Load the layer opacity selection of the painted squiggle line by Cmd(Ctrl)+clicking on the layer in the Layers palette.

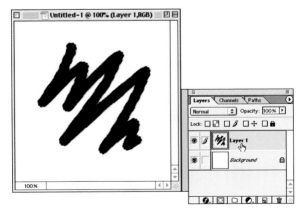

Paint a squiggle line on a new layer and load the layer opacity selection.

2 Make the Paths palette visible and select Make Work Path on the side pull-down menu.

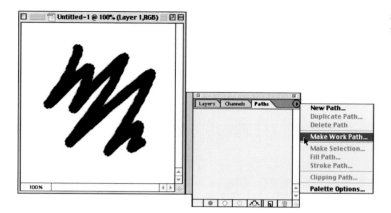

Select Make Work Path from the Paths palette.

3 Since the squiggle line was drawn with a hard-edged brush, set the Tolerance of the Work Path to **1.0** pixels.

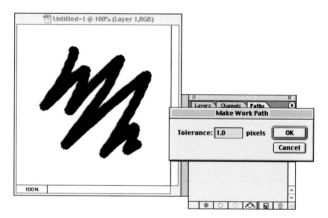

Set the Work Path Tolerance to 1.0 pixels.

4 Save and name the new Path as a Custom Shape by selecting the Define Custom Shape option from the Edit pull-down menu. Delete the Work Path after you have safely saved the Custom Shape.

5 Create a new layer and hide the original painted squiggle layer. Select the new Custom Shape from the Shape Tool option bar.

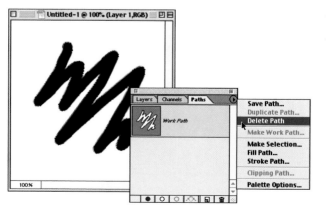

Save and name the new Path with the Define Custom Shape option, deleting the Work Path afterwards.

6 Test your new Custom Shape by drawing out various sizes with the Shape tool to see how it scales.

Draw out several copies of the new Custom Shape to see how it scales.

7 Hide the Shape tool outlines without rasterizing the layer by deselecting the Show Extras option from the View pull-down menu [or use Cmd(Ctrl)+H on your keyboard].

Hide the outlines of the Shape tool by selecting Cmd(Ctrl)+H.

8 Apply a Custom Style to the layer to see what the effect is on various sizes of the shape.

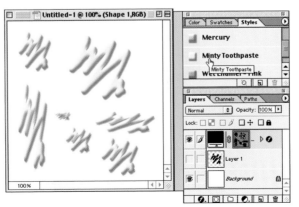

Apply a Custom Style to the shape layer to see its effect at different scales.

MODIFICATION

Have fun with the Custom Shapes when you're designing buttons or image maps for the Web. In just a few steps, a simple layout can take on a realistic new design for a "tasty" navigation panel. Life isn't always a box of chocolates.

1   Create a new file with the same dimensions as the test file. Draw out about four custom shapes resembling chocolate pieces, evenly-distributed inside the image window.

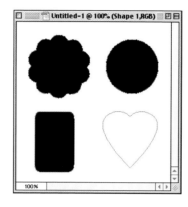

Create a new file and draw out four Custom Shapes to resemble chocolate pieces.

2   Apply one of the chocolate Custom Styles (available on the enclosed CD-ROM) to the Shape layer. In this case, the Crunch Bar Style was used. Rasterize the layer when you're done. (This can be done prior to applying the Custom Style if you prefer.)

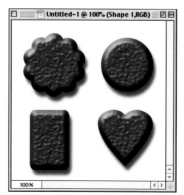

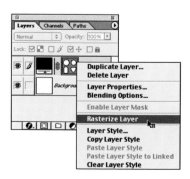

Apply a chocolate Custom Style to the shapes layer and rasterize the layer.

3 Create a new layer and load the transparency of the
   shapes layer. Fill the selection on the new layer with
   the foreground color.

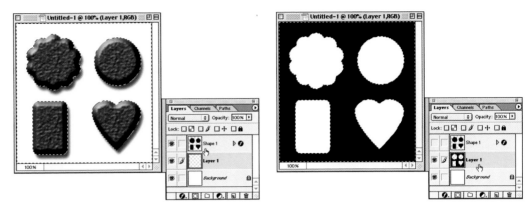

Create a new layer and load the transparency of the shapes layer.
Fill the selection on the new layer with the foreground color.

4 Apply the Gold Mylar Custom Style to the new layer
   to create a gold plastic insert for the chocolate box.
   The Style can be found on the enclosed CD-ROM.

Apply the Gold Mylar Custom Style (from the enclosed CD-ROM)
to the new layer to create the appearance of the chocolates
sitting in a gold plastic foil box insert.

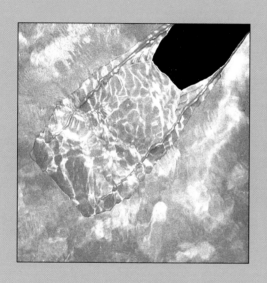

CREATING CUSTOM BRUSHES

"Do not go where the path may lead, go instead

where there is no path and leave a trail."

—RALPH WALDO EMERSON

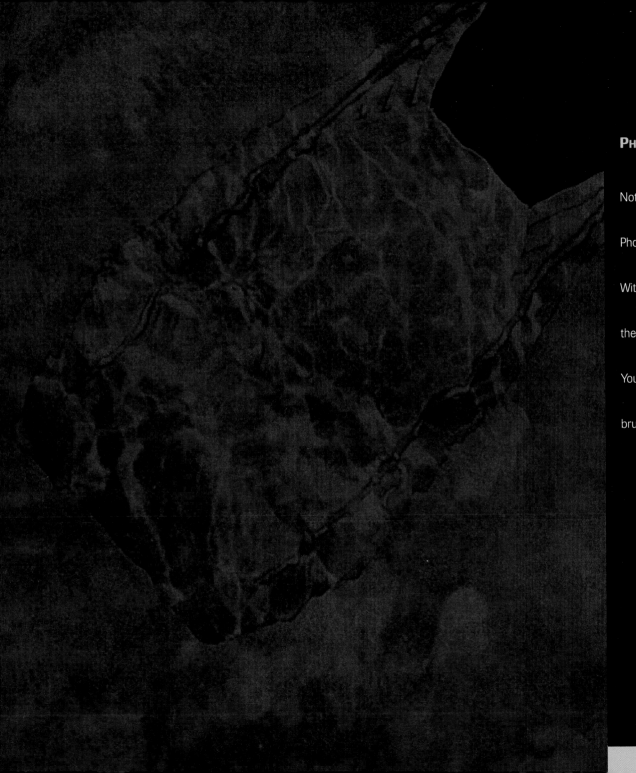

PHOTO BRUSHES

Not only has the Brush palette moved in

Photoshop 6, it's taken on a whole new look.

With this new look comes a new functionality—

the ability to define a custom brush any time.

You can turn almost any image into a custom

brush and save it to your custom library.

Project 7

Creating Custom Brushes

by Jeff Foster

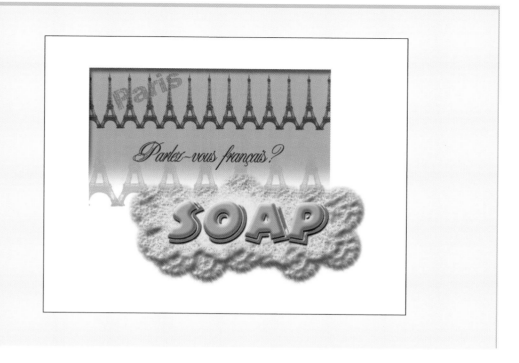

GETTING STARTED

Most of the brush features have remained the same; they've just been moved to the top Options bar. The Brush Selection palette itself is now a drop-down window in which literally hundreds of brushes can be available at any time. Custom brushes can be created with a single menu command, of whatever visible image is on the screen at the time, though it's converted to grayscale. There's more information about using the Brush Options bar and palette in Appendix A at the back of this book.

CREATING A CUSTOM BRUSH FROM AN IMAGE

Not all images are well suited to being used as a Custom Brush. Most images will need to be cropped or the object in the image will need to be isolated from the background in order to work well as a brush. We'll start with an image from the Samples folder that was installed with Photoshop 6 and then strip out an object from the image to use as a Custom Brush.

1   Open the file **EiffelTower.tif** from the Samples folder in Photoshop 6.

Note: Since the Define Brush command creates a grayscale image that will only "paint" the darkest areas (white is transparent), you will need to make sure the source image you are using has good detail and contrast. The basic shape of the image object needs to be dark because very dark shadows on the image will stand out more than the object itself.

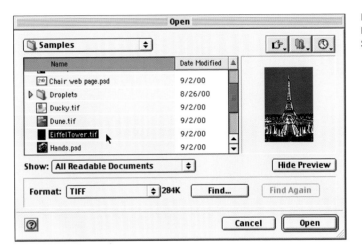

Locate and open the image EiffelTower.tif in the Photoshop 6 Samples folder.

2   Using the Lasso Selection tool with 0 pixel feathering, carefully outline the Eiffel Tower from the background image.

You can use the Option(Alt) key while holding down the mouse button to make the tool "snap" from point to point for smoother selection.

Select the Eiffel Tower from the background image.

3 Copy the selection, paste it to a new layer, and then hide the Background layer.

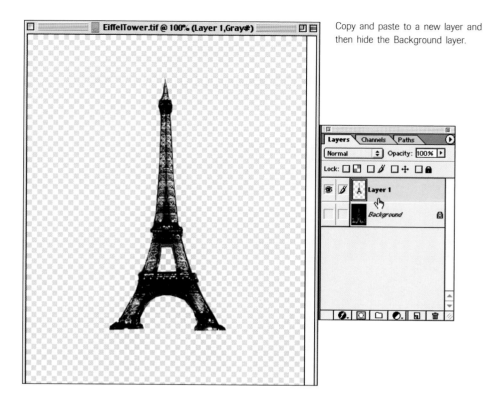

Copy and paste to a new layer and then hide the Background layer.

4 Select Define Brush to create a huge brush with the Eiffel Tower. This will demonstrate just how incredible this feature is!

Select Define Brush to create a huge Eiffel Tower brush.

5 Name the new Custom Brush.

Notice how the pixel size of the brush is displayed in the icon window of the brush. You will be prompted to set the spacing of the brush as well.

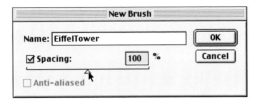

Set the spacing of the new Custom Brush.

6 Hide the pasted Eiffel Tower layer and create a new layer. Select the Paintbrush tool and choose the new Eiffel Tower brush.

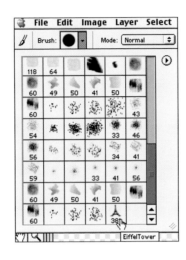

Select the new Eiffel Tower brush.

7 Test the brush on the new layer.

If you set the spacing of the brush to 100%, it should line up side by side automatically.

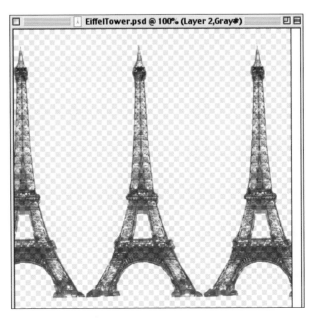

Apply the Custom Brush to the new layer to test it.

Note: You can edit the spacing of any brush by clicking on the icon in the Brush Options bar. Reset the spacing of the Eiffel Tower brush to 25% and apply the Paintbrush tool to the image again to see the effect that spacing has on the brush.

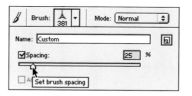

Edit the Custom Brush's spacing by clicking on the Brush icon in the Brush Options bar.

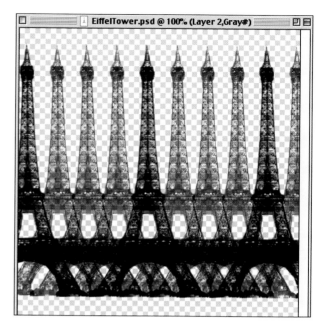

Apply the Custom Brush to the image again to see the change in spacing.

8   Duplicate the original Eiffel Tower layer. Using the Transform, Scale function, resize the duplicated image. Repeat the Define Brush process for each resizing to have a series of Eiffel Tower Custom Brushes.

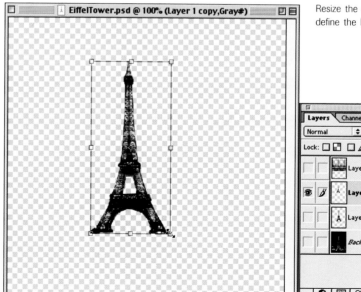

Resize the original Eiffel Tower layer and define the brushes for each resizing.

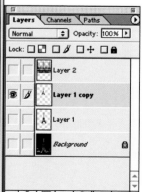

Experiment with different Custom Brush sizes and spacing on a blank layer or new file. Play with the brush fading options for unique effects as well. Imagine the cool borders and designs you can create using this technique!

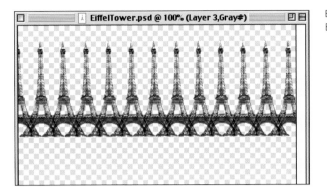

CREATING A RUBBER STAMP FROM ALTERED TEXT

You don't always need an image to create a Custom Brush. Brushes can be created from shapes but can also be created from text—or anything on a visible layer. In this section of the project, we'll create a "rubber stamp" from altered rasterized text.

1 Create a new file that's **300×200** pixels with a white background and place a large, block-text word in the center of the image window. For this example, use 72-point Arial Black.

Create a new 300×200-pixel file and insert 72-point Arial Black text in the middle.

2 Select Rasterize Layer by right-clicking on the text layer.

This will convert the text from an outline font to a rasterized pixel layer that can be easily modified.

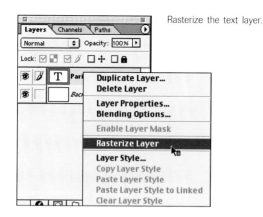

Rasterize the text layer.

3 Select the Eraser tool and choose the Rolled Rag – Cotton 120-pixel brush from the drop-down Brush Selection palette.

Note: The Rolled Rag-Cotton brush is not loaded with the default brushes. You will need to load Faux Finish Brushes.abr, which shipped with Photoshop 6.

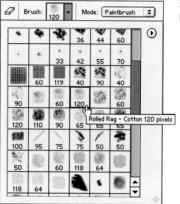

Select the Rolled Rag – Cotton 120-pixel brush Eraser tool.

4 Apply the Eraser tool to the rasterized text with only a couple of clicks.

The effect should look as if it were stamped onto a rough paper surface.

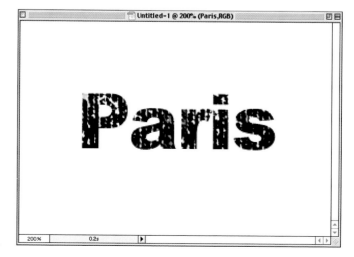

Apply the Eraser tool to the rasterized text.

5 Rotate the text layer about –30 degrees with the Transform, Rotate feature.

Rotate the text layer approximately –30 degrees.

6 Save the brush with the Define Brush option.

Using only the two Custom Brushes from this project, several designs can be derived—whether they're borders, backgrounds, buttons, or just graphic elements.

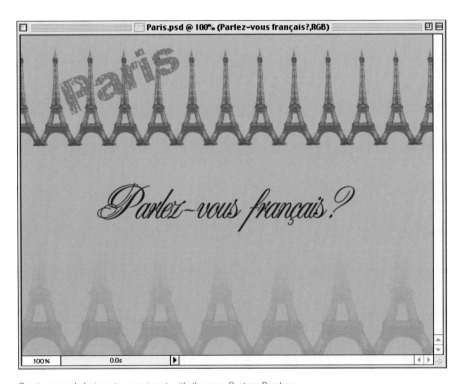

Create several designs to experiment with the new Custom Brushes.

MODIFICATION

Another "built-in" source for creating Custom Brushes is to use patterns.
Selecting a soft-edged sampling from a pattern will produce a wild new brush.
Apply a Custom Layer Style to the brush and get a 3D textured effect.

1   Create a new file that's **150×150** pixels. Fill the
    background with the built-in Wrinkles Pattern.

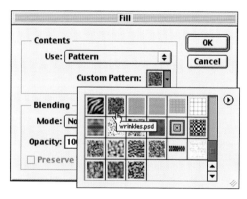

Create a new 150×150-pixel file and
fill it with the Wrinkles Pattern.

2   Using the Elliptical Selection tool with a 5-pixel
    Feathered edge, make a large circular selection in
    the center of the image window. Be sure to stay far
    enough away from the edges of the image window
    so as not to create a hard, flat edge.

Use the Elliptical Selection tool with a 5-pixel Feather to
select a circular selection in the middle of the image.

3   Copy and paste the selection to a new layer, hiding
    the Background layer, and select Define Brush.

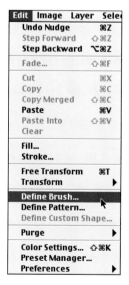

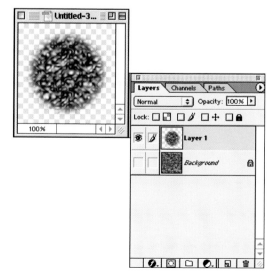

Copy and paste the selection to a
new layer and select Define Brush.

Experiment by painting with the new Custom Brush using different colors. Notice the transparency in the "white" spaces of the original pattern. Apply a Custom Layer Style to the brush on a layer and discover a whole new world of 3D brushes!

Use ImageReady to make the foam appear on the screen randomly or animate some text over it for a great opener to your Web site.

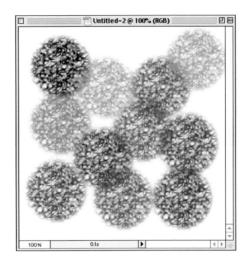

Painting with different colors using the Custom Brush.

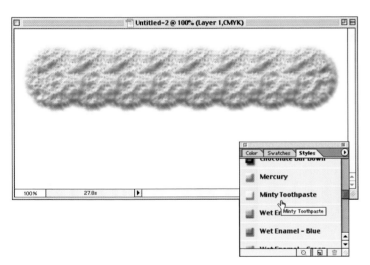

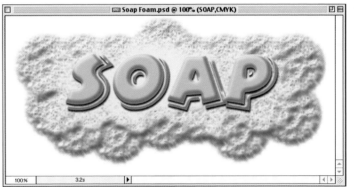

Experiment with different patterns, colors, and Custom Layer Styles to create new and exciting design elements.

Apply a Custom Layer Style to the brush on a layer.

WORKING WITH PHOTOS— RETOUCHING AND PAINTING WITH STYLES

"Old age is not so bad when

you consider the alternatives."

—MAURICE CHEVALIER

EVERYTHING NEW IS OLD AGAIN!

Sometimes a digital camera shot is so bad that

the only way to salvage it is by "aging" it. This

is a great effect to use when you have several

different sources providing photos of varying

quality and you need to provide consistency

while creating a mood for your composition.

Working with Photos— Retouching and Painting with Styles

by Jeff Foster

GETTING STARTED

With architectural shots in general, even professional photographers can't always get in the best position to capture a large building without it looking like it's a mile away. A couple of simple corrective "tweaks" in Photoshop can cure the tilting building syndrome!

CHANGING THE PERSPECTIVE (REPOSITIONING THE CAMERA)

In this case, the building is too far away and is "leaning in" toward the middle of the picture. To correct this image, you'll use the Transform Perspective and Scale tools.

1 Open your digital photo (or the one provided for you on the enclosed CD-ROM, titled **Theater.jpg**, in the Sample Images folder) and duplicate the background layer.

This will enable you to reference back to the original image as needed and will also enable you to apply Transformations to the layer.

Note: It's always a good idea to duplicate the original image to another layer—especially if you are working with an original image. This way, if anything goes wrong, you won't risk losing your original image.

Open your digital photo and duplicate the background.

2 Choose Edit, Transform, Perspective. Using the handles on the bounding box, click and drag them until the vertical lines of the building are aligned with the edges of the window.

You may choose to scale the image so the subject is centered inside the window frame. Resize the window of your image if necessary to give you room to pull the corners out past the outside edges.

Click and drag the Transform Perspective and Scale box to correct the image angle and size.

TRANSFORMING THE IMAGE TO SEPIA TONE

To give the photo image an aged look, we'll completely shift the color range over to a Sepia Tone. This will help make an oversaturated and contrasty photo look more natural in the aging process.

Note: If you are working with a digital camera, you may have noticed that there are a multitude of potential problems with the images you take, ranging from saturation to over/underexposure, contrast, color-shift, white point balance, and worst of all, JPEG compression damage. This technique might just help cover some of that up!

1   Choose Image, Adjust, Hue/Saturation.

2   To create the Sepia Tone effect, the colors need to be shifted from the original RGB. To do this, select Colorize and set the Hue to 30 and Saturation to 30.

3   Select the Burn tool. Choose the Soft Round 200-pixel brush; set the Range to Shadows and the Exposure to 50%.

Because this image was not evenly exposed, some minor corrections need to be made to the building to enhance the details and provide more contrast.

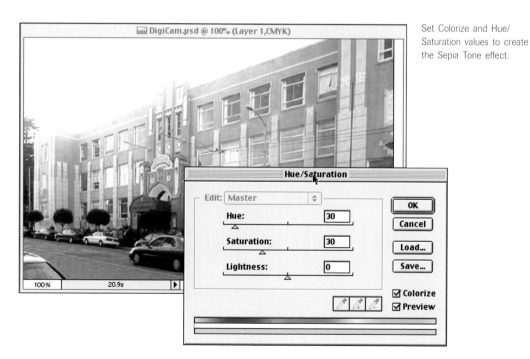

Set Colorize and Hue/ Saturation values to create the Sepia Tone effect.

4   Carefully and evenly apply the Burn tool to the image until you achieve the desired exposure effect.

5   With the Clone tool, do some final cleanup of the image.

Use this tool sparingly to get rid of imperfections in the image. It takes some practice to become proficient with the Clone tool and to create effects that can't be easily detected.

In this image, the car in the foreground can easily be removed. In addition, you need to clean up the top edges of the building.

Note: When cloning over an unwanted image, always plan your moves before executing. Look ahead to where you will sample your image material from and make sure you don't cause a worse problem by repeating a pattern over and over.

The Burn tool applied to the image.

Clean up the image using the Clone tool from the Tools palette.

AGE THE PHOTO AND CREATE A BORDER

To further enhance the aging effect, a border with emulsion cracks and folds
will be added to the image. This effect will appear as if the photo has seen many
years of handling. You'll start off this section by resizing the canvas so you
can add a border to the photo, and then you'll work with layer styles and a
paintbrush to add the aging.

1 On Layer 1, choose Select All and copy and paste to
   a new layer (Layer 2). Activate Layer 1 and fill the
   background with white.

2 Choose Image, Canvas Size and increase by at least
   50 pixels in both Width and Height, keeping the
   anchor point in the center of the image. This will
   create a white border around the image.

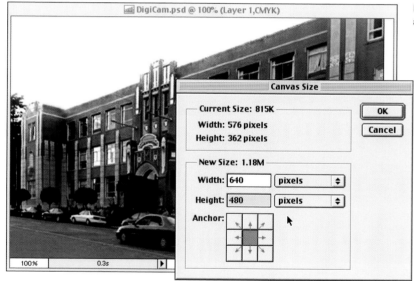

Resize the Canvas to create
a border around the image.

108

3   Activate Layer 2 (with the Sepia image on it). Open the Drop Shadow Layer Style and apply the default settings to the image edges.

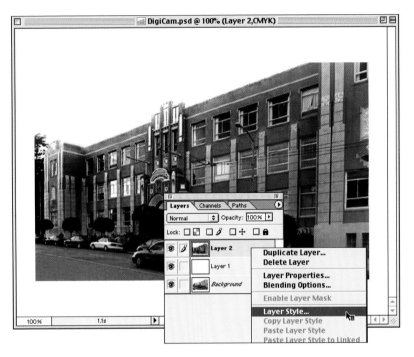

Select Layer Style on Layer 2.

4   Open the Bevel and Emboss Layer Style and use the following settings for the image edges:

Style: **Inner Bevel**

Technique: **Chisel Hard**

Depth: **100%**

Size: **1 px**

Shading Angle: **–160°**

Use Global Light: **Unchecked**

Shading Altitude: **70°**

5   Select the Eraser tool and choose the Chalk 60-pixel brush.

Note: The Chalk brush is not loaded with the default set of brushes. You will need to load Faux Finish Brushes.abr, which shipped with Photoshop 6.

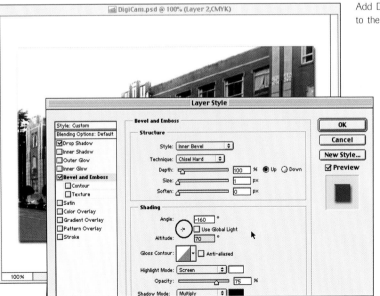

Add Drop Shadow and Bevel to the image edges.

6 Apply the Eraser brush sparingly around the edges of the image to produce a "worn" effect.

> **Note:** Since these steps are subjective in nature, a bit of practice will ensure the desired final effect along the edges. Don't remove too much material; otherwise, it will be too obvious that you overworked the image.

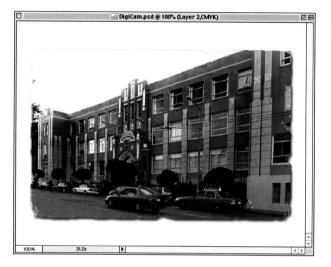

Apply the Eraser brush around the edges to achieve a "worn" effect.

7 Create and activate a new layer (Layer 3) above the Sepia image layer (Layer 2).

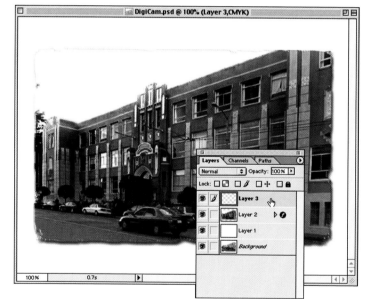

Create a new layer on top of the Sepia layer.

8   With the Hard Round 1-pixel paintbrush and the foreground set to White, draw some "cracked" lines across the image at varying angles.

Use some of the "worn" edges as a guide and draw your lines freehand.

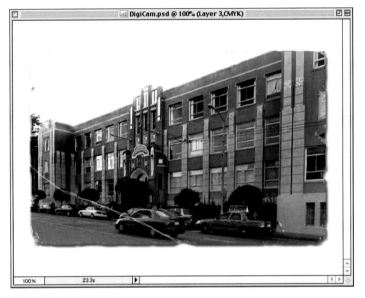

Draw "cracks" in the emulsion with the Paintbrush tool.

9   Select the Lasso tool with the Feather set to 0 and Anti-Aliased turned on. Draw a selection around one of the "corners" you've outlined with the 1-pixel Paintbrush tool.

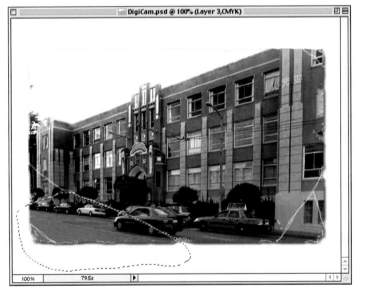

Draw a selection around a corner with the Lasso tool.

10 Select the Airbrush tool and choose a 100–200 pixel Soft Round brush in Normal mode with 7% Pressure and the color set to White. Airbrush along the inside edges of the selected area to achieve a lighting effect on the cracked corner. Do this for all cracked corners.

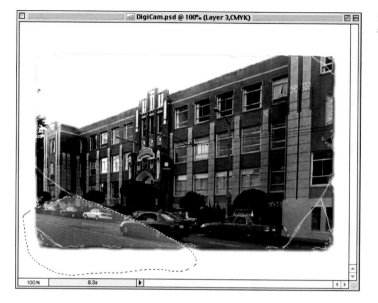

Paint with a 100-pixel soft Airbrush to achieve a cracked-corner effect.

11 Set the layer's Opacity to approximately 50%.

This will soften the effect of the cracked emulsion and make it appear more realistic.

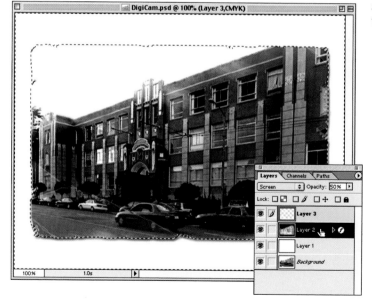

Set the Layer 3 Opacity to 50% for a more subtle effect.

12 Load the selection of the transparency of Layer 2. With Layer 3 activated, delete the contents of the selected area on Layer 3.

This will remove any white Paintbrush or Airbrush "overspray" that was applied outside of the Sepia image area (painting outside the lines).

13 Deselect the live selection. Create a new layer on top of the layers in the Layers palette.

Remove the "overspray" from the outside area of the image.

14 Select a Soft 17-pixel paintbrush. Apply the Emulsion Wrinkle style, which can be found in the Custom Styles library on the accompanying CD-ROM or can be downloaded from the book's Web site: **http://www.photoshopwebmagic.com**.

Selecting the Emulsion Wrinkle Custom Style.

113

Be careful to apply very little amounts to the image because this Style has a very wide spread on it—about 200% of the size of the brush. Also, pay attention not to get outside the "card" image area.

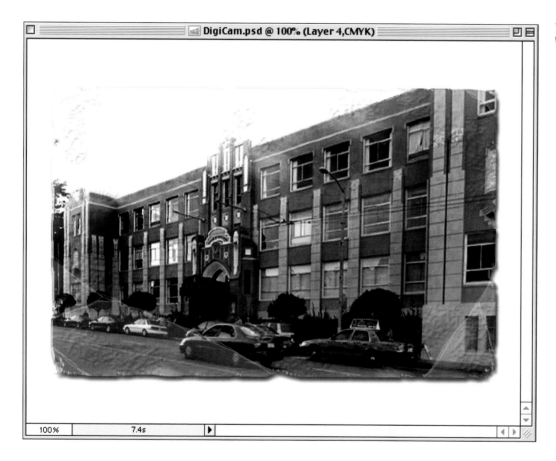

The final image with the Emulsion Wrinkle Custom Style applied.

DigiCam.psd @ 100% (Layer 4,CMYK)

100%   7.4s

MODIFICATIONS

With a bit of practice and additional photos, you can make a composite image using antique cars and figures if you so desire. Apply this technique to old family photos or very modern images to create an artistic, "museum-quality" effect.

These images were created using the same effects layers as the image in this project, but adding the car photos underneath the effects layers and colorizing them disguises the digital camera effect.

WARPED IMAGES FOR
IMAGE MAP ANIMATION

"Reality is merely an illusion,

albeit a very persistent one."

—ALBERT EINSTEIN

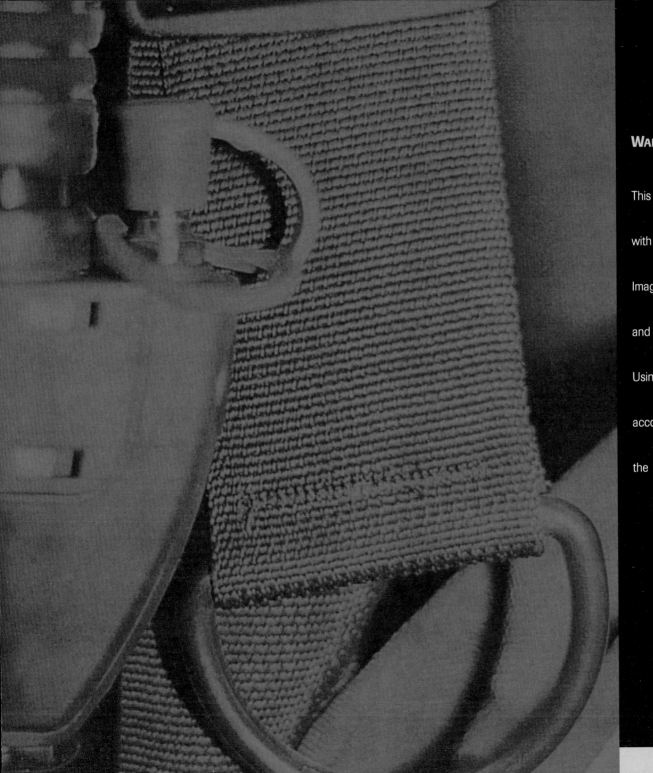

WARPING IMAGES FOR ANIMATION

This is a fun way to create an image map

with rollovers and animation. Using Adobe

ImageReady, you can slice up a larger image

and specify animation slices and rollovers.

Using the sample "Carnival" image on the

accompanying CD-ROM, you'll want to get off

the rides once you're done with this project!

Project 9

Warped Images for Image Map Animation

by Jeff Foster

GETTING STARTED

Although this project in its entirety is most likely way too busy to actually use on a Web site, it will get you to think about how you can apply individual techniques from it to your own design. It incorporates the Liquify command and Custom Layer Styles effects to make bubbles warp when you roll over them and "pop" when you click on them.

CREATING THE BUBBLES FOR THE HOT SPOTS

The first part of this project is to create the bubbles on the rollover points of the image. This will be done by filling circular shapes on layers and applying the Custom Layer Styles effects. The Liquify command will be applied to each area on the main image to create various warping techniques.

118

1　Open the sample image **Carnival.tif** on the enclosed CD-ROM and create a new layer. Using the Elliptical Marquee tool, draw a circle large enough to cover an area on the photo where you want to place a hot spot.

Open the sample "Carnival" image on the CD-ROM and create a circular selection on a new layer.

2　Fill the selection on the new layer with the foreground color. (The color doesn't matter at this point, as it will be overwritten with a Custom Style later.) Don't deselect the selection.

Fill the selection on the new layer with the foreground color.

3 Using the Marquee tool, continue creating new layers and filling new hot spots. When completed, deselect the active selection.

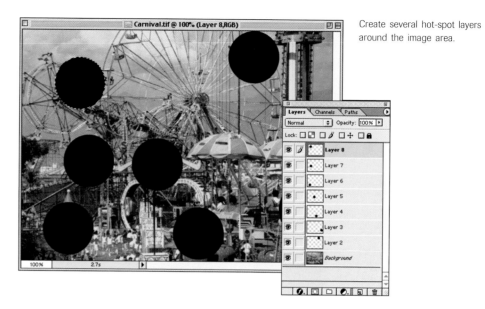

Create several hot-spot layers around the image area.

4 Apply the Clear Glass Tubing Style from the Custom Styles library to each of the circular shapes on the hot-spot layers.

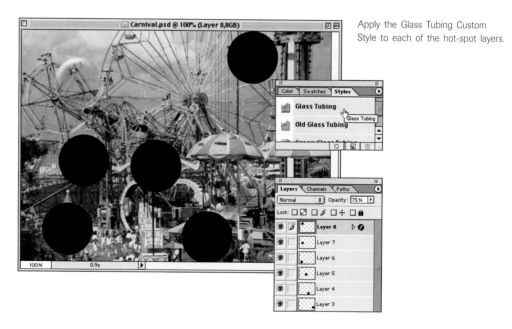

Apply the Glass Tubing Custom Style to each of the hot-spot layers.

5 Continue applying the Glass Tubing Style until all the spots are covered.

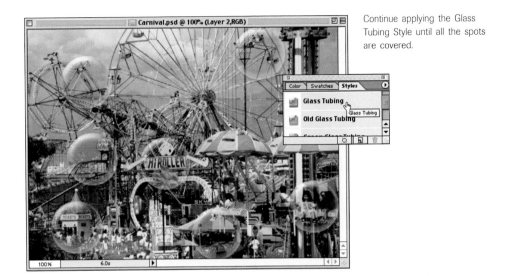

Continue applying the Glass Tubing Style until all the spots are covered.

6 Hide all of the spot layers except one. Duplicate the Background layer and select the Liquify command.

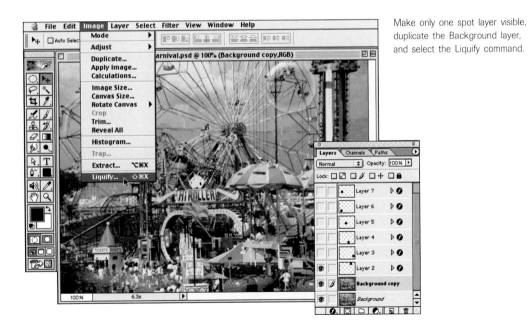

Make only one spot layer visible, duplicate the Background layer, and select the Liquify command.

7 Select one of the Warping tools and apply it in stages in the area where the spot layer sits.

In this example, the Bloat tool is being used with a 100-pixel brush.

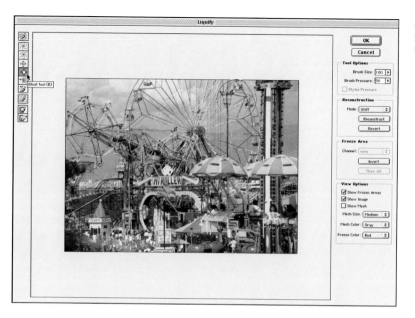

Apply the warping tool to the areas directly beneath the hot spots.

8 Repeat the process in the same area—first duplicating the Background Copy layer and then applying a little more of the Warping tool.

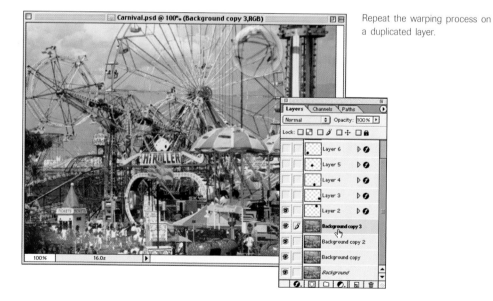

Repeat the warping process on a duplicated layer.

9　Clean up each of the warped layers, removing the unnecessary image areas, to help keep the file size down. Choose Select All and then use the Rectangular Marquee tool to deselect just outside the warped area. Press the Delete key when ready.

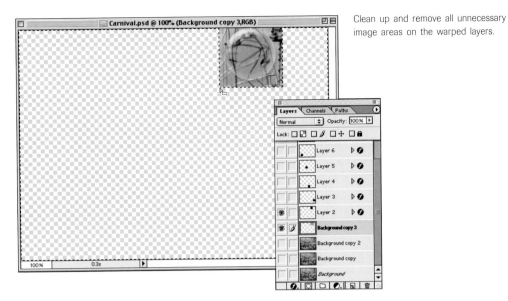

Clean up and remove all unnecessary image areas on the warped layers.

ORGANIZING THE LAYERS INTO GROUPS

Because you will be creating lots of similar-looking layers in this project, it is a good idea to take a moment to start organizing them into groups. They all will be individually selected later in Adobe ImageReady, so it's important to know which is which at that time. You will want to keep the warped image layers together with their associated bubble layer. The first step will be to start naming the layers in each group with something meaningful to the project—and its layer order in an animation sequence.

1 Name the bubble hot-spot layer to which you just applied the image warping.

In this example, I used a spelled-out number for my hot spots (one–seven) and numeric naming for the warp layer order in its animation sequence (1–3). So the first frame of animation sequence (the first warped image layer on the first hot-spot bubble layer that I used) would be called "one–1."

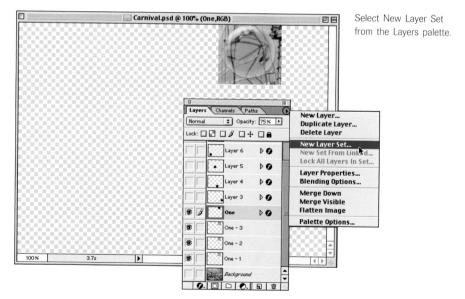

Name the layers so you can figure out in what animation sequence the layer order will be.

2 After you've named a "set" of layers (the animation sequences to the hot-spot layer), select New Layer Set from the side pull-down menu on the Layers palette. This will create a folder on the Layers palette to make organizing sets of layers much easier.

Select New Layer Set from the Layers palette.

3 Drag all of the layers into the new Layer Set folder on the Layers palette.

You can now turn all of the layers in the Layer Set on or off (making them visible or invisible, respectively) by clicking the Eye icon on the Layers palette.

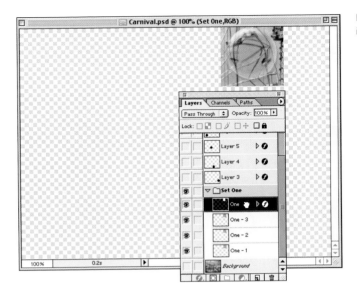

Drag all of the associated layers into the new Layer Set folder.

4 Continue the warp/distortion process by repeating Steps 6–9 of the preceding section for each hot-spot layer. Make the effect interesting by mixing up the Warp tool styles on each selection.

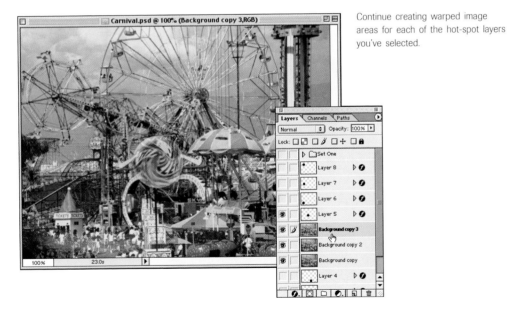

Continue creating warped image areas for each of the hot-spot layers you've selected.

5 When each hot-spot area is completed, remove the excess image area and organize the layers in the associated Layer Sets.

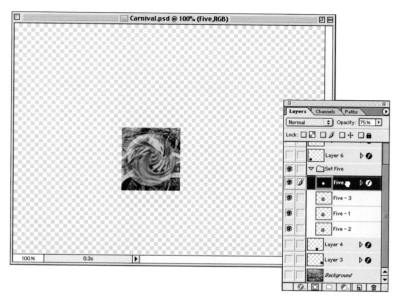

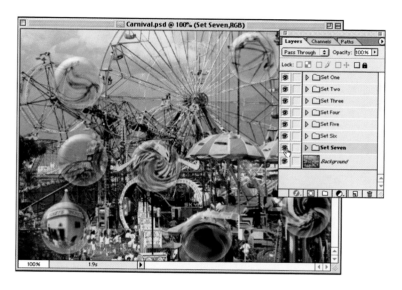

Remove excess image areas and coordinate layers in their Layer Sets.

6 After all the hot spots and their associated warped image layers are organized into corresponding Layer Sets, choose Jump to, Adobe ImageReady 3.0.

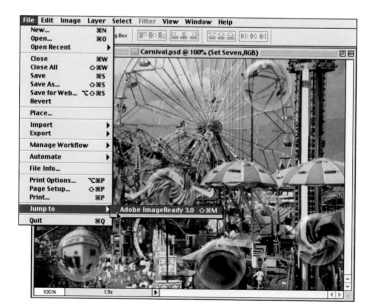

Jump to Adobe ImageReady 3.0 after all files are completed and organized.

CREATING AN IMAGE MAP WITH ROLLOVERS AND SLICES

It used to be a painstaking process to align all the images and rollovers necessary for making a seamless-looking Image Map in table form. The difference between this process and an actual Image Map is that, while an Image Map is one image with hot spots coded into it, this process is several images built into a table with rollover sequences assigned to each slice you choose. The end product is then saved out as an incredible array of images with an HTML document to drive it.

1   Once the image is open in ImageReady, select the Slice tool and draw a square around each of the hot spots.

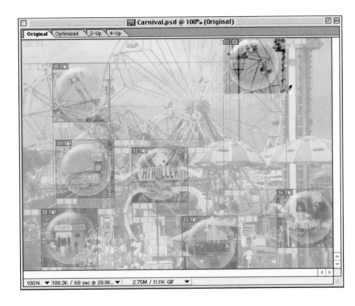

Draw areas around the hot spots with the Slice tool.

2 Name each of the Slices that correspond to the hot-spot names. Enter the name in the Slice options bar and enter the corresponding URL if applicable. (A URL is not needed to test the animation or rollover sequences.)

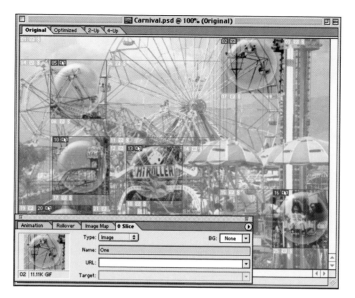

Name each of the hot-spot Slices.

3 For each rollover, click inside the Slice with the Slice Selector tool. Open the Rollover Options bar and make the corresponding layers visible for the normal (mouse off) mode.

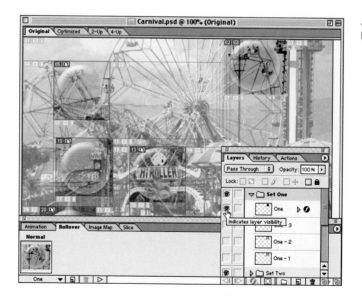

Assign the corresponding "mouse off" layers to the rollover Slice.

4   Add a rollover state on the Options bar and select the image layers associated with that state.

In this example, I only used the Normal, Over, and Down rollover states.

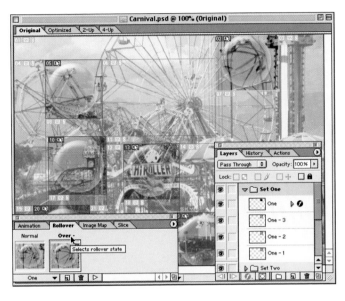

Assign the corresponding rollover image layers to the Over state.

5   Add another rollover state and select the corresponding Down state image layers.

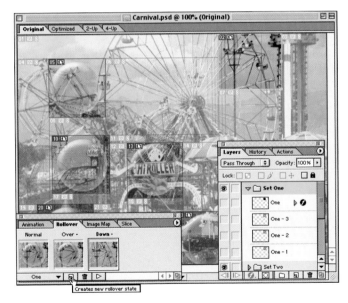

Assign the corresponding "mouse down" image layers to the Down state.

6 Preview the rollover actions for each state in the browser of your choice by selecting Preview In and then selecting a browser.

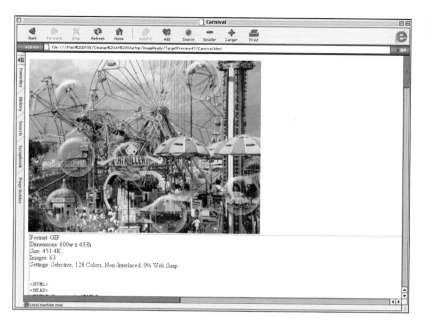

Preview the rollover states in the browser of your choice.

7 Once satisfied with the functionality of the rollovers, repeat the layer-assignment process with the remaining Slices and rollover states. Save your finished work as an HTML (HTM) file. Run locally from your hard drive in your browser to make sure all the pieces are saved correctly and are in working order.

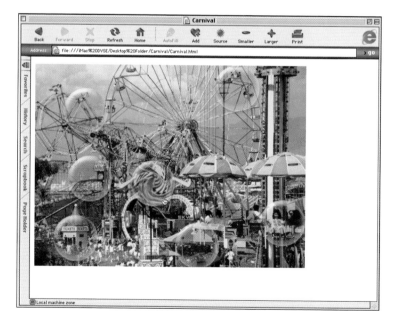

View locally in a browser to do a final check.

MODIFICATION

I struggled with leaving this portion of the chapter in, but I decided to at the last minute for those of you who dare to venture into no man's land. On a smaller scale, this would actually be a nice touch. It proved to be quite a task for the browser to run animations *and* follow the rollovers at the same time—though it still looked pretty cool (albeit not for the queasy). Animation frames were added to the image, and by selecting different animation sequences to be visible at alternating times, it appeared as though the image was "bubbling" when there were no mouse-over events.

The final project is on the enclosed CD-ROM, as is the final HTML document should you want to investigate this process further and apply it in a subtler manner.

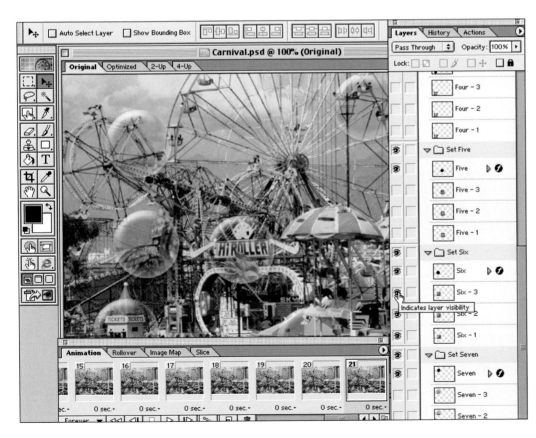

Creating a mass of animations concurrently with the rollovers—quite a woozy effect!

ANIMATING WITH LIGHT

"Each problem that I solved became a rule which

served afterwards to solve other problems."

—RENE DESCARTES

USING STYLES TO ANIMATE 3D TEXT

Animation doesn't always have to involve

moving objects, patterns, or text. Sometimes

the animation can come from the light source

in the scene. This is useful for creating a

catchy logo treatment, making announcements,

building image map rollovers, or just plain fun!

Project 10

Animating with Light

by Jeff Foster

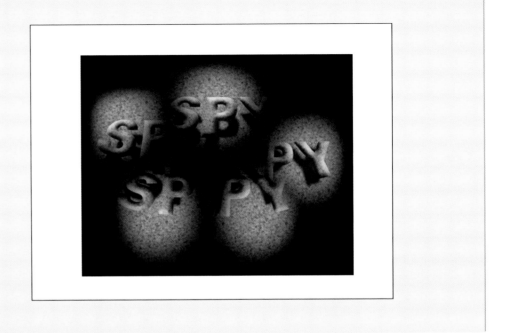

GETTING STARTED

The purpose of this project is to create an animated effect using the "light source" in the Layer Styles effects option. Text will be created with a custom pattern background of similar material, but when the Style is applied—and then modified with ImageReady and animated—the effect is spectacular! This effect works on large and small text as well as any 3D object.

CREATING THE TEXT TO BE ANIMATED

The font you choose for this exercise will be a critical part of making the effect work.

1   Create a new **300×300**-pixel file. Select the Text tool; choose a large, bold font; and type a short word in the middle of the file.

Create a 300-pixel image and add large, bold text.

2   Click the Create Warped Text button in the Text options bar to apply a text warp. Set the Style to Shell Lower and the Bend to +35%.

3   On the new text layer, add a Drop Shadow Layer Style:

Blend Mode: **Multiply, Black**

Opacity: **75%**

Angle: **130°**

Use Global Light: **Checked**

Distance: **35 px**

Spread: **0%**

Size: **5 px**

Warp the text for an enhanced 3D effect.

Selecting the Layer Style option on the text layer.

4   To create the illusion that the text is floating above the background, the shadow should be created a lengthy distance beneath the text.

Note: Most of your shadow settings will move and follow the "light source" when you start the animation process in ImageReady, so make sure your shadows look visually appropriate for the text to which you're applying them.

Create a Drop Shadow for a "floating text" effect.

5   With the Layer Style window still active, enable Pattern Overlay and choose a custom texture that has a tight pattern to it so that, when applied to the text, it is still legible.

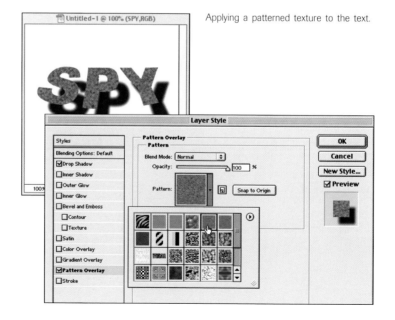

Applying a patterned texture to the text.

6 Enable the Bevel and Emboss option and apply a broad, smooth Inner Bevel. Click OK when you're satisfied with the effects, but do not Rasterize the layer.

The amounts shown here may be too much or too little, depending on the font, size, and style of text you've chosen. You will have to make adjustments to your size and soften amounts.

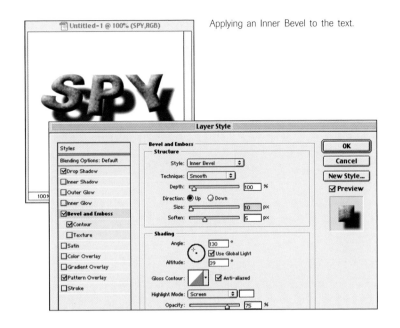

Applying an Inner Bevel to the text.

7 Activate the Background layer. Choose Edit, Fill, Use Pattern and choose a pattern or texture.

The same pattern as applied to the text was used in this example.

The 3D text now appears as if it is floating above the background with the light source coming from the upper-left corner of the screen.

The text appears as if it's floating off the background.

CREATING THE LIGHT SOURCE

To make this effect more intriguing and believable, a mock light source will be added to simulate a flashlight moving around on the image.

1   Create a new **600×600**-pixel file with a transparent background.

2   Fill the background with black. Select the Eraser tool and choose the Soft Round 200-pixel brush set to 100% Opacity.

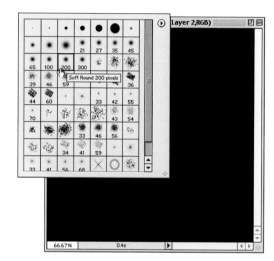

Fill with black and select the Eraser tool.

3   With the Eraser tool, simply click once or twice in the very center of the image screen.

This will create a soft transparent "hole" in the middle of the image.

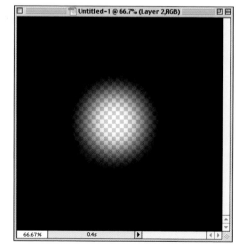

Use the Eraser tool to create a "hole" in the image.

4   Copy the entire layer to the clipboard and return to
    the original 3D text file.

    Paste the image onto the top of the text layer and
    center the "flashlight" in the middle of the image
    window. Save your file in Photoshop (PSD) format,
    keeping the Layers.

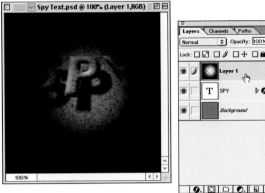

Copy the image layer and return
to the 3D text file.

MAKING IT ALL "MOVE"

Thanks to Adobe for making ImageReady work in harmony with Photoshop!
All your Style settings and layer options stay attached and ready to modify in
this animation.

1   Jump to Adobe ImageReady 3.0.

Note: Because this process is really straight forward
and can be used to create just a few frames of
animation for a rollover or a continuous loop, you might
experiment with smaller animations until you get the
hang of coordinating the light layer with the angle of
light/shadow on the Style option.

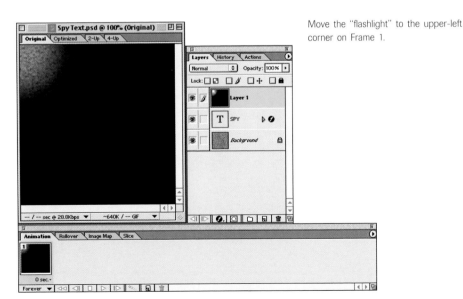

Move the "flashlight" to the upper-left
corner on Frame 1.

2   On Frame 1 of the animation, select the Move tool
    and click and drag the top "flashlight" layer to the
    upper-left corner as shown.

3   For each new frame of your animation, select New
    Frame from the side arrow pull-down menu on the
    Animation palette.

4 Slowly move the "flashlight" layer with the Move tool toward the type on the text layer.

The amount of movement you make will dictate the speed of the animation, but be careful of the file size if you add too many frames.

In addition to moving the "flashlight" layer on each frame, you will need to move the highlights and shadows on the type in the text layer.

5 For the first frame, select the Drop Shadow Layer Style from the Layers palette. Change the angle of the light source so that it follows the movement of the "flashlight" layer.

6 Continue this process of going back and forth between the "flashlight" layer and the Global Angle setting on the text layer, making sure to adjust both for each frame of the animation.

You can click on other frames to quickly check that the motion between frames is smooth.

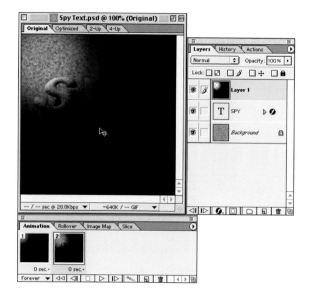

Moving the "flashlight" layer toward the center of the type for each frame in the animation.

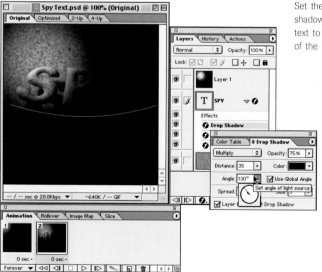

Set the Global Angle of the shadow/light source on the text to follow the movement of the "flashlight" layer.

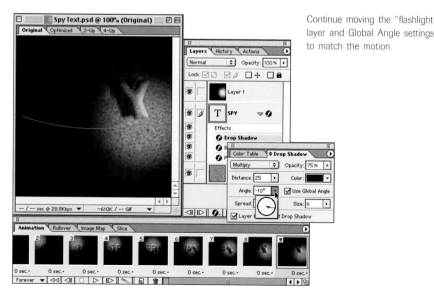

Continue moving the "flashlight" layer and Global Angle settings to match the motion.

7   Select Preview in Browser to view your animation.

You can make adjustments to motion, angle, color depth, and even timing of each frame. Simply jump back to the Browser Preview to see the updates live.

8   Once you've made all the modifications and timing adjustments, select Save Optimized As with the file type and compression settings on the Options palette.

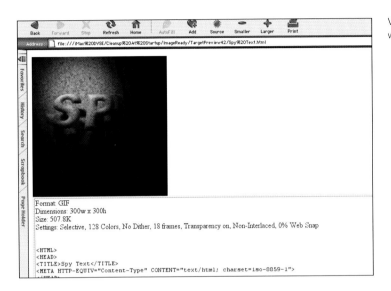

Viewing the final animation with modifications.

MODIFICATION

There are so many variations you can apply this effect process to. From animated spotlights to highlights, the possibilities are truly endless!

In this modification, I used the Big sky.psd image from the Adobe Photoshop 6.0 Samples folder. The Lens Flair plug-in was applied to the image and text was added, with the Warp Text Flag style applied. The Custom Layer Style, Glass Jar was applied, from the PS6WM Styles.asl library in the Custom Presets folder on the enclosed CD-ROM. The Drop Shadow and Emboss highlight angles were changed to match the light source in the image to create a "heavenly" appearance in the design.

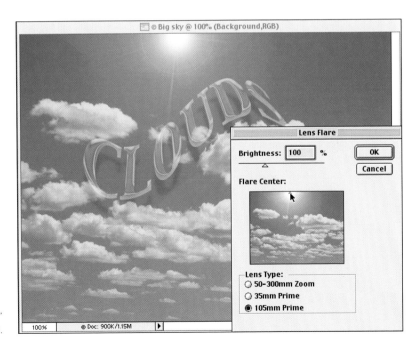

Using the Lens Flair plug-in to determine the "light source" in an image will lend a sense of realism to the design.

ANIMATING TEXT
ON A CURVE

"Whenever you are asked if you can do

a job, tell 'em, 'Certainly, I can!' Then

get busy and find out how to do it."

—THEODORE ROOSEVELT

RUBBER BAND TEXT

One of the coolest new features in the Text

Tool palette is the capability to put text on a

curve and then distort it. Because it works

with the outline data of the font, it remains a

clean vector image until it is rasterized after

it's warped. This project will explore the Warp

Text features and provide a snappy 3D

animation sequence!

Animating Text on a Curve

by Jeff Foster

GETTING STARTED

There are many ways to use the Warp Text feature, but this project will focus primarily on one. You'll have a blast experimenting with all of them!

WARPING THE TEXT

In this project, we will warp the text in different stages to prepare it for animation in ImageReady. The effect will be that of a rubber band stretching and then letting go with a snap.

1   Create a new file that is **500×200** pixels and fill the
    background with black.

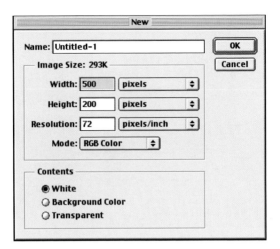

Create a new file that's 500×200 pixels.

2   Select the Text tool and a large sans-serif font. Type
    in your message, centered in the screen, and allow for
    plenty of room on all sides to warp the text.

    (48-point Arial Black was used in this project.)

3   Click the Create Warped Text icon and set the Style
    to Bulge and the Bend amount to 50%.

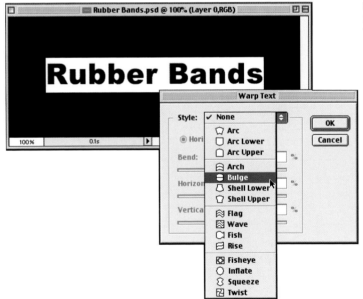

Select a large font and type
in a word, and select a Warp
Text tool from the Text bar.

To create the desired animation, several sequences need to be created on separate layers. This first image will be the extreme outward distortion of the animation sequence, so only change the amount of Bend (not the Horizontal or Vertical Distortion modes).

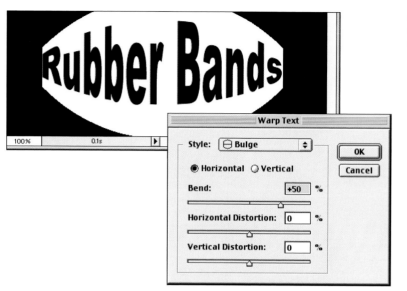

Adjust the amount of distortion for a frame of animation.

4 Select "Rubber Band" from the Custom Layer Styles library.

Note: The Custom Layer Styles library can be found on the accompanying CD-ROM or can be downloaded from the *Photoshop 6 Web Magic* Web site at **http://www.photoshopwebmagic.com**.

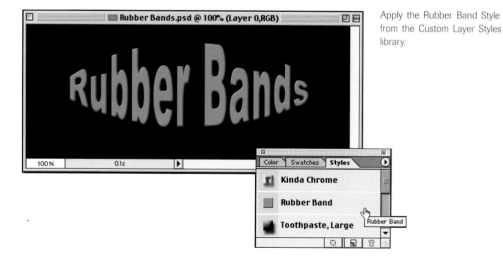

Apply the Rubber Band Style from the Custom Layer Styles library.

5 Duplicate the text layer, select the text on the new layer, and with the Warp Text tool, set the Bend to +30%.

This will be the next step of distortion in the animation sequence.

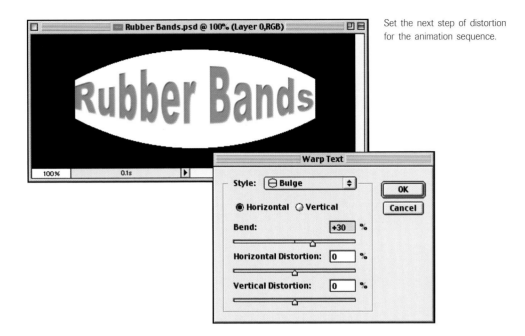

Set the next step of distortion for the animation sequence.

6 Repeat Step 6 but set the Bend to +10%.

This will be another step in the sequence.

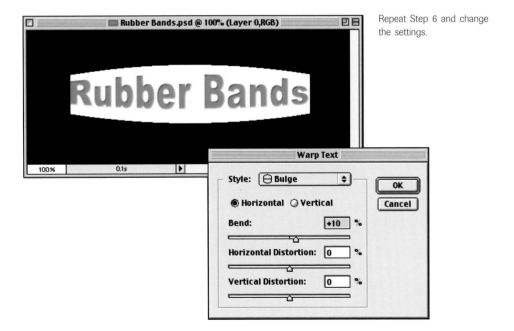

Repeat Step 6 and change the settings.

7 Repeat Step 7 but set Warp Text to None.

8 Duplicate the layer in Step 7 and set the Bend amount to −10%.

Repeat Step 7 and set Warp Text to None.

9 Repeat Step 7 one more time and set the Bend amount to −30%.

10 Duplicate the −10% distorted layer and select Motion Blur. When prompted to Rasterize the duplicated text layer, click Yes.

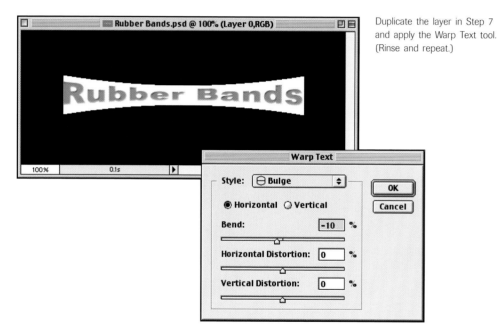

Duplicate the layer in Step 7 and apply the Warp Text tool. (Rinse and repeat.)

148

11 Set the Motion Blur with an Angle of 90° and a Distance of 30 pixels.

This creates an effect of vertical vibration, which will be layered with other layers (frames) when creating the animation in ImageReady.

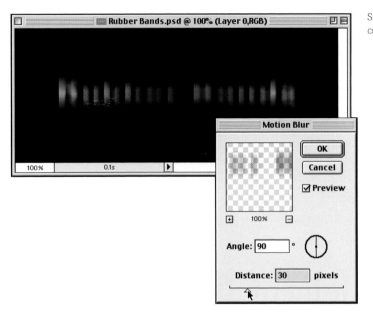

Set the Motion Blur filter to create a motion effect.

12 Duplicate the +30% distorted text layer and repeat Step 12.

By now you've created a few layers or frames that are necessary for the following animation sequence in ImageReady.

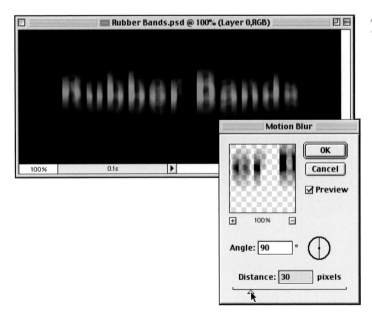

Apply Motion Blur to a duplicated +30% distorted text layer.

ANIMATING THE TEXT

By using the handful of frames in the Photoshop 6 file, you can create a multi-frame animation by simply making the individual layers visible in each frame sequence. Combine with the blurred layers and set the timing of the animation for the final "Rubber Band Snap" effect.

1   With only the black background layer and the undistorted text layer visible, jump to Adobe ImageReady. The first frame on the Animation bar is selected, and the image appears in the project window.

2   Add the next frame in the animation. Click New Frame in the Animation bar's side pull-down menu.

3   After a new frame has been added, simply shuffle through the Layers palette and make each distorted layer visible in succession according to the distortion amounts. Refer to the frame number chart in the sidebar for the proper sequence in this first animation.

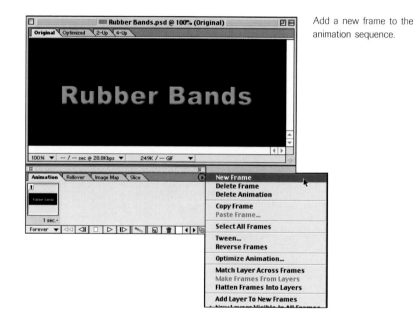

Add a new frame to the animation sequence.

BACKGROUND BLACK IS VISIBLE FOR ALL FRAMES

Frame 1:   0%   Distortion (Warp) Layer   1 Second

Frame 2:   +10%   Warp Layer   No Delay

Frame 3:   +30%   Warp Layer   No Delay

Frame 4:   +50%   Warp Layer   No Delay

Frame 5:   +30%   Warp Layer, +30%   Blur Layer
            No Delay

Frame 6:   +10% Warp Layer, +30% Blur Layer
            No Delay

Frame 7:   0% Warp Layer, +30% Blur Layer
            No Delay

Frame 8:   0% Warp Layer, +30% Blur Layer,
            −10% Blur Layer   No Delay

Frame 9:   −10% Warp Layer, +30% Blur Layer,
            −10% Blur Layer   No Delay

Frame 10:   −30% Warp Layer,
            +30% Blur Layer(50% Opacity),
            −10% Blur Layer   No Delay

Frame 11:   −10% Warp Layer,
            +30% Blur Layer(50% Opacity),
            −10% Blur Layer   No Delay

Frame 12:   0% Warp Layer, −10% Blur Layer
            No Delay

Frame 13:   −10% Warp Layer, −10% Blur Layer
            No Delay

Frame 14:   0% Warp Layer,
            −10% Blur Layer(50% Opacity)
            No Delay

Selecting visible layers in sequence from the Layers palette.

After you have created the animation sequence, you can preview it in Internet Explorer or Netscape Communicator by selecting the Preview in Browser button on the toolbar.

MODIFICATIONS

One of many modifications that can be made to this animation style is a simple rubbery, twisting motion. This can be achieved with just a few simple steps and only one Warp Text option.

1 Duplicate the 0% distorted text layer (or create a new one). Click on the Warp Text tool and select the Flag Style.

> Apply opposing distortion in equal increments.
>
> Bend: **+15%**
>
> Horizontal Distortion: **−15%**
>
> Vertical Distortion: **+5%**
>
> This creates a waving twist to the text for the animation sequences.

2 Duplicate the text layer and set the Warp Text tool as follows:

> Bend: **+30%**
>
> Horizontal Distortion: **−30%**
>
> Vertical Distortion: **+10%**

Repeat the text layer again *twice* and make the Warp Text settings listed here:

> Bend: **+45%**
>
> Horizontal Distortion: **−45%**
>
> Vertical Distortion: **+15%**

Fourth distorted layer

> Bend: **+60%**
>
> Horizontal Distortion: **−60%**
>
> Vertical Distortion: **−15%**

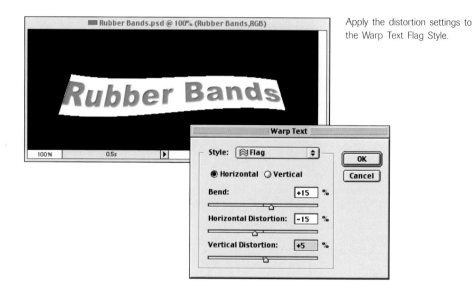

Apply the distortion settings to the Warp Text Flag Style.

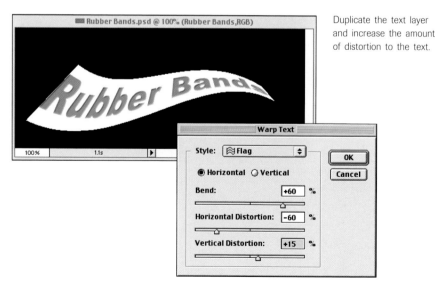

Duplicate the text layer and increase the amount of distortion to the text.

3 Repeat Steps 1 and 2, only move the Warp Text settings equally in the opposite directions.

First Distorted Layer

Bend: **−15%**

Horizontal Distortion: **+15%**

Vertical Distortion: **−5%**

Second Distorted Layer

Bend: **−30%**

Horizontal Distortion: **+30%**

Vertical Distortion: **−10%**

Third Distorted Layer

Bend: **−45%**

Horizontal Distortion: **+45%**

Vertical Distortion: **−15%**

Fourth Distorted Layer

Bend: **−60%**

Horizontal Distortion: **+60%**

Vertical Distortion: **−5%**

4 Once all your layers are created, use ImageReady and create your looping animation to the sidebar table.

You can view these finished sample animations on the included CD-ROM for comparison if necessary.

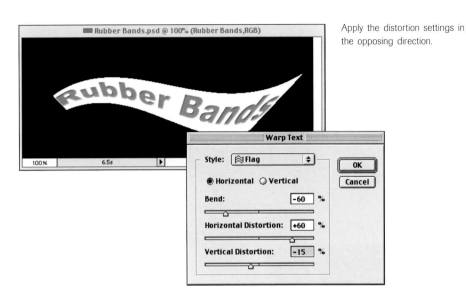

Apply the distortion settings in the opposing direction.

The distorted text will animate in a rubbery, twisting motion.

BACKGROUND BLACK IS LEFT VISIBLE FOR ALL FRAMES— TIMING IS SET FOR NO DELAY FOR ALL FRAMES

Frame 1:   0% Distortion Layer

Frame 2:   +15% Bend Layer

Frame 3:   +30% Bend Layer

Frame 4:   +45% Bend Layer

Frame 5:   +60% Bend Layer

Frame 6:   +45% Bend Layer

Frame 7:   +30% Bend Layer

Frame 8:   +15% Bend Layer

Frame 9:   0% Distortion Layer

Frame 10:   −15% Bend Layer

Frame 11:   −30% Bend Layer

Frame 12:   −45% Bend Layer

Frame 13:   −60% Bend Layer

Frame 14:   −45% Bend Layer

Frame 15:   −30% Bend Layer

Frame 16:   −15% Bend Layer

WARPING WET
TEXT ANIMATION

"You cannot acquire experience by making experiments. You cannot create experience. You must undergo it."

—ALBERT CAMUS

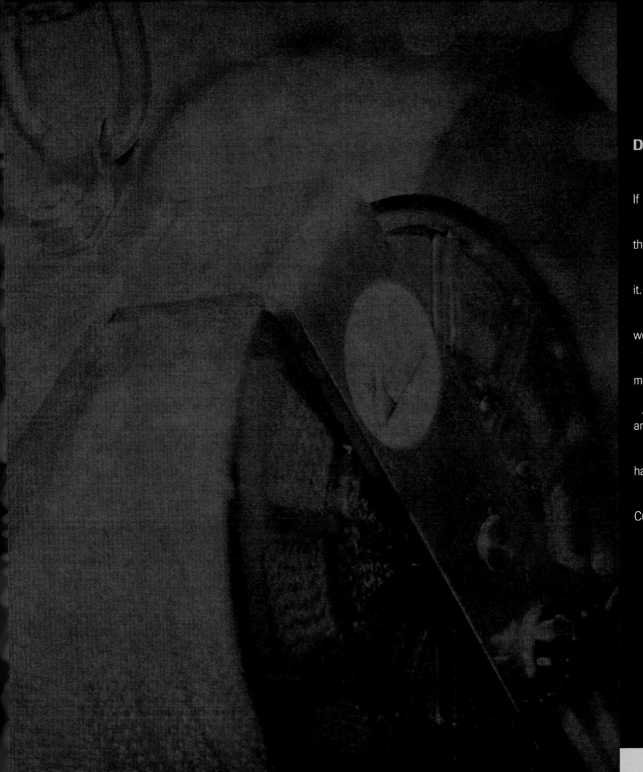

DRIPS AND DROPS

If you don't want your title text to be static, there are several ways to add a little "life" to it. Whether it's bubbling, warping, or dripping wet, it will still be very legible because it's not moving all over the page (like most Flash animations seem to do these days!). Plus it has the benefit of the photorealistic look of Custom Layer Styles.

Project 12

Warping Wet Text Animation

by Jeff Foster

GETTING STARTED

There are many "fluid motion" animation techniques you can now create in Photoshop 6.0 with ImageReady 3.0. For this project, only some Custom Layer Styles and a Custom Paintbrush tool will help you create wet, dripping text effects—and hone your painting skills at the same time!

CREATING THE TEXT

Text is created, and a liquidy Custom Layer Style is applied. The drips will be created with simple Paintbrush tools applied to the text layers that have the Custom Layer Style. This will give you a gauge as to how much of the painting effect you will need in each step.

1 Start by creating a new file that's **400×200** pixels.

2 Select a large, fat font like Arial Rounded or Comic Sans Bold and type your word or title in the upper third of the image window.

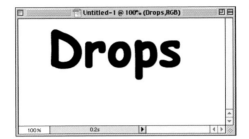

Type in your message with a bold font.

3 Apply a liquid-like Style to the text from the Custom Layer Styles library found on the enclosed CD-ROM. For this example, Blue Wet Enamel was chosen.

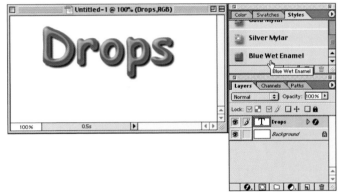

Apply a liquid-like Style to the text from the Styles Palette.

4 Duplicate the text layer and rasterize the duplicated layer in the Layers palette.

This layer will become the first frame of the animation sequence, so name it Layer 1 or a name that makes sense for your sequence.

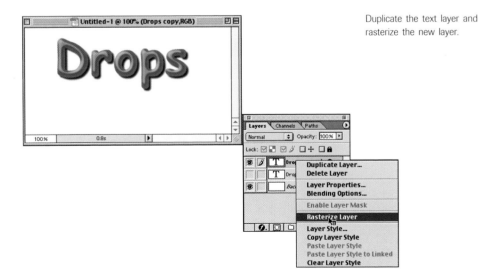

Duplicate the text layer and rasterize the new layer.

5 Select one of the Raindrop brushes from the Custom Brushes library found on the accompanying CD-ROM.

Depending on the size of your text and the resolution of the file, choose the brush size that fits your design.

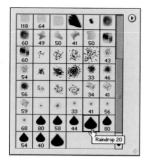

Select a Raindrop brush from the Custom Brushes library.

Note: Since this project is going to simulate dripping-wet paint or liquid, you have to determine how gravity would work, especially on the rounded edges of the letters. This animation sequence will start with the letter farthest to the left and work one letter at a time to the right.

6 Duplicate the rasterized text layer (Layer 1). On this duplicated layer, use the Paintbrush tool to make the first letter slightly sag as if it were made of wet paint or liquid. Notice the slight deformation of the letter "D" in the figure.

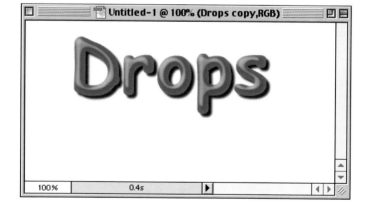

Duplicate the rasterized layer and start "sagging" the letters one at a time with the Paintbrush tool.

7 Continue duplicating the Layer 1 (frame 1) layer and moving it to the top of the list in the Layers palette. Name each frame layer in the animation sequence appropriately, as this will help when assembling the frames in ImageReady.

Each time you duplicate a layer, use the Paintbrush tool to add the droplet, distorting the letters to create an illusion that there is going to be a drop formation from the "heaviest" part of the letter (think gravity).

If you can, try to picture how a dewdrop slowly falls down the surface of a leaf until it drips off the end. More frames and more steps will make the animation slower and smoother.

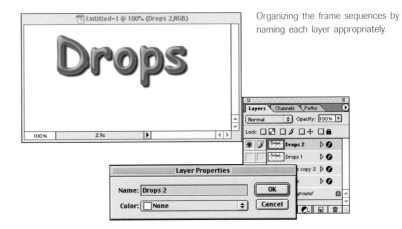

Organizing the frame sequences by naming each layer appropriately.

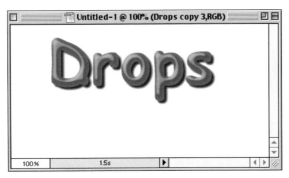

Duplicate the first frame sequence layer and apply the Paintbrush tool again.

8   Once the "droplet" has fallen from the bottom-most part of the letter, it will move rapidly—probably in only three frames of the sequence.

Always compare the frame layer you're working on to the frame layer just below it. Be sure not to move too fast or too far in any one step. This will get easier with practice, and you'll be an animator in no time!

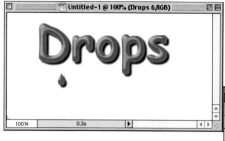

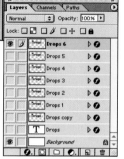

Make the droplets fall faster after they've fallen from the surface of the letter.

9   Once a droplet has fallen from the surface of the letter, start distorting the next letter, choosing a path that the next droplet will fall from that letter.

Keep your droplets falling straight down by keeping the previous frame layer visible while you are applying the Paintbrush tool. Reference back several layers as needed to make sure you aren't forgetting to advance a droplet on any one layer.

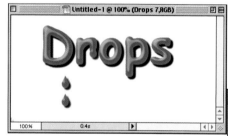

Compare the steps in the animation by keeping the previous frame layer visible while applying the Paintbrush tool.

10 Continue this process until you've reached the last frame on the end of the work or title.

It's a good idea to save your Photoshop document at this point, just in case you need to go back and fix any frame sequences later.

11 Make only the background layer and Layer 1 (frame 1) of the sequence visible and select Jump To Adobe ImageReady from the File pull-down menu.

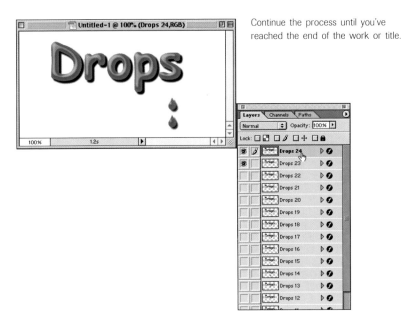

Continue the process until you've reached the end of the work or title.

ANIMATING THE "DROPLETS"

Now you get to test your animation skills. Because this project is highly subjective in the manner in which you apply the Paintbrush tool to get the desired effect, you may have to re-create a few frame layer sequences or add/delete some to either slow down or speed up the animation. Jump back and forth between Photoshop and ImageReady as necessary.

1 Open the Animation options bar and duplicate the first frame. Hide the Layer 1 (frame 1) layer and make the frame 2 layer visible. Repeat this process until all the layers in your animation have been assigned to a frame in the animation.

Go back and check to see that the number of frames in your animation matches the number of layers in your file.

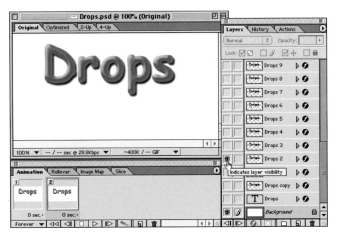

Make the layers visible to coincide with the frame sequence in the animation.

161

2   Preview the animation in your favorite browser from the File pull-down menu. Make any necessary adjustments you see in either the ImageReady sequence or the Photoshop file.

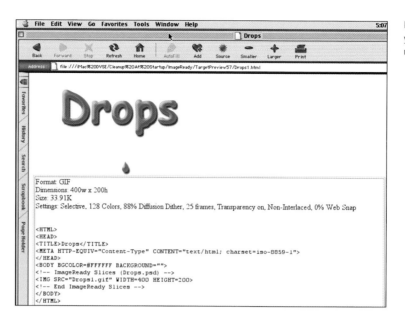

Preview the animation sequence in your favorite browser and make any necessary adjustments you see.

MAKING A "SPLASH" FOR YOUR DROPLETS

This step will create a small splash as the droplet nears the end of its cycle within the edges of the frame, using a brush from Photoshop's built-in library.

1   Open the Photoshop file and create a new layer. Apply the same Style that you applied earlier to the text layer.

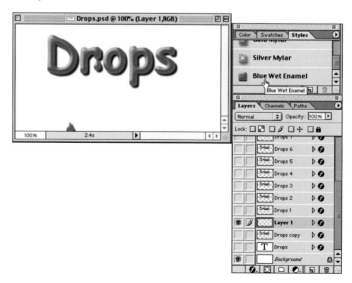

Create a new layer in the Photoshop file and apply the same Style that you applied to the text layer.

2   Select the Paintbrush tool and choose the Star 70-pixel brush from the Paintbrush options palette.

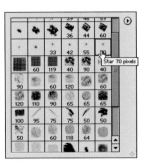

Select the Star 70-pixel brush from the Paintbrush options palette.

3   Apply the brush at the bottom edge of the image window as shown in the figure.

This layer will be aligned in the correct position for each splash occurrence in ImageReady.

Apply the Star brush at the bottom of the image window to create the droplet Splash effect.

4   Choose the Jump to ImageReady option again. Using the Move tool, click and drag the "splash" layer to the appropriate exit point where the droplet falls for each occurrence.

In some cases in which the droplet is partially out of frame, leave the splash layer visible for two frames. In cases in which the droplet is either completely in frame or out, just make the splash visible on the first frame in which the droplet is gone.

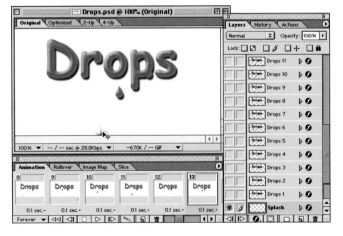

Jump to ImageReady and use the Move tool to position the "splash" layer into alignment with the falling droplets.

MODIFICATION

Instead of creating free-falling drops, imagine that the text is actually on the surface of the background, and the liquid starts running down the surface like wet paint. Using a similar technique and a layer-by-layer process of animation, this project has a completely different end effect. This effect works great for "oozing" effects like dripping cheese or even (gulp!) fake blood.

1   Start with Steps 1–3 in the first section of this project. Create a new file, add text, and apply the Red Wet Enamel Style from the CD-ROM to the text layer.

Create a new file in Photoshop and apply the Red Wet Enamel Style on the text layer.

2   Continue duplicating and organizing/naming the layers as in the previous animation, only this time you can simply duplicate each previous frame and apply a small amount to each drip. Using a round Paintbrush (slightly smaller than the diameter of the stroke of the text you're using), paint the drips slowly and evenly for each stage of the animation. Use the Shift key to keep your painted lines straight.

Unlike the first animation, these drips will all run simultaneously, though some may run faster than others.

Use the Paintbrush tool to draw the drips on each sequence of the animation.

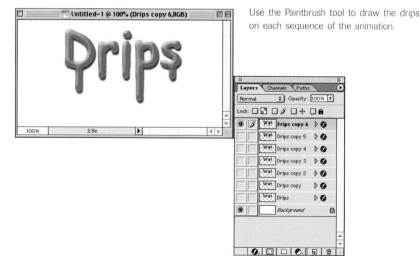

164

3 Jump to ImageReady when you are satisfied with the amount of drips you've created from your text. This time, simply select Make Frames From Layers from the right pull-down menu on the Animation options bar.

You will most likely need to make the background visible for each frame of the animation unless you are creating a transparent GIF. Preview in your browser to see the animation in motion (but note that this animation doesn't "loop" like the droplets do).

Jump to ImageReady to create the animation and preview in the browser.

JITTER BUG TEXT

"Insanity in individuals is something rare—but in

groups, parties, nations, and epochs, it is the rule."

—FRIEDRICH NIETZSCHE

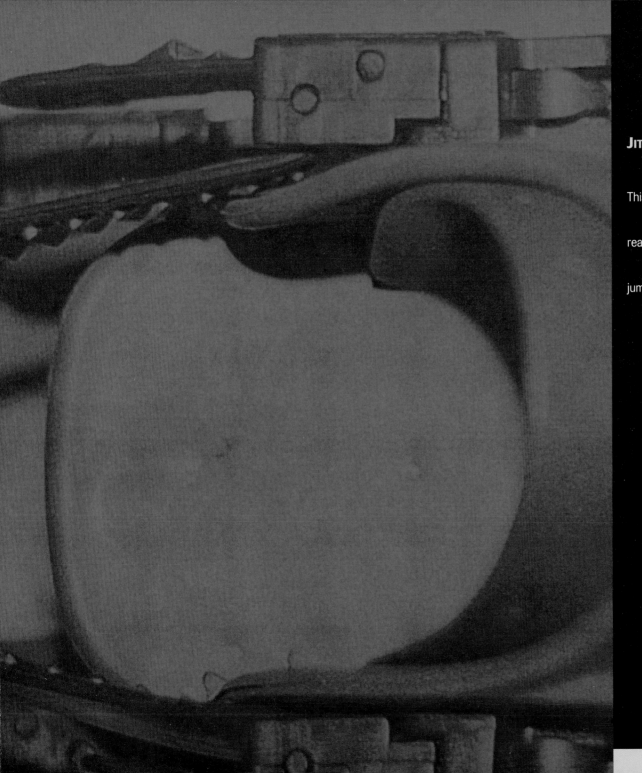

JITTERING ANIMATED TEXT

This effect is almost creepy. The motion is so

realistic that you'd swear the text is going to

jump off the screen and up your arm!

Project 13

Jitter Bug Text

by Jeff Foster

GETTING STARTED

This project will explore the use of Custom Styles and the Liquify feature to add a life-like "jittering" motion to the text layer and to create a simple four-frame looping animated GIF in ImageReady.

PREPARING THE BACKGROUND TEXTURE

The background texture in this technique helps give the text its realistic appeal. If you choose to skip this section, simply start with the file **Sandtile.jpg** in the Sample Images folder on the accompanying CD-ROM. You'll use filters and Hue/Saturation to create this sandy texture. Starting with a blank slate, you'll be sticking your toes in the sand in just a few steps.

Note: You can shortcut past the first section by starting with the **Sandtile.jpg** in the Sample Images folder on the accompanying CD-ROM.

168

1 Create a new file using these settings (or adapt the settings to your needs):

Width: **300 pixels**

Height: **300 pixels**

Resolution: **72 pixel/inch**

Background: **White**

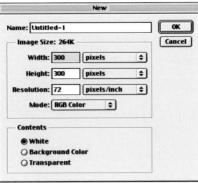

Create a new file that's 300×300 pixels.

2 Select the Background layer and then, from the Menu bar, choose Filter, Noise, Add Noise and use these settings:

Amount: **15%**

Distribution: **Gaussian**

Monochromatic: **Checked**

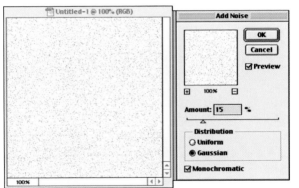

Add Noise to the Background layer.

3 From the Menu bar, choose Filter, Blur, Gaussian Blur and set Radius to .5 pixels.

The Radius setting smoothes out the noise.

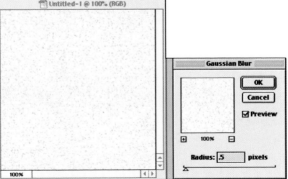

Smooth out the noise slightly with the Gaussian Blur filter.

4   From the Menu bar, choose Image, Adjust, Hue/Saturation and use the following settings:

Colorize: **Selected**

Hue: **30**

Saturation: **40**

Lightness: **−25**

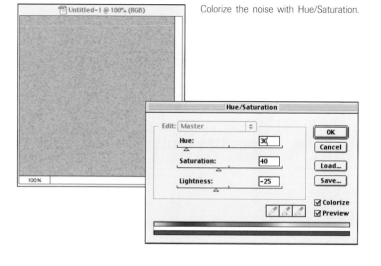

Colorize the noise with Hue/Saturation.

5   From the Menu bar, choose Filter, Noise, Add Noise. Using a smaller amount than you did in Step 2, use these settings:

Amount: **8%**

Distribution: **Gaussian**

Monochromatic: **Checked**

Applying the Add Noise filter at this point in the process adds depth to the sand.

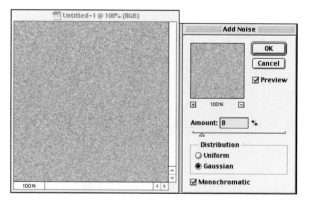

Complete the texture and create the illusion of depth by adding a small amount of noise.

CREATING THE JITTER BUG TEXT

It's important to choose a font that has a lot of character and detail to achieve the best effect. At a minimum, choose a sharply serifed or handwritten font. In this example, I've chosen Jokerman LET. If you use a blocky, straight-sided font like Arial, the effect will just appear wavy and lumpy instead of "jittering" and bug-like.

1. In the Toolbox, select the Text tool and a black foreground color, type the text you want to use, and then center the text in the image window.

   Once you're satisfied with the text in the window, it's time to rasterize the type so it can be distorted and stylized for animating. If you choose to Liquify the text without rasterizing, it will prompt you to do so upon opening the Liquify window.

Place text in the center of the image window using the Text tool.

Note: It's still not too late to change the font, the type style, or even what you want the word to say, but after you rasterize the type layer, you can't make text changes.

2. From the Menu bar, choose Layer, Rasterize, Type.

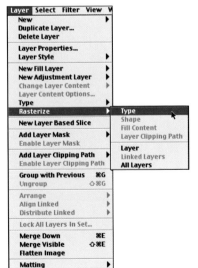

Rasterize the text prior to applying Styles and distortion.

3 From the Menu bar, choose Image, Liquify.

The Liquify screen opens, giving you access to a variety of tools and settings specific to the Liquify command.

Select Liquify from the Image pull-down menu.

4 Select the Warp tool, choose a 150-pixel brush with a pressure of 10, and then, using a long, horizontal sweeping motion, gently "nudge" the text.

Brush Size: **150 pixels**

Brush Pressure: **10**

Warning: Don't go over an area of text that you already "nudged;" you will move it back to where it started (or it might distort the text too much at one time). Overworking an area will also feather out the edges and make the effect look fuzzy.

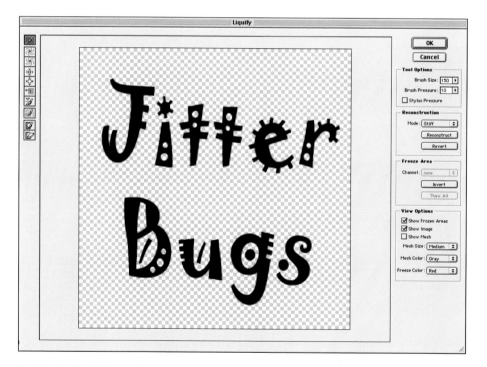

Applying the Liquify Warp tool to the text layer.

5   Duplicate the text layer and repeat Steps 3 and 4, working the Warp tool in the opposite direction as you did previously.

Changing directions makes the text "jitter."

6   Repeat Steps 3-5 at least two more times.

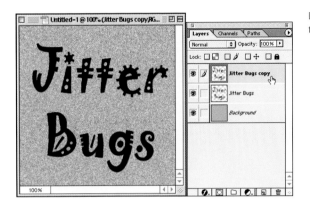

Duplicate the text layer and apply the Liquify Warp tool.

7   From the pull-down menu on the Layers palette, select Layer Style.

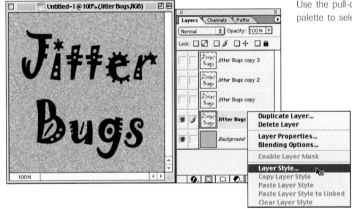

Use the pull-down menu on the Layers palette to select Layer Style.

8 Apply the following effects using these settings:

Drop Shadow: **Default settings**

Bevel Style: **Inner Bevel**

Technique: **Chisel Hard**

Depth: **150%**

Size: **3 px**

Soften: **0 px**

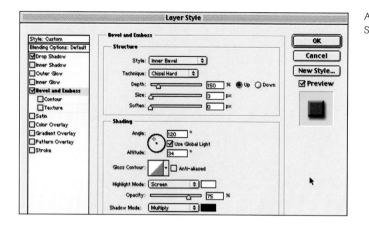

Apply the Shadow and Bevel
Style to the text layer.

9 Using the pull-down menu on the Layers palette,
copy the Layer Style of the text layer.

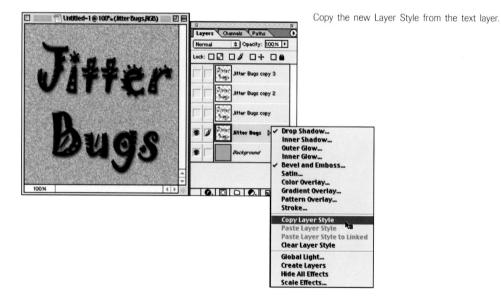

Copy the new Layer Style from the text layer.

174

10 Using the pull-down menu on the Layers palette, paste the Layer Style onto the remaining text layers.

You should now have at least four layers of "jittered" text with the 3D effect applied and ready for animating.

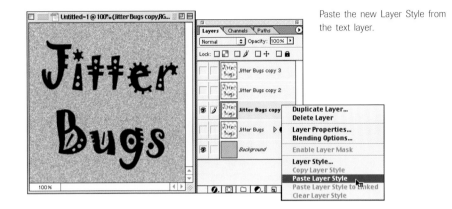

Paste the new Layer Style from the text layer.

USING ADOBE IMAGEREADY TO ANIMATE THE TEXT LAYERS

Get ready to start jittering the "buggy" text! By converting the layers created in Photoshop to frames of animation in ImageReady, you will create an animated GIF that will loop the jittering text.

1 From the Menu bar, choose File, Jump to, Adobe ImageReady 3.0.

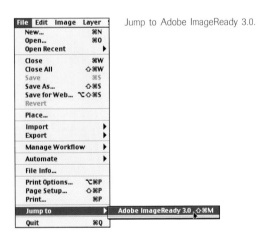

Jump to Adobe ImageReady 3.0.

2 Make sure the first text layer and background texture are visible and then start the first frame of animation.

Make sure there is no delay set in the frame duration by checking the number at the bottom of the first frame of animation. The default is 0 seconds.

3 Create a New Frame and make the second text layer visible. Hide the first text layer and make sure the duration is set to 0.

4 Repeat the process in Step 3 for the remainder of the text layers.

Make the first text layer and background visible on Frame 1.

5 Click the Play button at the bottom of the Animation palette to test your animation.

Continue creating new frames and sequencing the text animation until you are ready to test the animation by clicking the Play button.

6 From the Menu bar, choose File, Preview In and then select your Web browser.

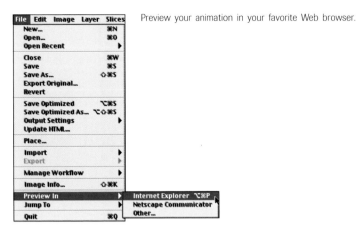

Preview your animation in your favorite Web browser.

MODIFICATIONS

You can apply this effect to just about any shape or text and achieve fun (and creepy) results. This variation shows that you can use the Paintbrush tool or Shapes on layers to apply the effect.

Check out the finished animations on the CD-ROM that accompanies this book.

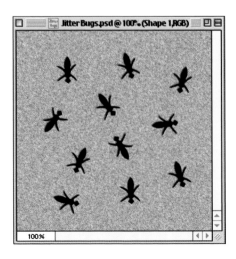

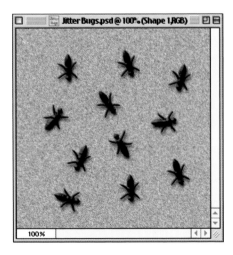

You can apply this creepy effect to just about any shape on a layer—just be ready with the bug spray!

MOTION TEXT

"The artist is nothing without the gift,

but the gift is nothing without work."

—EMILE ZOLA

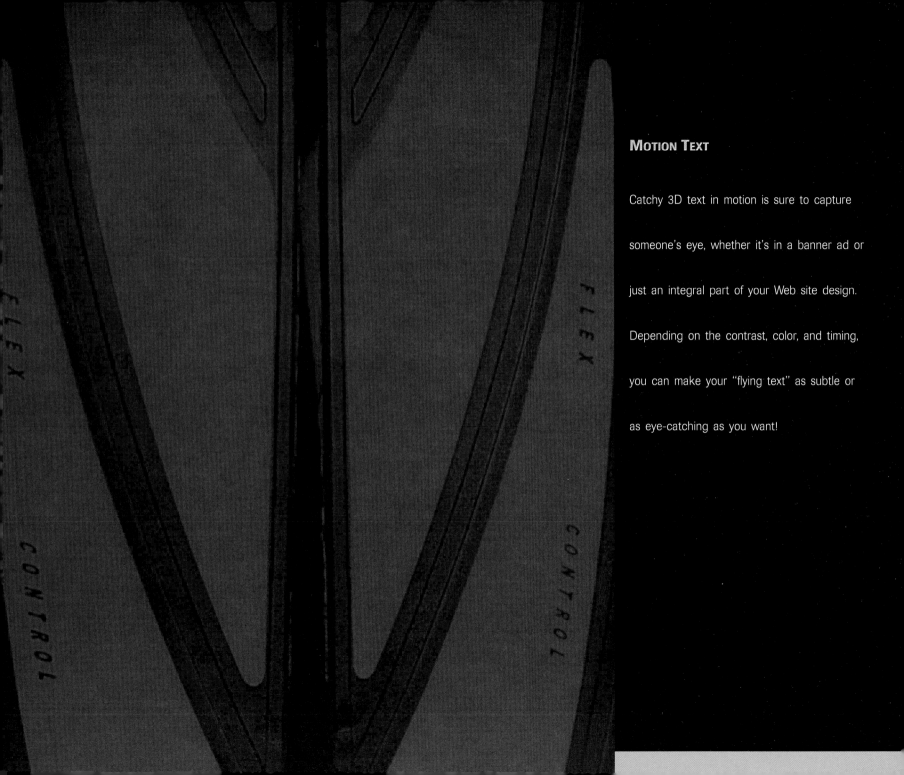

MOTION TEXT

Catchy 3D text in motion is sure to capture

someone's eye, whether it's in a banner ad or

just an integral part of your Web site design.

Depending on the contrast, color, and timing,

you can make your "flying text" as subtle or

as eye-catching as you want!

Project 14

Motion Text

by Jeff Foster

GETTING STARTED

In this exercise, the text is a single word created with a large, bold font and then stretched out to fill most of the window. It's duplicated, skewed, and slightly blurred and then set into motion using Adobe ImageReady 3.0.

SIZING UP THE TEXT

Unless you happen to choose a word or line of text that perfectly fits in your window area, you're going to have to tweak it a little to make it fit. Before skewing or moving the text, you'll need to use the Transform tool to stretch it out to fit.

180

1   Create a new file that's **500×72** pixels.

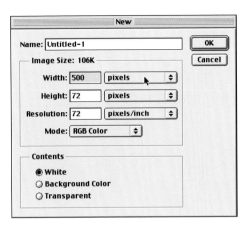

Create a new file that's 500×72 pixels.

2   Select a foreground color (other than white or black). Using the Text tool, select 48-point Arial Black font and type a single word.

Select a large font and type a word.

3   Select Edit, Transform, Scale. Using the handles on the bounding box, click and drag them until your text is the desired size inside the window.

Click-drag the Transform Scale box to the desired text size.

GIVING THE TEXT DIMENSION

It's one thing to just move text around on the screen, but if you give it a 3D effect, you'll definitely have a "Wow!" factor that can't be ignored!

1   Select Layer Style from the Layers palette.

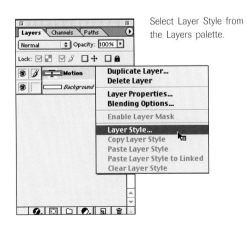

Select Layer Style from the Layers palette.

2 Select Drop Shadow and Bevel and Emboss in the following configuration to get a slick, wet enamel look:

Shadow Opacity: **50%**

Bevel Style: **Inner Bevel**

Technique: **Smooth**

Depth: **250%, Up**

Size: **10 px**

Soften: **5 px**

Shading Angle: **153°**

Altitude: **65**

Gloss Contour: **Gaussian**

Contour Shape: **Gaussian**

Anti-Aliased: **Checked**

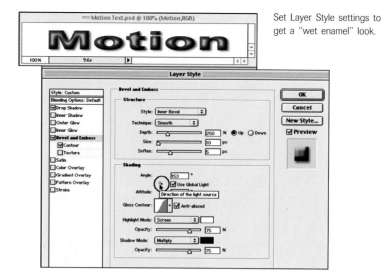

Set Layer Style settings to get a "wet enamel" look.

3 When you're satisfied with the text in the window, rasterize the type so it can be filtered and distorted for animating.

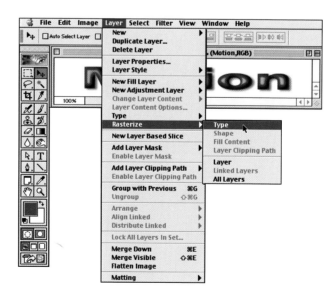

Rasterize the text prior to applying filters and distortion.

4   Duplicate the text layer and hide the original in
    the Layers palette. Choose Transform, Skew from the
    Edit menu.

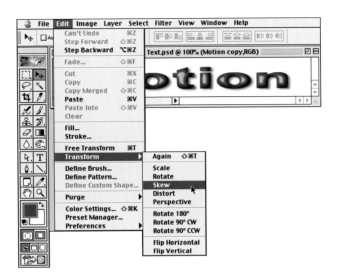

Duplicate the text layer and
apply a Skew Transform.

5   Click the top center handle of the bounding text box
    and drag it off to the left side to skew the text.

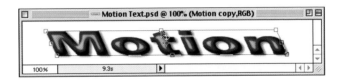

Click and drag the text to skew
it to the left.

6   Duplicate the second layer and repeat Steps 4 and 5,
    only skew the text to the right.

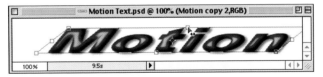

Duplicate the second text layer and
skew it to the right.

7 Duplicate the third text layer and hide the previous layer. Select Filter, Blur, Motion Blur and set Angle to 0° and Distance to 10 pixels for the new layer.

Note: If you are going to use your animation floating on a white background in your Web page design, it might be a good idea to make the text "blend" into the frame by adding an additional layer with white blended in on the entrance and exit points.

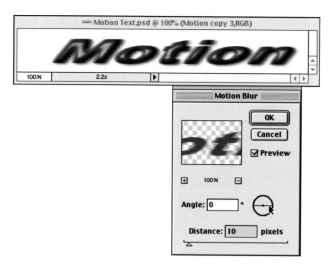

Duplicate the third text layer and apply Motion Blur.

8 Create a new layer and fill it with 100% white. Select the Rectangular Marquee tool, set the feather to 15 pixels, select an area in the middle of the layer, and delete the selection.

This leaves a soft "window" that will frame the animation and make it blend into the white background on your Web page.

Note: Be sure to make the layer visible at all times when creating the animation in ImageReady so that the effect is seamless.

Create an outline layer of white to smooth out the entrance and exit of the animation frame.

USING ADOBE IMAGEREADY
TO ANIMATE THE TEXT LAYERS

Using only these four text layers, you can create a looping "flying text" effect that zooms into the screen, screeches to a halt, and then zips right back off the screen!

1   Jump to Adobe ImageReady 3.0.

2   Start the first frame of animation with only the white background visible.

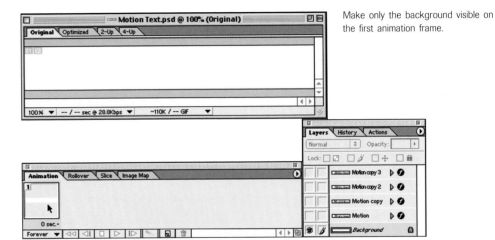

Make only the background visible on the first animation frame.

3   Create a new frame. Shift+click and drag the blurred text layer to the right side of window.

Make the blurred text layer visible. Click and drag the layer off to the right side of the window until it's just barely visible. Hold down the Shift key and make sure it doesn't move up or down in the process.

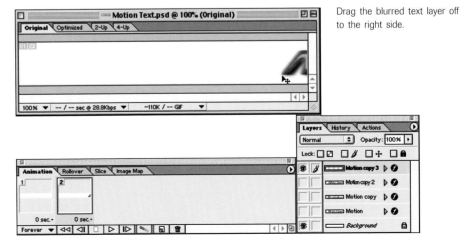

Drag the blurred text layer off to the right side.

4 Repeat Step 3 until the text reaches the center of the window. When the blurred text layer is back in the center of the window, create a new frame and hide the text. Make the first text layer visible (the unskewed original text layer).

Note that smaller increments make for a longer, smoother animation, but they also make the final animation file size larger.

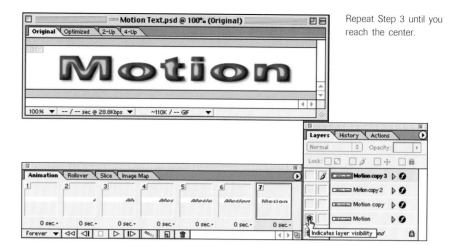

Repeat Step 3 until you reach the center.

5 Create a new frame, hide the original text layer, and make the left-skewed layer visible.

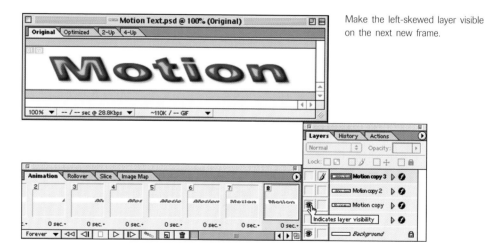

Make the left-skewed layer visible on the next new frame.

6 Create a new frame, hide the skewed layer, and then make the original text layer visible.

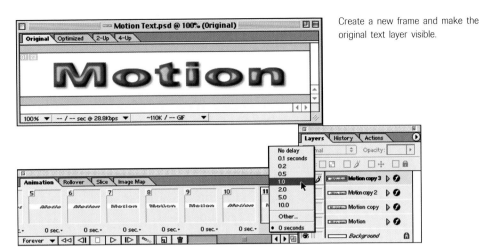

Create a new frame and make the original text layer visible.

7 Create a new frame, hide the original text layer again, and make the right-skewed layer visible. Repeat Step 6 and set the Duration to 1 second.

Note: You can choose to skip some of these steps if you do not want to have a "recoil" effect on the text. Simply exclude the left-skewed text back to right-skewed text layers when creating the animation, and the text will just stop in the middle before taking off again.

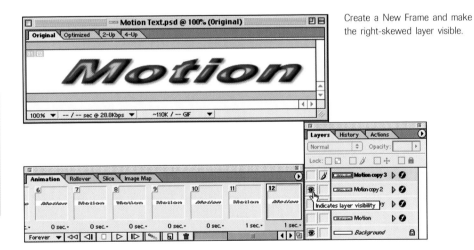

Create a New Frame and make the right-skewed layer visible.

8 Create a new frame, hide the original text layer, and make the blurred text layer visible.

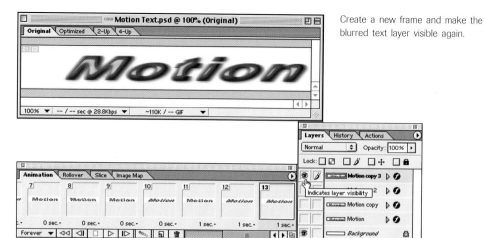

Create a new frame and make the blurred text layer visible again.

9 Continue to make new frames. Shift+click to move the blurred layer off to the left side of the window until it's no longer visible—similar to the first stages of the animation sequence.

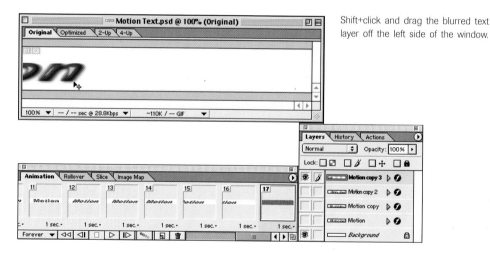

Shift+click and drag the blurred text layer off the left side of the window.

10 Click the Play button at the bottom of the Animation palette to test the animation.

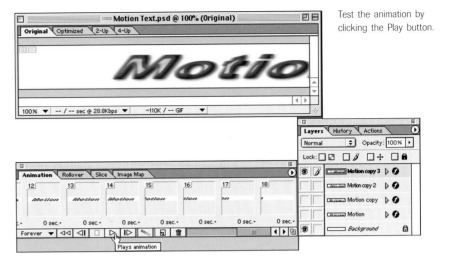

Test the animation by clicking the Play button.

11 You can preview your animation in your favorite Web browser by selecting Preview in Internet Explorer or Netscape Communicator.

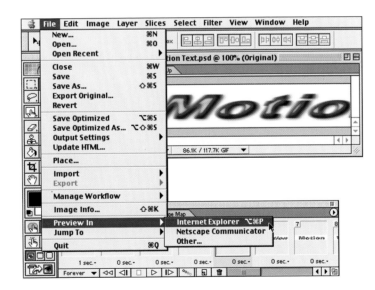

Preview your animation in your favorite Web browser.

MODIFICATIONS

You can put your animated text inside a three-dimensional frame as well. This modification shows how to create a simple frame with a glass window inside of which the animated text flies by.

1 Hide the White layer and create a new layer on the top level in the Layers palette. Select All, choose the Rectangular Marquee tool, and deselect an equal middle section of the layer, leaving just a thin frame on the outside edge of the layer.

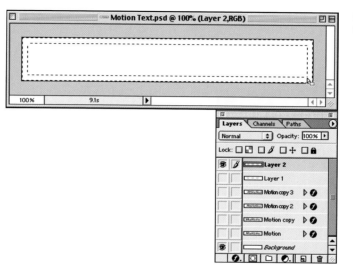

Create a new layer and select a frame border around the edge.

2 Fill the selection on the new layer and deselect. Apply a solid-filled Custom Style to the layer to create a solid frame along the outside edge. For this example, the Custom Style "Lead" was used.

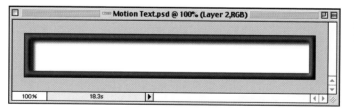

Fill the selection and apply a Custom Style to create a frame border.

3   Create one more new layer on top and select just the
inside of the frame. Fill this selection on the new
layer and apply a transparent texture (preferably
"Glass"). For this example, the Custom Style
"Antique Glass" was applied.

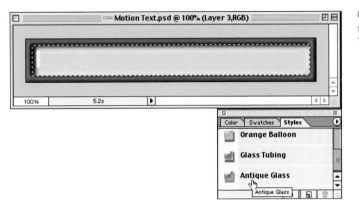

Create another layer, fill the middle
selection, and apply a transparent
"Glass" Custom Style.

4   As with the original technique, arrange the animation sequence. Keep the new frame and window
layers visible for each frame of animation in
ImageReady.

The finished sample animations are available for
preview on the CD-ROM included with this book.

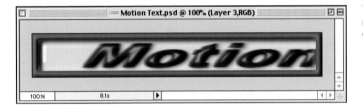

The completed animation sequence
appears to be inside a see-through
window.

SPLASH ANNOUNCEMENT—
SPRAYED TEXT

"If you can't annoy somebody,

there's little point in writing."

—KINGSLEY AMIS

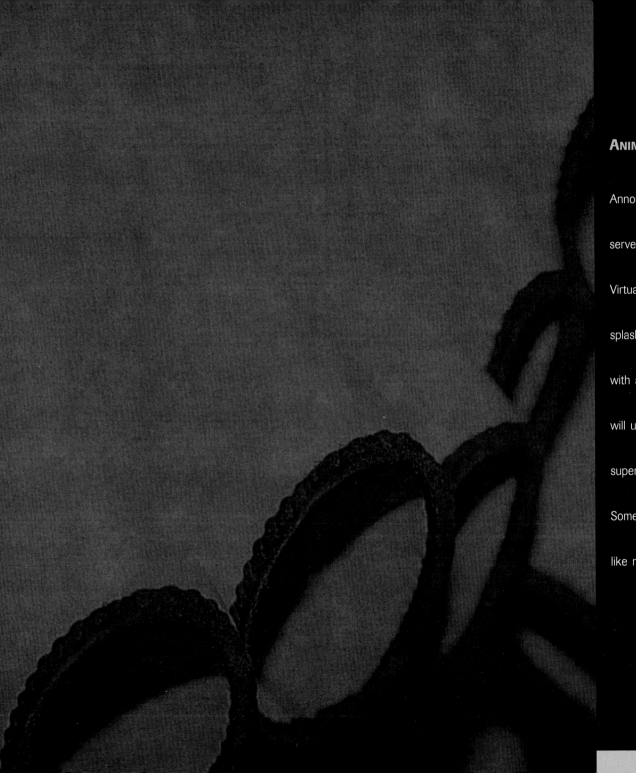

ANIMATED SPRAY CAN

Announcements, banners, and splashes all

serve the purpose of being attention grabbers.

Virtually any color scheme can use a bit of

splash color or animation to pack a punch

with a message or announcement. This project

will utilize red, white, and yellow to create a

supermarket-style splash announcement.

Sometimes "cheesy" will get people's attention

like nothing else will!

Project 15

Splash Announcement— Sprayed Text

by Jeff Foster

GETTING STARTED

This project can be created very quickly once you have created your Custom Styles for varying sizes and resolutions. Because each announcement or text splash is going to vary in size, you will have to adjust the Style you're using to better match; too much or too little bevel or sprayed outline can ruin the effect. The resulting animation sequence will be your message popping out of the center and springing into position.

CREATING THE TEXT AND CUSTOM STYLE

Depending on the background image you use, this effect can look 3D when animated or 2D as static on a texture or photo. For this part of the project, we will want to animate the text, so a solid-color background is desirable.

1 Start by creating a new file that's **200×200**, **72** pixels/inch.

2 Fill the background with a bright red. (Keep in mind that the colors on your screen will be dramatically brighter than what can be displayed on paper in this book.)

Fill the background with a bright red.

3 Using the Type tool, insert text in the middle of the image area, rotating or skewing it if desired.

Make sure to select a contrasting color (like white) for your text. Though the color will be overwritten when the Style is applied, it will be easier to position the text if you can see it!

Add text with the Type tool and rotate or skew for the desired angle.

4 Select the Layer Style Editor from the Layers palette. Choose the Bevel and Emboss option and make only the setting changes listed:

Depth: **100%**

Size: **5px**

Soften: **0px**

Angle: **130°**

Altitude: **45°**

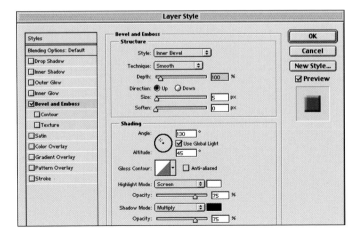

Using the Layer Style Editor, choose Bevel and Emboss.

5 Choose the Contour option and set the range to 50%. Keep the default linear contour shape and select the Anti-aliased option.

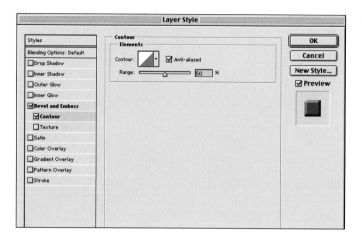

Choose Contour and set Range to 50%.

6 Select Blending Options and set the Fill Opacity to 0%.

This will make the foreground color of the text disappear, and all you will see is the highlights and shading on the letters.

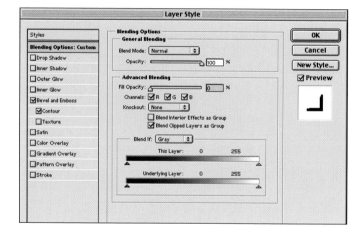

Select Blending Options and set the Fill Opacity to 0%.

7 Select the Outer Glow option and change the solid color glow to a bright yellow. Change only the settings listed:

Blend Mode: **Screen**

Opacity: **100%**

Noise: **3%**

Technique: **Precise**

Spread: **50%**

Size: **35px**

The amount of spread and the size will determine how far out the "spray" will reach. Obviously, use more spread for larger text, less for smaller.

Apply the Outer Glow option and adjust the spread and size to match the text size.

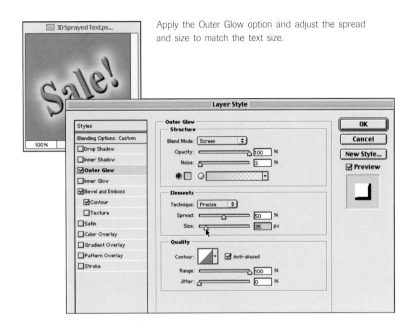

8 Select the Stroke option and set the Gradient Fill from White to Transparent. Make other changes only as listed:

Size: **1px**

Position: **Outside**

Fill Type: **Gradient (set White to Transparent)**

Style: **Shape Burst**

Select the Stroke option and set the Gradient Fill from White to Transparent.

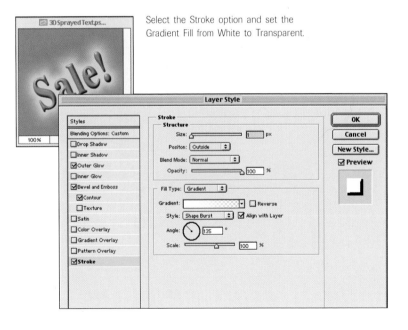

9 Save your Custom Style for later use. Duplicate the text layer and hide the original.

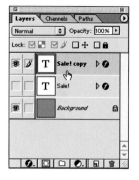

Duplicate the text layer with the Custom Layer Style applied to it.

10 With the duplicated text layer active, choose the Transform, Scale option from the Edit pull-down menu.

The purpose of transforming the text in this step is to create a reverse-zoom of the text, starting with the largest (closest) text first.

11 Scale the text down slightly, holding the Shift+Option(Alt) keys to make the text scale down exactly in the center of the selection.

Scale down the text to create a reverse-zoom effect.

12 Duplicate the transformed text layer and repeat Steps 10 and 11.

Continue repeating the process until you have several stages of the reverse-zoom created.

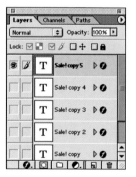

Duplicate the scaled text layer and repeat the process.

13 Starting with the smallest text layer, set the Layer Opacity to 50% and progressively work up to 100% with the largest text layer.

This will reinforce the zooming effect out of the background color.

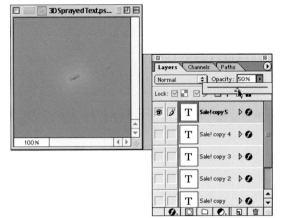

Set the Layer Opacity of the smallest text layer to 50% and progressively increase the opacity of larger text layers.

14 Select the largest text layer and duplicate it twice, rasterizing the newly duplicated layers.

15 Select one of the rasterized text layers and choose the Distort, Pinch filter.

Make two duplicates of the original large text layer and rasterize them.

16 Apply a −25% Amount of the Pinch filter to the layer.

This makes the text animation appear as if it's springing out toward the viewer by creating a bulging and pinching image sequence.

17 Apply a 25% Amount of the Pinch filter to the layer to create the pinching effect.

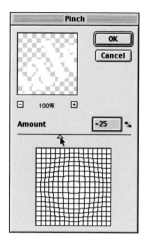

Set the Amount of Pinch to −25% to create a bulging effect.

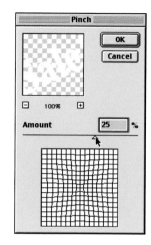

Set the Amount of Pinch to +25% to create a pinching effect.

ANIMATING THE SPRAYED TEXT EFFECT

Depending on whether you want your text to loop continuously or just pop up once and then remain static, you can get several effects out of the few layers that were created in Photoshop—just by the sequence you put them in ImageReady.

1 Make only the background layer visible and select Jump to ImageReady.

2 The first frame of the animation sequence will automatically be visible in the Animation Options bar. Duplicate the first frame by clicking on the duplicate icon and then make the smallest text layer visible in the Layers palette.

Repeat the process until you've reached the largest text layer that hasn't been distorted.

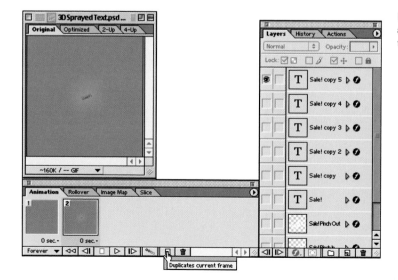

Duplicate the first frame and make the smallest text layer visible.

200

3 To make the text appear to spring out, create four
more frames and make the bulged-text layer visible.
Then make the large text layer visible, followed by
the pinched text layer, and finally the large text layer.

Reverse the process to make it zoom back in. It
might take a few attempts to get the timing just right
for the springing effect.

Organize the text layers to
create a spring-out, zooming
effect. Reverse the process
to make it zoom back in.

4 Preview your animation in your favorite browser
and make adjustments to timing, length, or looping
as necessary. Compare your project to the sample
animated GIF file for this project on the accompanying CD-ROM, 3D Sprayed Text.gif. This will help
you understand the animation process in detail.

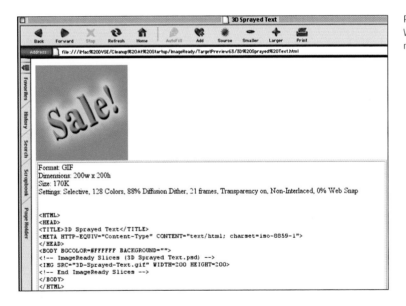

Preview the animation in your
Web browser and make any
necessary adjustments.

MODIFICATION

Another effective way to use the sprayed text effect is with a simple static image with a bold statement. This part of the project covers applying the Custom Layer Style created earlier in Step 9 and a background texture. You might also want to use one of the Custom Patterns on the accompanying CD-ROM.

1   Create a new file that's **200×200** pixels.

2   Select a pattern and fill the background layer with it. In this example, I used the built-in Stucco Pattern that can be found in Patterns 2.pat which ships with Photoshop 6.

3   Add some text with the Type tool and center it in the window. Be sure to leave room around the edges of the text to allow for the sprayed effect.

Add text and center in the window.

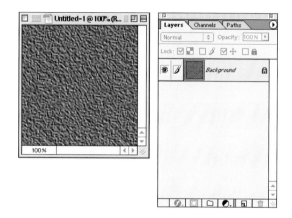

Create a new file and fill the background layer with a textured pattern.

4   Apply the Custom Layer Style created and saved earlier in this project in Step 9.

5   Double-click the text layer to open the Layer Style Editor.

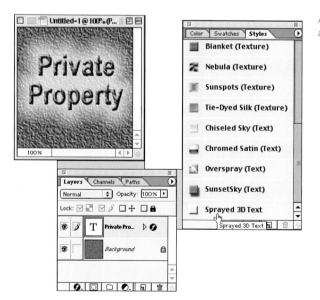

Apply the Custom Layer Style created and saved in Step 9 of this project.

6 Deselect the Bevel and Emboss option and the Contour option. Double-click the Outer Glow to white.

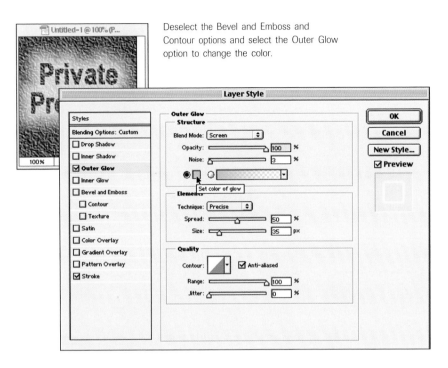

Deselect the Bevel and Emboss and Contour options and select the Outer Glow option to change the color.

7 Set the Noise level to 35% and adjust the Size according to your text size—just enough so it isn't touching the edges of the window.

The end result should appear as if the text has been stenciled on the wall with white spray paint.

You can save this Custom Style for future use on other textured patterns or photos. Try experimenting with variations of color and transparency for other realistic effects.

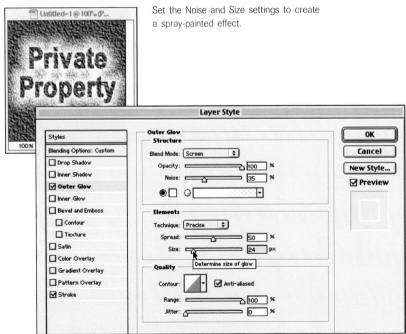

Set the Noise and Size settings to create a spray-painted effect.

RUBBER ROLLOVER
BUTTONS WITH TEXT

"There's nothing remarkable about it.

All one has to do is hit the right keys at the

right time and the instrument plays itself."

—JOHANN SEBASTIAN BACH

ANIMATED BUTTONS WITH TEXT

Three-dimensional, "rubberized" rollover buttons

are a snap in Photoshop 6. With the addition

of Warping Text and Custom Styles, what used

to take about 10–15 steps can now be done in

about three mouse clicks! The best part is that,

once you've created your button profile, you

can save the Style for use at any time with

just the click of a button.

Rubber Rollover Buttons with Text

by Jeff Foster

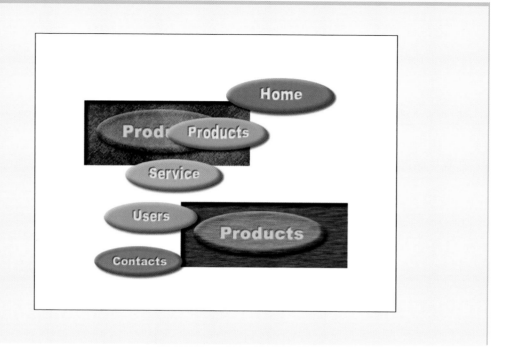

GETTING STARTED

After you have built the basic button Style, it can be saved in the Custom Styles library for later retrieval at the click of a button. Once the "up" and "down" button Styles are created and saved, you can apply them with a single mouse click on any object on a layer.

This simple button will have the effect of being physically pushed in when rolled over on your Web page. This effect is a basic element for most of your rollover animations, so it's important to understand the process so you can apply it in other shapes and sizes.

BUILDING THE BUTTON

In this project, the button size is intentionally huge for display in this book, but you can adjust and create the buttons at any size you want. The basic principles will apply to any shape or size button. We will create a basic oval-shaped button to which a simple Custom Layer Style will be applied to create an illusion of the button actually being pressed down. This Custom Layer Style then can be applied to other shapes or buttons and modified for its height, depth, size, gloss, and more.

1   Create a new file in Photoshop, just slightly larger than the size of the button you want to create, with a white background. Use the Elliptical Marquee tool to draw out a wide oval selection.

2   Create a new layer, fill the selection with a solid color, and then deselect.

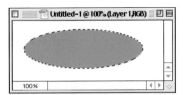

Create a new layer and fill the selection with a solid color.

3   Select the Layer Style Editor from the Layers palette. Choose the Drop Shadow option and apply these settings:

Blend Mode: **Multiply**

Opacity: **50%**

Angle: **120°**

Use Global Light: **On**

Distance: **5 px**

Spread: **0%**

Size: **5 px**

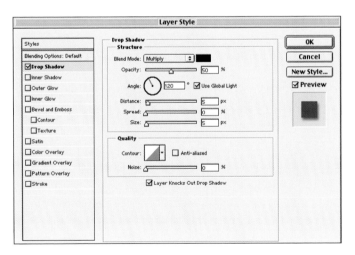

Make the settings for the drop shadow.

Note: Remember that the settings in this example are for a fairly large button. You might want to choose smaller percentages and measurements.

4 Select Bevel and Emboss, Contour, and set Range at 50%. Click on the Contour icon to open the Contour Editor. Adjust the Linear setting by click-adding a point in the center of the line and dragging up to create an "arc." Save the new shape as Button Up.

Make sure not to move the line too far up; otherwise, the contour will have a flat top. The image on the screen will automatically update as you move the line.

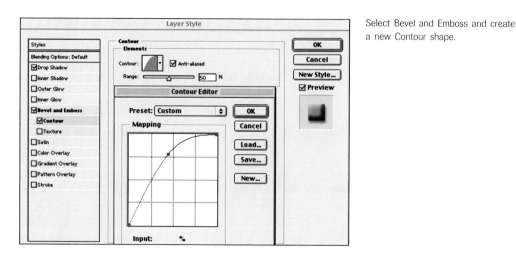

Select Bevel and Emboss and create a new Contour shape.

5 Select Bevel and Emboss and make changes to the Structure and Shading, as shown in the corresponding figure. Save the finished settings Style as Button Up for later reference.

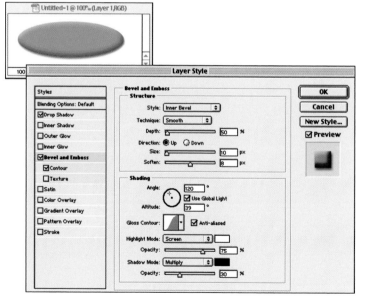

Change the settings of the Bevel and Emboss options and save the new Style as Button Up.

6 Duplicate the layer and open the Layer Style Editor to create Button Down.

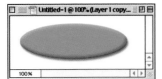

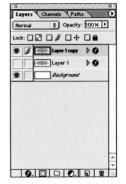

Duplicate the layer and open the Layer Style Editor.

7 Open the Contour Editor and select the Custom Contour to edit. Pull down the far-right handle just below the level of the center handle on the arc line. Save the edited new Style as Button Down for later retrieval. Save the Contour as Button Dn.

The effect can be seen as the image is updated in the project window.

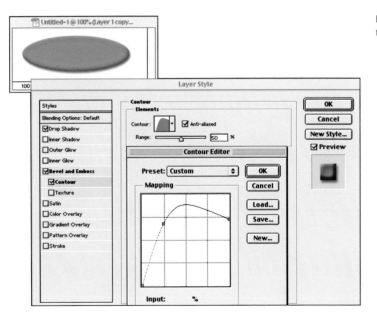

Edit the Contour shape in the Contour Editor.

ADDING TEXT TO THE BUTTON

Because you can apply Custom Styles to text, there will be no need to rasterize the text on these buttons. The Warp Text tool will be used to modify the up/down button features and can be applied globally.

1   Select a contrasting color and the Text tool. Place Text over the center of the "up" button.

Place text over the center of the "up" button.

2   Select the Layer Style Editor for the new text layer and choose Bevel and Emboss. Leave all default settings except for the Emboss Depth, Direction, and Size.

Depth: **50%**

Direction: **Down**

Size: **1 px**

This creates a slight embossing on the text to give it a 3D effect.

3   Select the text again with the Text tool and click on the Warp Text tool icon in the top bar. Select the Bulge effect and set the Bend to +15%.

The warped text should closely match the contour of the button on which you are placing it. Some adjustments of the distortion might need to be made for your project.

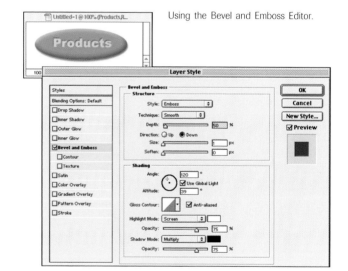

Using the Bevel and Emboss Editor.

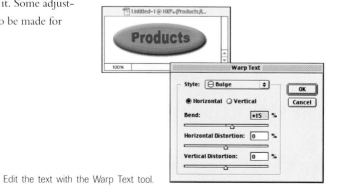

Warped Text on the button surface.

Edit the text with the Warp Text tool.

4   Using the Move tool, nudge the Down button text
    down and to the right a few pixels.

    The text on the "down" button surface in this
    project will be left undistorted, but there should
    be a sense of downward motion when the rollover
    is animated.

    Save the up/down button sequences as GIFs or
    JPGs and use in your HTML JavaScript rollovers.
    You can also test the button rollovers by jumping to
    ImageReady and watching the animation sequence.

Moving text on the "down"
button surface.

MODIFICATIONS

Now that you have the simple button basics done, you can crank out buttons
with just a few simple steps. Grouping the button "sets" and duplicating the sets
saves time and keeps organization of the layers easy.

1   Click on the Layers palette right pull-down menu
    and select New Layer Set. Save the set with a
    meaningful name and apply an identifying color
    for better organization.

    After the Layer Set is created, select both the Up
    Button text and the Up Button graphic layers and
    drag them into the Layer set. Repeat for the Down
    Button set.

2   To create more buttons, simply duplicate the Layer
    Sets. Make sure to name the sets so that you will be
    able to recognize what they are in the Layers palette.

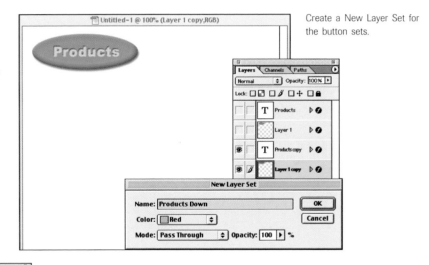

Create a New Layer Set for
the button sets.

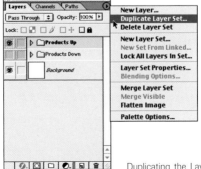

Duplicating the Layer Sets to create more buttons.

3 Simply change the color in the duplicated button's color layer, make the associated text layer active, and just retype the new text. It's that easy to create a new button—all the Styles and Warp Text effects remain intact!

Changing the color and text on the duplicated button in two steps.

4 Reorganize the buttons any way you want, but make sure that the button groups stay linked together. For each up button, there should be a linked down button.

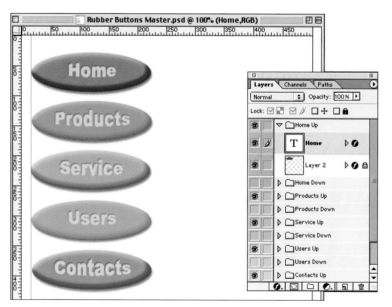

Reorganizing the duplicated buttons.

212

5   Keep each of the up/down buttons linked together at all times. That way, wherever one is moved or resized, the other will take on the same changes and not be out of sync—even if a transformation is applied to the Layer Set.

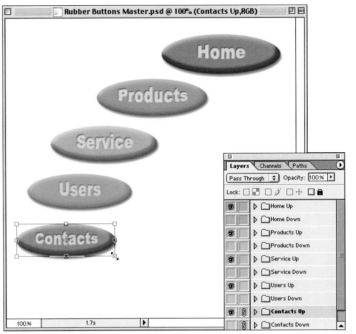

Applying a transformation to an entire button group.

You will be able to apply this technique to virtually any button shape. Make sure to save your up/down Styles each time, noting size and texture differences.

For even more variety, you can set the Fill Opacity of the button layer's Blending Options to 0% and place a texture on a layer below the button layer. Voila! Instant textured buttons!

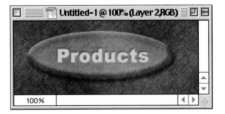

Transparent buttons over textured backgrounds.

TRANSPARENT PLASTIC WINDOWS

"It's kind of fun to do the impossible."

—WALT DISNEY

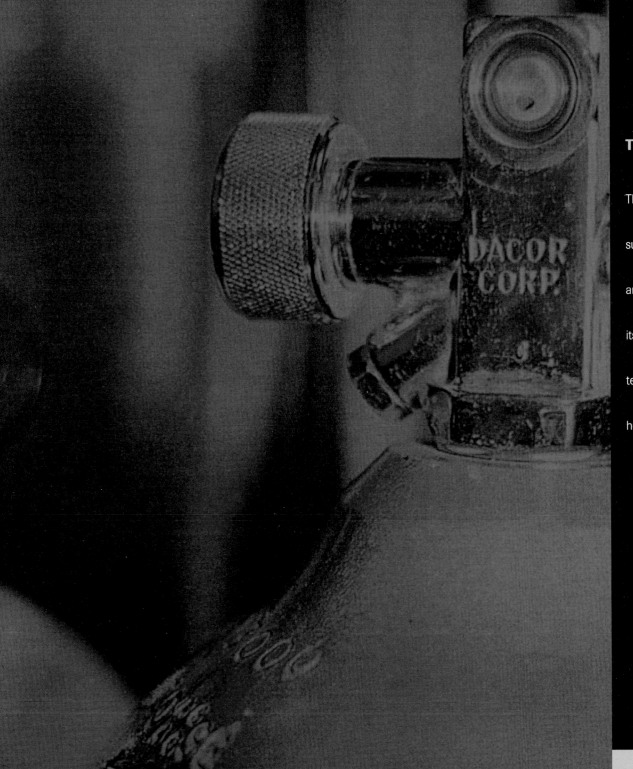

TRANSPARENT PLASTIC WINDOWS

These Navigation bars and control panels are sure to give your Web design a high-tech and classy look. The beauty of this effect is its flexibility. Just about any shape or size of text window will work for rollover buttons or hot spots in an image map.

Transparent Plastic Windows

by Jeff Foster

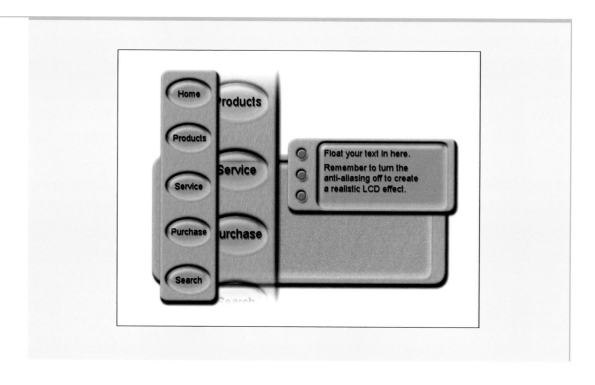

CREATING A NAVIGATION BAR
WITH WINDOWS

There are many ways to create a Navigation bar, with variations in style, shape, texture, size, and so on.... This first project will show you the basics of building a simple yet effective five-button Navigation bar with text windows over small LCD screens. One variation is to create an "Indiglo" style screen rollover.

1   Create a new vertical file that is **150×500** pixels, **72** pixels/inch with a White background.

2   Select a Rounded Square shape from the Custom Shapes palette to create the Navigation bar bezel.

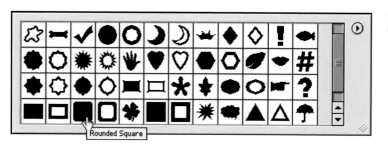

Select the Rounded Square custom shape to begin construction on the Navigation bar beze

3   Draw a square shape, keeping the corners at quarter-round. This shape will be duplicated several times on the same layer to create the final desired shape, so choose to rasterize the layer in the Layers palette.

To keep the corners of the square perfectly quarter-round, hold down the Shift key while dragging the Shape tool.

Draw a perfect square with the Shape tool and rasterize the layer.

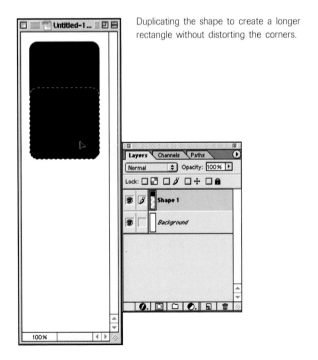

4   Load the selection of the rasterized shape layer and select the Move tool. Hold down the Option (Alt) key and click and drag the duplicated shape down to create an extended rectangle.

Holding the Shift key down while moving the duplicated shape will keep it vertically aligned with the original shape.

Duplicating the shape to create a longer rectangle without distorting the corners.

5 Repeat the duplication process until a full-length rectangle has been created. Be sure to leave an equal distance from the bottom edge of the shape as from the top. Deselect the selection when completed.

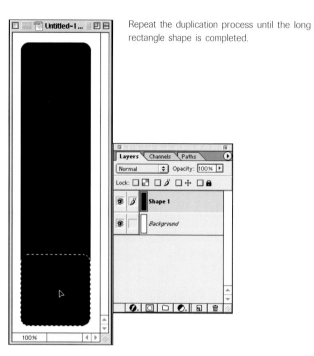

Repeat the duplication process until the long rectangle shape is completed.

6 Select the Brushed Aluminum Custom Style and apply it to the rectangle shape layer.

The Custom Styles library can be loaded from the enclosed CD-ROM.

Apply the Brushed Aluminum Custom Style to the shape layer.

7   Using the Elliptical Marquee tool with Feather set to
    0 pixels, draw out a selection large enough for a text
    window. It should be toward the top but not too
    close to the edges of the bezel.

    After you've drawn it, you can move your selection
    around by clicking inside the selected area with the
    Marquee tool.

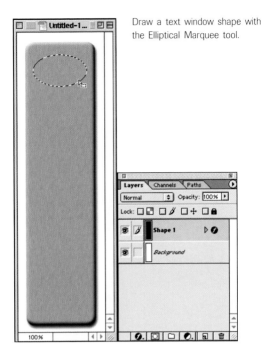

Draw a text window shape with
the Elliptical Marquee tool.

8   When the selection is centered exactly where
    you want it, press the Delete key to remove the
    material from the bezel. Without deselecting, use
    the Marquee tool to move the selection down to an
    equal distance from the bottom edge of the bezel.

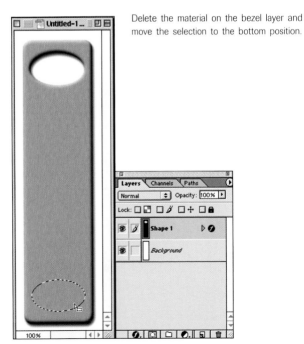

Delete the material on the bezel layer and
move the selection to the bottom position.

9 Repeat the process of deleting material from the bezel and moving the selection around to form the Navigation bar windows.

Note: To create the windows in a perfectly aligned pattern, turn View Rulers on and use guides to pattern your spacing. If you are intent on eyeballing the spacing, then cut the distance between the top and bottom shapes in half by placing the center window shape before filling in with the fourth and fifth shapes.

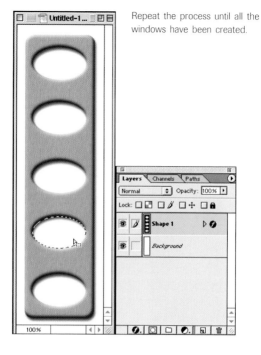

Repeat the process until all the windows have been created.

10 Load the selection of the bezel shape layer and choose Inverse Selection option. Use the Rectangular Marquee tool to deselect the outer edges of the inverted selection so that only the window "portals" are selected.

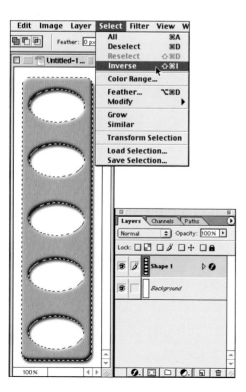

Load the bezel layer selection and choose Inverse Selection.

11 Create a new layer and fill the selection on that layer with the foreground color. (The color itself doesn't matter at this point because it will be replaced by the Layer Style later on.)

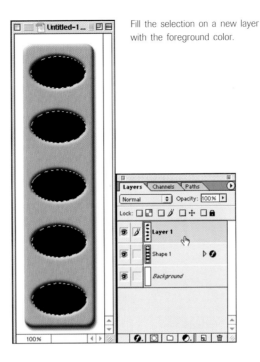

Fill the selection on a new layer with the foreground color.

12 Select and apply the Clear Glass Tubing style from the Styles palette to the new shape layer.

The Custom Styles library can be found on the accompanying CD-ROM. You can always experiment with other Styles or play with the Layer Style settings to tweak the look of the glass window.

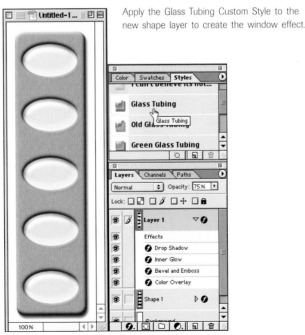

Apply the Glass Tubing Custom Style to the new shape layer to create the window effect.

13 Create a new layer underneath the bezel shape layer and draw a selection with the Rectangular Marquee tool, just inside the edges of the bezel shape.

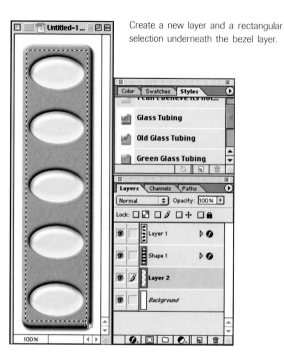

Create a new layer and a rectangular selection underneath the bezel layer.

14 Fill the selection on the new layer with the LCD Pattern from the Custom Patterns library found on the accompanying CD-ROM.

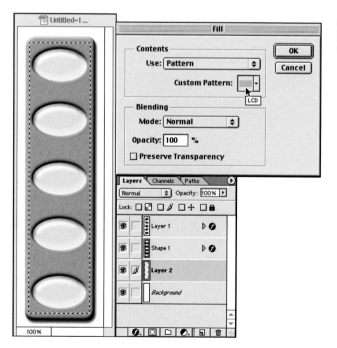

Fill the selection on a new layer with the LCD Pattern from the Custom Patterns library on the accompanying CD-ROM.

15 Duplicate the LCD layer and fill the selection of the new layer with the Indiglo Pattern from the Custom Patterns library.

You now have a base for the LCD Navigation bar, ready for placing text or graphic images "under" the glass buttons.

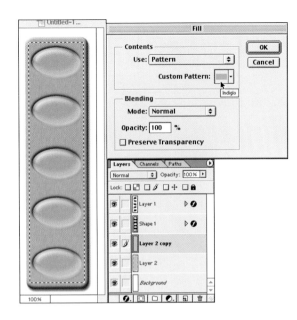

Fill the selection on a new layer with the Indiglo Pattern from the Custom Patterns library.

ADDING THE LCD TEXT LAYERS

This is a very simple process to which you can apply almost any font and have believable results. Arial will be used for this project, but feel free to experiment with other fonts to get the effect you desire. Make sure you always have the Anti-aliased option turned off to get the best result.

1 Using the Type tool directly below the bezel layer, type in a word or message in the top window area.

Be sure to choose None in the Anti-aliasing pull-down menu from the Tool Options bar.

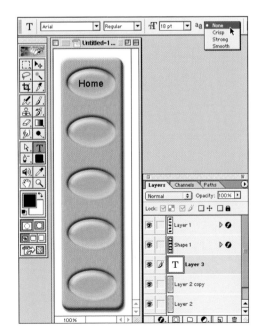

Add text just below the bezel layer, making sure anti-aliasing is turned off.

2   Select the Layer Style Editor from the Layers palette
    and choose the Drop Shadow option. Change only a
    few of the default settings:

    Opacity: **30%**

    Distance: **2px**

    Size: **0px**

    The drop shadow effect will make the LCD text
    appear as if it's on a glass plane above the textured
    surface.

Apply a slight drop shadow to the text to make it
appear as if it's floating on a glass panel inside.

3   Add a text layer in another window area and copy
    the Layer Style of the first text layer from the Layers
    palette.

Create another text layer and copy
the Layer Style form the first.

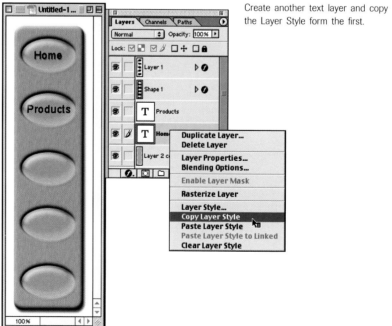

4　Paste the Layer Style to the new text layer in the Layers palette.

By selecting portions of the Indigo texture, you can create rollover animated buttons that "light up." You can learn more about how to do this in Adobe ImageReady in Project 20, "Image Maps, Tables, and Rollovers in ImageReady."

You can vary the look of the entire project just by eliminating or changing the pattern or Style on the texture behind the windows.

Create rollover highlights with the Indiglo layer and more simply by eliminating or changing the texture behind the windows.

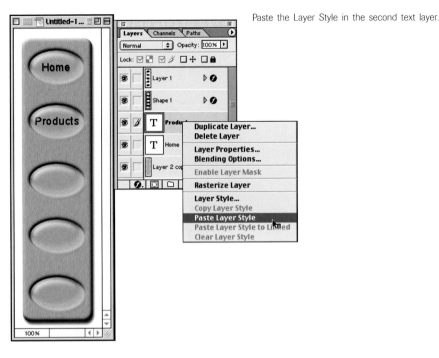

Paste the Layer Style in the second text layer.

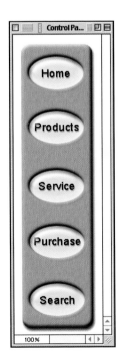

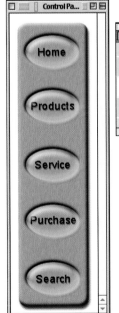

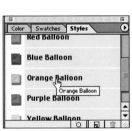

MODIFICATIONS

With so many variations in shape and textures, it's often hard to choose what will work best with your project or design. This variation shows you a few flexibility features that you can further explore on your own design. A small control panel with "floating" text can appear as you program the buttons as rollovers or down-clicks in ImageReady.

1   Create a new file and a modular shape using the Shape tool, Paths, or just by painting on a layer with the Paintbrush tool. Apply the Brushed Aluminum Style to the shape (or any texture/Style you want to use).

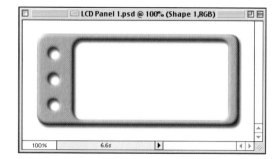

Create a new file and shape layer to which to apply a Custom Style.

2   Create additional layers and apply the techniques you learned earlier in this chapter to these new shapes to achieve the desired look.

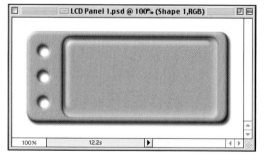

Create additional layers and apply the steps from earlier in this chapter to the new shapes.

3   Add in the text layer(s) where appropriate for your needs. Remember to apply the drop shadow and to keep anti-aliasing turned off for this project.

Add the text layers and apply the Layer Style drop shadow.

4 To add small rubber buttons, simply create a new layer and "paint" them in the appropriate positions with the Paintbrush tool. Then apply the Sm Button Up Style from the Custom Styles library.

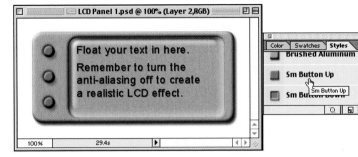

Create small rubber buttons with the Paintbrush tool and add the Sm Button Up Style from the Custom Styles library.

5 To create a down position for the buttons, apply the Sm Button Down Style from the Custom Styles library. You can choose to have the buttons act as rollovers that will advance a string of text or activate the Indiglo backlight panel.

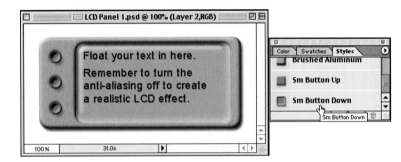

Apply the Sm Button Down Style from the Custom Styles library for a pushed-in effect that can act as a rollover state.

Note: Working examples can be viewed in the Examples area of the accompanying CD-ROM, as well as at this Web site: **www.photoshopwebmagic.com**.

ANIMATED
ATTENTION-GETTERS!

"Is not life a hundred times too short

for us to bore ourselves?"

—FRIEDRICH NIETZSCHE

STRYPER ANIMATIONS

One of those 1980s "hair bands" inspired this

eye-catching yellow and black animation effect...

and since it's created using only the Styles

palette, you can apply it to any layered object—

painted lines, text, bullets, arrows, whatever!

Project 18

Animated Attention-Getters!

by Jeff Foster

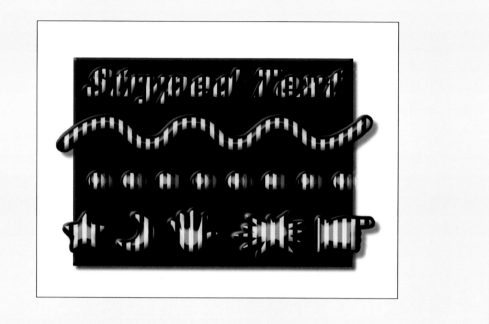

GETTING STARTED

For this exercise, we'll create a long, snake-like line that the animation effect will run inside. This accentuates the effect when it's animated. A couple of variations at the end of the chapter will show you how to add this same effect to bullets and text for truly eye-catching results!

CREATE A PATH FOR THE STRIPED BRUSH

To create a smooth line that doesn't have any jagged or distorted curves in it, a path is created along points on a grid. The grid will be laid out first, and the Path tool will be applied with a brushstroke that creates the final curved line.

1 Select File, New and create a new file that's wide enough for a long smooth line.

Width: **600 pixels**

Height: **100 pixels**

Resolution: **72 pixels/inch**

Background color: **Black**

2 Select Show Rulers and drag out guides to create a smooth line. In this example, the guides were placed at 75-pixel horizontal increments and two equidistant vertical increments.

Set up rulers and guides for an even, smooth line.

3 Select the Pen tool from the Tool palette. A path will be created to draw a smooth line. This will ultimately become the wide shape that the striped animation will run inside.

Click and drag the Pen tool to alternate guide intersections to create a smooth, snake-like line.

4 Click on the intersection of the bottom-left guides. Then click and drag the Pen tool alternately on upper/lower intersections to create a smooth, snake-like line until you reach the farthest right guide intersection.

5 Create a new layer (Layer 1) and select the Hard Round 19-pixel paintbrush from the Brush palette.

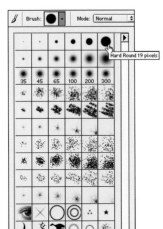

Select the Hard Round 19-pixel paintbrush.

6 Select the Paths palette and choose Stroke Path from the side pull-down menu.

7 Select the Paintbrush tool from the pop-up menu.

   Layer 1 will now have a smooth white paintbrush line following the path line.

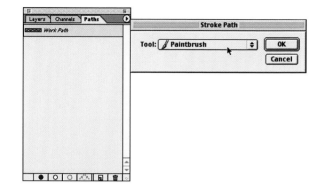

Select Stroke Path from the Paths palette pull-down menu.

Select the Paintbrush tool from the pop-up menu. Layer 1 will have a smooth paintbrush line that follows the path line.

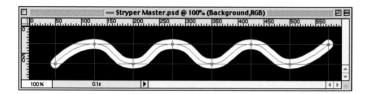

APPLY STYLES TO THE LINES

Make sure you have the custom Styles library loaded from the CD-ROM. You will duplicate Layer 1 three times and apply the animation sequence Styles in order 1 through 4 to achieve the desired effect.

1 With Layer 1 active in the Layers palette, choose B&Y V Stripe Bar 1 from the Styles palette.

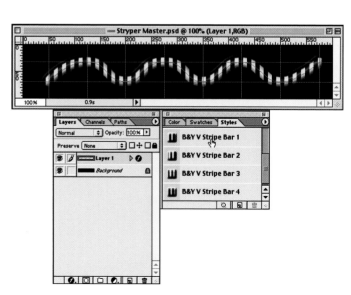

Select B&Y V Stripe Bar 1 from the Styles palette.

2 Duplicate Layer 1 and then apply the Style B&Y V Stripe Bar 2 to the Layer 1 copy.

3 Repeat Step 2 twice more, selecting the sequential Styles for the third and fourth animation frames.

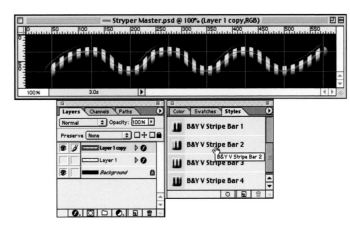

Apply the second animation sequence Style to the duplicated layer.

4 Select Turn Off Path from the Paths palette. Hide the guides and you're ready to start animating the layers with ImageReady!

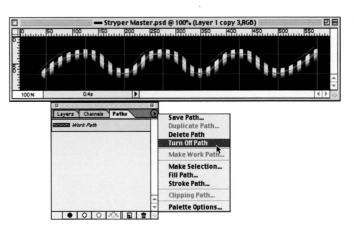

Turn off the path and you're ready to start animating the layers in ImageReady!

CREATE AN ANIMATION OF THE LAYERS IN ADOBE IMAGEREADY

Adobe ImageReady is an application that comes with Photoshop 6 for creating animation sequences and image maps. No need to use third-party utilities and save several layers out as sequenced files. With just a few clicks of the mouse, you'll be animating your project in no time!

1. Select Jump to Adobe ImageReady 3.0 from the File menu.

2. In the Animation palette, select Make Frames From Layers.

3. Click on each frame in the Animation palette and make the Background layer visible by clicking on the Eye icon.

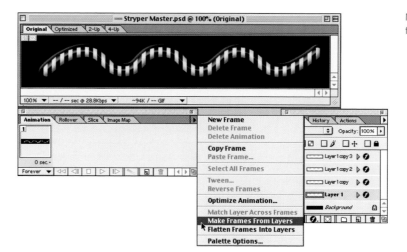

Make frames for the animation from the Photoshop layers.

4. Preview the animation sequence by clicking on the Play button at the bottom of the Animation palette.

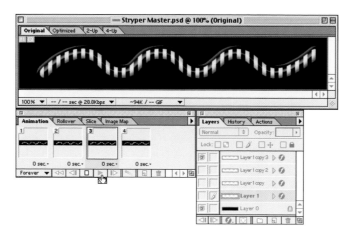

Preview the animation by selecting Play in the Animation palette.

5   Preview how the animation will run in your Web browser by selecting Preview In Internet Explorer or Netscape Navigator.

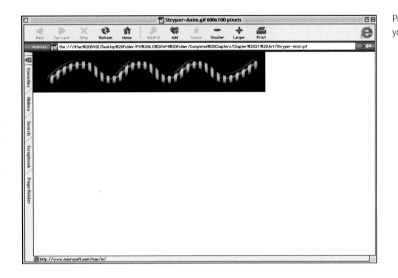

Preview the animation in your favorite Web browser.

Note: This preview option may require more memory than your computer has available because most Web browsers require as much memory as Photoshop or ImageReady alone.

6   Make any necessary timing adjustments on the Animation palette to speed up or slow down your animation before saving the optimized file.

MODIFICATIONS

By simply changing the images, brushes, or shapes, or by using type, you can create countless animations with this simple four-step animation Style.

You can also view these animation examples located on the accompanying CD-ROM.

The Stryper animation applied to text.

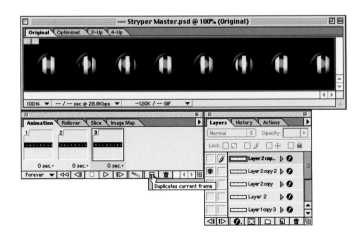

The Stryper animation applied to round buttons.

The Stryper animation applied to shapes.

BOING! POP-UP
ANNOUNCEMENT SPLASH

"Do not trust the horse, Trojans!

Whatever it is, I fear the Greeks,

even though they bring gifts."

—VIRGIL, FROM *THE AENEID*

POP-UP ANNOUNCEMENT SPLASH

A fun way to encourage click-throughs on

a Web site or banner ad is with a clever

animated announcement. This pop-up splash

announcement is a perfect way to let the visitor

know you have a message they just shouldn't

ignore! Variations can be added to photos

or other artwork and used as rollovers or

click-down animations.

Project 19

BOING! Pop-Up
Announcement Splash

by Jeff Foster

GETTING STARTED

Although the process of creating this project seems quite simple, the "magic" in
the effect is the timing of the animation in ImageReady. If you don't achieve the
"bounce" in the final animation, it won't have as much impact—or get enough of the
people's attention. Using the new Shapes tool and the Text tool, you can quickly lay
out scaleable image layers that will cleanly rasterize at varying sizes without aliased
edges or blurry pixelation. The Custom Layer Styles give the shapes and text substance
and shadowing, and with the Liquify command, both type and shapes can be warped
to appear as if they are springing up off the page.

CREATING THE SHAPE ANIMATION SEQUENCE

For this project, a variety of tools and options will be used to create the springing
"pop-up" effect, including the Shape and Text tools, Warp Text option, Custom
Layer Styles for a 3D effect, and the Liquify command. First, the layered stages of
the animation are created in Photoshop. Then the timing of the animation will
occur in ImageReady.

1 Create a new file that's **300×300** pixels, **72** pixels/inch.

2 Select the Shapes tool and choose the 10 Point Star Custom Shape.

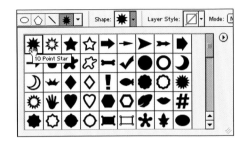

Select the 10 Point Star Custom Shape.

3 With a bright foreground color selected, draw a wide star in the window.

You want the star to be slightly wider than tall because it will be rotated.

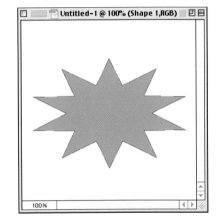

Draw a wide star shape in the window.

4 Using the Transform command, rotate the star shape to an approximate angle of −15 to −20 degrees.

This will be the largest size in the animation sequence, and we will work backwards through the pop-up animation.

5 Double-click on the star shape layer to launch the Layer Styles Editor. Select the Bevel and Emboss option and increase the Bevel Size to 10.

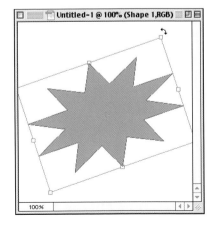

Rotate the star shape approximately −15 to −20 degrees.

6 Apply the Drop Shadow option and set the Distance to 25 pixels and the Size to 15 pixels.

7 Duplicate the shape layer. Hide the original layer and make the copy layer active.

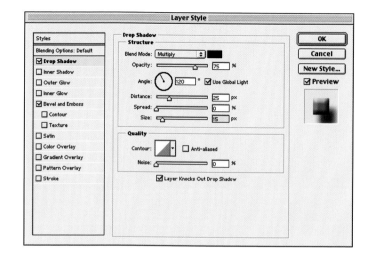

Apply the Custom Layer Styles to create dimension and shadows.

8 Choose the Direct Selection Tool from the Tool palette.

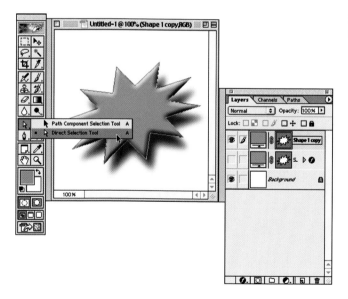

Duplicate the shape layer and choose the Direct Selection Tool.

9   Draw out a selection area that selects only the inside points of the star shape.

10   Select the Transform Points Scale tool.

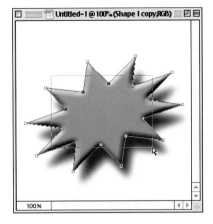

Select only the inside points of the star shape.

11   Hold down the Shift key and pull out the scale handles to create a "bulge" effect to the star shape.

This will become the closest frame in the animation sequence.

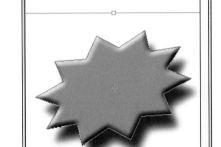

Using the Transform Points Scale tool, scale up the inner points to create a bulge effect.

12   Hide the bulged layer and duplicate the original layer. Use the Transform tool to decrease the size of the duplicated layer slightly and rotate approximately 5 degrees (clockwise).

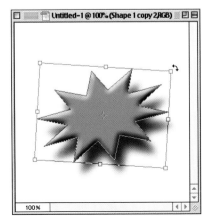

Duplicate the original layer again and decrease its size while slightly rotating clockwise.

13 Open the Layer Styles Editor, decrease the Bevel and Emboss option a couple of pixels, and decrease the size of the Drop Shadow slightly.

Repeat Steps 12 and 13 so you'll have a total of four shape layers in ascending size and rotation.

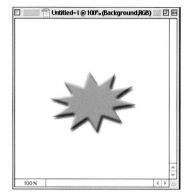

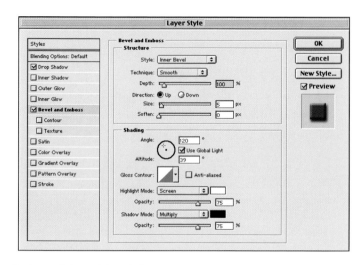

Decrease the amount of Bevel and Emboss, Drop Shadow, and size and then duplicate once more.

14 Duplicate the smallest star shape layer and rasterize it in the Layers palette.

Duplicate the smallest star shape layer and rasterize it.

CREATING THE TEXT ANIMATION SEQUENCE

Now that there's a pattern of shapes to guide the process, the text can be quickly added to the sequence. The result will be that the text actually pops up toward the viewer slightly more than the star shape, creating a disconnected springy effect.

1 Select the Type tool and apply text with a complementary color. Make sure the text's size keeps the word inside the edges of the smallest star layer. Select the Transform Rotate tool to match the angle of the star shape.

Apply text in a complementary color that fits inside the smallest star shape and rotate to match the star's angle.

2 Open the Layer Style Editor on the text layer and apply the Drop Shadow option with the Distance set to 3 pixels and the Size set to 2 pixels. Check that the angle is set at the default 120 degrees. Select the Bevel and Emboss option and set the Depth to 100% and the Size to 3 pixels.

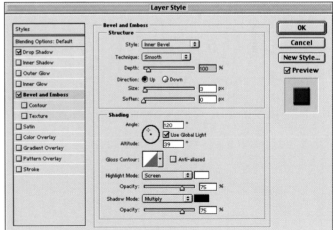

Apply Bevel and Emboss with Drop Shadow to the text to give it a 3D appearance.

3 Hide the current layers and make the next-larger-size star shape visible. Duplicate the text layer, increase the Scale, and rotate a couple of pixels counterclockwise to follow the angle of the star shape. Repeat the process two more times, increasing the amount of Drop Shadow and Bevel and Emboss for each step.

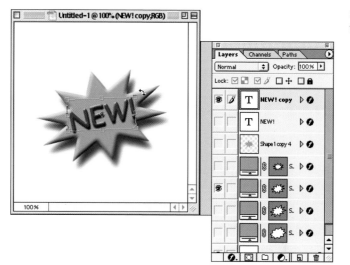

Duplicate the text layer and adjust for the increasing sizes of each star layer.

4 Make the bulged star layer visible. Duplicate the largest text layer and make it active. Select the Warp Text option and choose the Bulge Style. Set the Bend to +25%. Duplicate the text layer again, apply the Warp Text option, and set the Bend to −12%.

You will have two new warped text layers that will be used to enhance the pop-up spring effect.

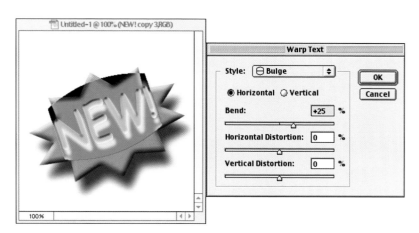

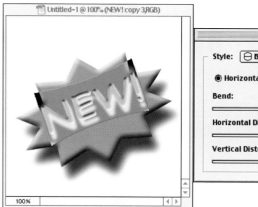

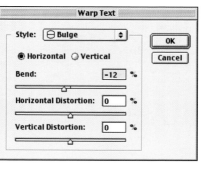

Duplicate the largest text layer twice and apply the Warp Text option to create a springing mode at the center of the text.

5 Duplicate the largest bulge text layer and increase its scale slightly as well as the Drop Shadow Distance.

This will be the sequence frame that will be the closest to the viewer during the pop-up animation.

Duplicate the largest bulge text layer and scale it up to appear as if it's closer to the screen.

Animating the Sequence in ImageReady

This part of the project is where it all comes together. Because most of the work has already been done in the Photoshop layers, it will just be a matter of making the layers visible along the animation timeline. This is the suggestive part of the project, so some adjusting will be necessary to achieve the effect you're looking for. Make sure to check out the sample animation in the folder for this project on the enclosed CD-ROM.

1 Make the smallest star and text layers visible, choose Jump to ImageReady, and select the Animation bar. Duplicate the first frame of animation and make the next larger star and text layers visible—while hiding the original layers.

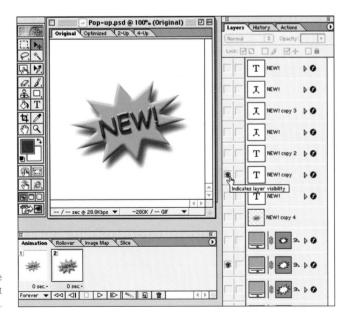

Jump to ImageReady and start the animation sequence from the smallest layers to the largest.

2 Repeat the process until you've reached the large bulged star layer. Hold the bulge layer in place (keep the layer visible) as you create more frames using the warped text frames.

The text will bulge out and then bulge in and out again, depending on how much "spring action" you want to give it. As the text reverses in order back down to the original size, make sure to follow with the star shape layers.

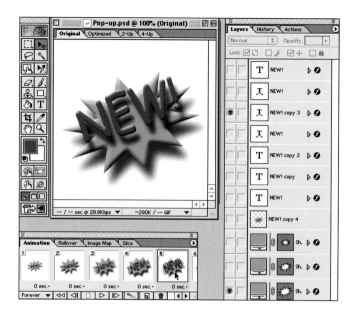

Repeat the process, working up to the bulged layers and back down to the original layers.

You will need to test the animation while you are creating the order. To do so, select the Preview in Browser option. You can make changes to the ImageReady file without selecting Save Optimized As while testing. It might help to study the motion sequence of the samples in the chapter folder on the enclosed CD-ROM or at the **www.photoshopwebmagic.com** Web site.

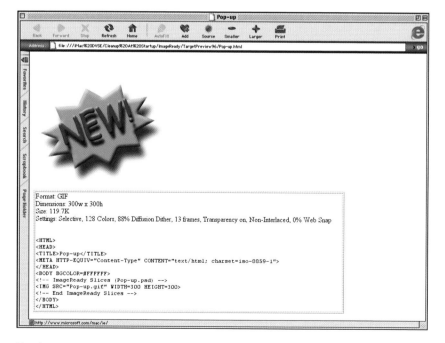

Test the animation in your Web browser or study the completed animation on the CD-ROM.

MODIFICATION

Using only a couple of passes of the Liquify command brush, a simple rollover technique can be made from this sequence.

1　Duplicate the smallest star layer and the smallest text layer visible and make the copies active. Choose the Rasterize command on both layers, link them together, and merge them using Merge Linked.

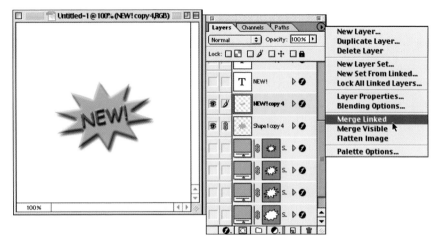

Duplicate and then rasterize the smallest star and text layers and merge them.

2　Select the Liquify command and apply the Pucker tool to the center of the star shape. The effect should appear; the star with the text is being pushed in.

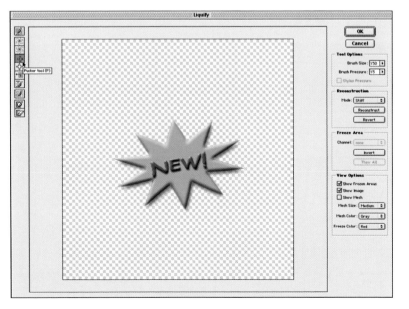

Apply the Liquify command to pinch the merged star and text layer to give it the appearance of being pushed in.

3   Make the smallest star layer and the next-to-smallest
    text layer visible and choose Jump to ImageReady.

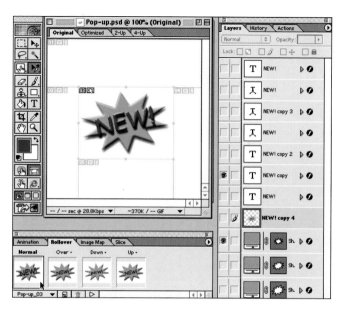

Jump to ImageReady and organize
the layers in the Rollover bar.

4   Use the Slice tool to draw out a slice selection
    around the star shape. Make the slice active with
    the Slice Selector tool and open the Rollover bar.

5   Choose the Add Rollover button and make the
    smallest text layer visible. Repeat for the Down-click
    state, only make just the Pinched layer visible. Make
    an Up state that matches the rollover state.

Test the rollover in your Web browser. You can choose to save the HTML table with all the separate images or just the selected slice with images out of ImageReady.

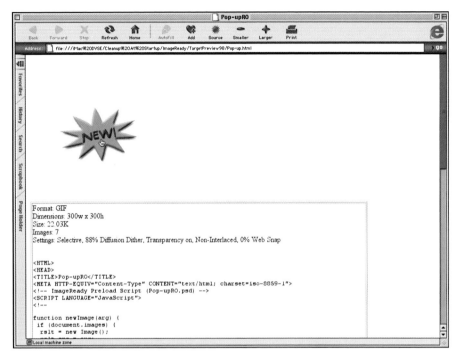

Test the rollover in your Web browser and save the optimized HTML and images when you're finished.

IMAGE MAPS, TABLES, AND ROLLOVERS IN IMAGEREADY

"Hey, you can't fight in here!

This is the war room!"

—DR. STRANGELOVE

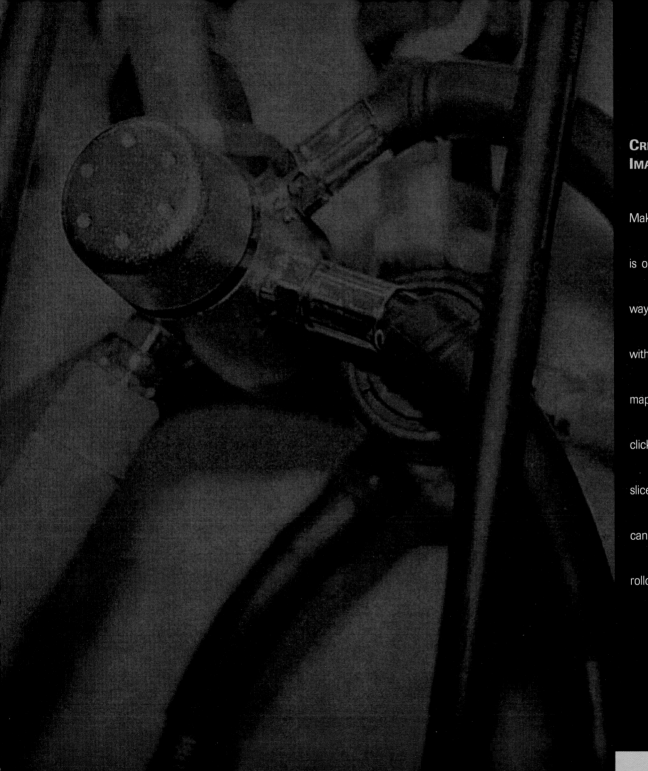

CREATING IMAGE MAPS AND TABLES WITH IMAGEREADY

Making your Web page design appear as if it

is one continuous image can be done several

ways—right out of ImageReady. A single image

with "hot spots" for rollovers is called an image

map. If you want animations or rollover and

click-down actions to take place, you'll need to

slice up your image and create a table. You

can create an easy image map or table with

rollovers very quickly in ImageReady.

Image Maps, Tables, and Rollovers in ImageReady

by Jeff Foster

GETTING STARTED

Image maps can be quickly created using ImageReady without the necessity of using an external HTML editor. Tables are just as easily created with great rollovers without much knowledge of HTML. ImageReady does create some pretty hefty HTML code (especially its JavaScript commands), so if you're used to using Adobe® GoLive® or Macromedia® DreamWeaver®, you may want to export only the image slices and build the HTML using another application. If you're new to Web page authoring (or just in a hurry), ImageReady will crank out what you need, pronto!

CREATING AN IMAGE MAP WITH IMAGEREADY

In this part of the project, a simple image map with five rollover "hot spots" will be created. These hot spots could link to any URL you give them, whether they're linking to page anchors, linking to documents elsewhere on the Web, or residing locally on an intranet hard drive. You can even have it open a new window or a document inside another frame on your page.

1 Launch ImageReady and open any image
file you want or follow along with the file
WasherDrum.jpg in the Sample Images folder on
the enclosed CD-ROM. Make the Image Map bar
active and select the Polygon Image Map Tool.

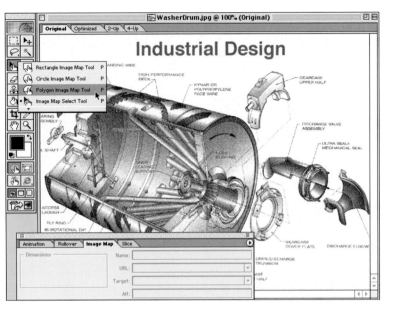

Open the image file inside
ImageReady and select the
Polygon Image Map Tool.

2 Draw a coarse outline around a detailed part of the
image with the Polygon Image Map Tool, joining the
line at the endpoint with the beginning point. At this
point, you can select the link URL, Alt tags, and
Target frames/windows.

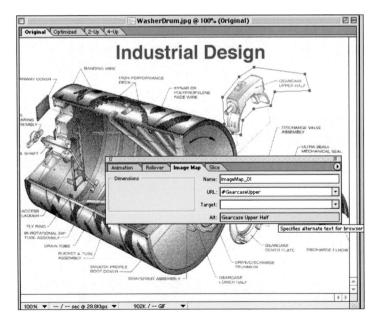

Draw the image map outline around
a detail in the image and set the
parameters of the hot spot.

3 Continue with as many hot spots as you want on the image. Be careful not to overlap any of the areas.

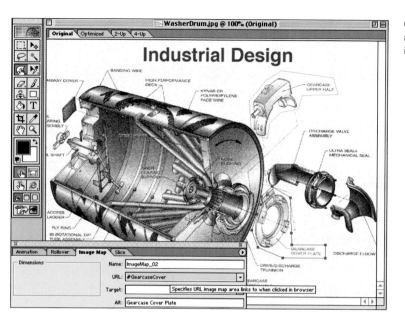

Continue the process of adding hot spots to the image map.

4 Preview the image map in a Web browser to check the hot spot links and rollover areas.

Note: Internet Explorer will show the actual image map hot spot borders when clicked on (as shown in this figure). Refer to the special HTML code section on the photoshopwebmagic.com Web site for tips on creating code that hides the outlines in Internet Explorer. Netscape Communicator users can enjoy an outline-free experience.

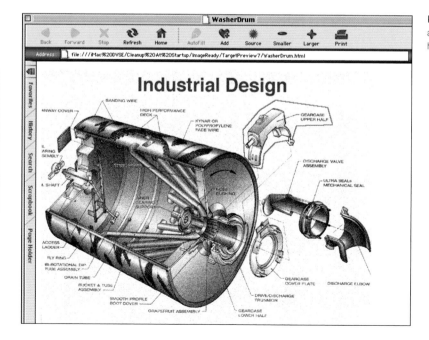

Preview the image map in a Web browser to check hot spot links.

CREATING FRAMES WITH ROLLOVERS IN IMAGEREADY

This part of the project will show you how to quickly add rollovers to your project. We will start with a Photoshop document that has the rollover layers already created for you, but the slices and rollover actions have been left for you to do.

1   Launch ImageReady and open the file **PointwareBoxes.psd** from the Sample Images folder on the enclosed CD-ROM. Turn on View Rulers and drag a guide line out about halfway down the horizontal center of the image.

    This will be used to guide the slices so that they match up cleanly and evenly.

2   Using the Slice tool, draw out your first Rollover Slice around the first box as shown. You can also select the link URL and Target frame at this point if you want.

3   Continue this process with the remaining four boxes. Make sure the edges of each slice butt up to the preceding slice so as not to create unwanted slices in between them.

Open the image file PointwareBoxes.psd inside ImageReady and draw a selection with the Slice tool around the first box.

Continue the process of creating slices with the remaining boxes.

4 Activate the Rollover bar and select the first box slice with the Slice Selector tool. Create a Rollover state on the Rollover bar and make the first Buy Now layer visible on the Layers palette.

5 Continue this process with the remaining four boxes, making each successive layer visible for each slice's matching Rollover state.

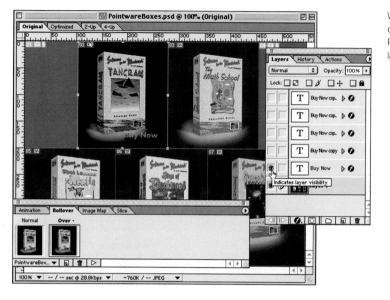

With the first box slice selected, create a Rollover state on the Rollover bar and make the first layer visible.

Preview in a Web browser to check the rollovers and the links. When you are satisfied with the progress, select Save Optimized As and select the option HTML and Images. You can use ImageReady Options to set the background color as well as many other optimized file and HTML features.

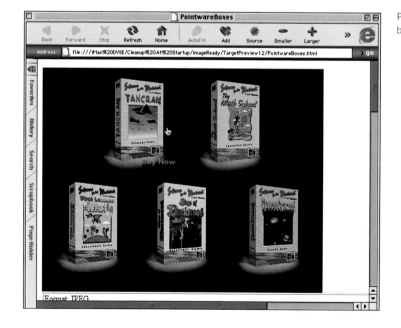

Preview the file in a Web browser to check the rollovers.

SAVING OUT THE ROLLOVER IMAGES FOR USE IN AN HTML EDITOR

If you already are HTML savvy or are using a text editor or a WYSIWYG (What You See Is What You Get) application, you may want to just save out the sliced images to put into your own table. This is a method chosen by professional Web site developers who don't want to deal with the incompatible code that ImageReady produces. In this part of the project, you will only rename the slices and save them into a folder to use in your own table in the WYSIWYG HTML editor.

1 After completing the preceding Steps 1 and 2, be sure to rename the slices to a meaningful image name that you can later use with your preferred JavaScript code. The slices will first be the "off" state.

Complete the preceding Steps 1 and 2 and then rename the slices to JavaScript-compatible image names for the "off" state.

2 Set the Options for Saving Optimized Files so that the slice name only is exported without any extraneous information. Select Save Optimized As and choose Images Only.

This will create images from your slices that only have the slice name and the .jpg or .gif extensions.

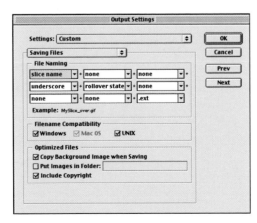

Make the File Naming changes in the Save File Options window to reflect only the slice names and then Save Optimized As and Images Only.

3 Make the subsequent Buy Now layers visible and change the slice names to reflect the need naming for the JavaScript code you will be using (for example, _on, _over, _RO, and so on). Repeat for the remaining layers and choose Save Optimized As and Images Only to the same directory as you did in Step 2. You are now ready to reassemble the images in your HTML editor.

Make the subsequent rollover images visible for each slice and rename the slices for the Rollover state in the JavaScript code you're using. Save the images to the same directory as in Step 2.

MODIFICATION

This is a quick way to modify an image to have interaction with the visitor by simply rolling over the image and clicking on it to produce a reaction to the visitor's motions. Using the Liquify command and the rollover slice sequences, this can be easily done in just a few steps.

1 Launch ImageReady and open the built-in Photoshop file **Bear.psd** from the Photoshop Samples folder on your hard drive.

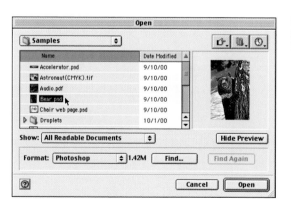

Open the Bear.psd file from the Samples folder in Photoshop from inside ImageReady.

2 Using the Rectangular Marquee tool, make a selection around the bear's head. Copy the selection and paste it to a new layer, twice. Make the first copied layer active and then launch the Liquify command.

Make sure to stay far enough away from the edges of his head so that you don't get bitten!

Make a rectangular selection around the bear's head, copy and paste it to two new layers, and then launch the Liquify command.

3 Select the Bloat tool and apply it to his eyes and tongue, creating the effect that his eyes are bugging out and he's sticking out his tongue.

You may need to practice with brush sizes and pressure a bit to get a feel for what works best for you. Use this figure as a guide.

Use the Bloat tool to make the bear's eyes and tongue bug out.

4 Make the second copied layer active and launch the Liquify command. Use the Pucker tool to squint his eyes and mouth closed and to pucker up his nose.

5 Using the Slice tool, create a slice around the bear's head, just inside the edges of the copied layers. Make the copied layers invisible and activate the Rollover bar. The Normal state will just have the background image layer visible.

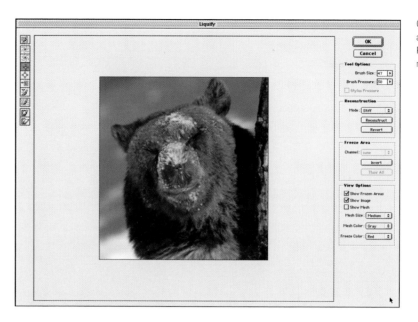

On the second copied layer, apply the Liquify command's Pucker tool to his eyes, mouth, and nose.

6 Create a Rollover state (Over) and make the big eyes layer visible. Create a Down state, making the squinted face layer visible. For an Up state, just make the background image visible.

Use the Slice tool to create a rollover area and set the Rollover and Down states as shown in the figure.

Preview in a Web browser and click on the bear's nose. It
will appear as if he's taunting you when you roll over his
face, then you can poke him in the nose and show him!
Imagine how fun this would be to do with a picture of
your boss.

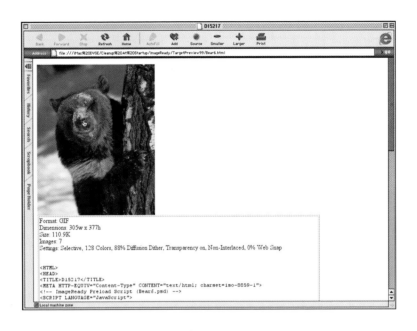

IMAGE OPTIMIZATION
IN IMAGEREADY

"The life so short,

the craft so long to learn."

—HIPPOCRATES

COMPRESSING IMAGES FOR THE WEB

The smaller an image file, the faster it will download to the viewer's computer. The faster an image downloads, the less the viewer waits. The less the viewer waits, the more pleasant the visit.

Unfortunately, smaller image files often require compromises in quality. Finding the right balance, however, between reduced size and high quality is not as difficult as it might seem. Photoshop 6's improved Web tools make it easier than ever.

Project 21

Image Optimization in ImageReady

by Peter Bauer

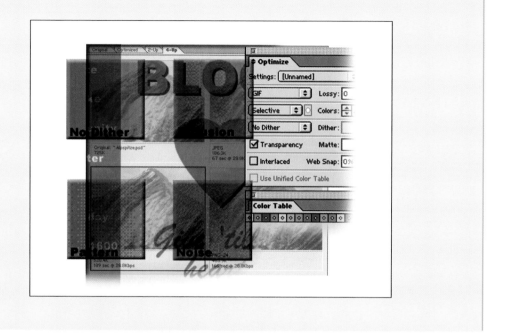

GETTING STARTED

This project is different from other projects in this book, not only in its subject matter but in the style in which it is presented. This is a very important topic that shouldn't be overlooked, though it is often misunderstood in Web design. That is why we've turned to the expertise of imaging guru Peter Bauer to help us understand image optimization.

Dozens of different file formats are available for saving images. Many are proprietary—they work only with a specific program or perhaps some related programs. The .psd format for Photoshop is an example. Few programs can open these files. Images saved for the Web must be opened by the visitors' Web browsers. Internet Explorer and Netscape Communicator can't open .psd files. In fact, they can open only a few image file types, but they do accept plug-ins for several more. Knowing what file formats are available—and for what they should be used—is the first step toward optimal file size.

THE WEB FILE FORMATS

The ImageReady compression techniques that we'll look at can also be performed, for the most part, through Photoshop's Save for Web command (found under the File menu). There are some minor differences in the palette layouts as well as a few minor functional differences.

Warning: There is one major difference between working in ImageReady and using the Save for Web command: There is no Undo in Save for Web. Although this might sound insignificant to people who rarely make mistakes, it's a huge loss for those of us who rely on trial and error to achieve perfection.

There is a way to work around the lack of Undo. With the Save for Web window open, press Option(Alt). The OK button changes to Remember, and the Cancel button switches to Reset. Remember saves the current optimization settings for that image with the image. (It will have no effect on other images.) Reset restores the optimization settings to those saved by Remember or, if no settings have been saved, to the default settings. When working in the 2-Up or 4-Up views, Reset will restore only the active window.

Compressing any image requires selection of a file format. The rule of thumb is that images with large areas of solid color (such as this one) should be saved as GIFs (graphic interchange format). Let's prove it using ImageReady and the blood drive announcement.

1　Open the image **BloodDrive.psd** from the accompanying CD-ROM. (You can see the difference on your screen by choosing the settings shown.)

2　Click the 4-Up tab. By default, the upper-left image is the original (although this can be changed). ImageReady enables you to view up to four variations as you make your choices. For this image, a file size of 10KB or smaller is acceptable.

JPEG (Joint Photographic Experts Group) requires extreme compression to reach the target file size, which results in a badly dithered and pixilated image. GIF with a maximum of 256 colors in the Color Table reaches the target size and provides an acceptable image. When the image is reduced to the original three colors (red, maroon, and white), the lack of anti-aliasing produces an unacceptably jagged image.

Note: Normally, optimization options should be viewed at 100% zoom. By viewing the actual pixels, you get a better indication of what the Web browsers will show your site's visitors. For the purposes of illustration, higher zoom ratios will occasionally be employed in this section.

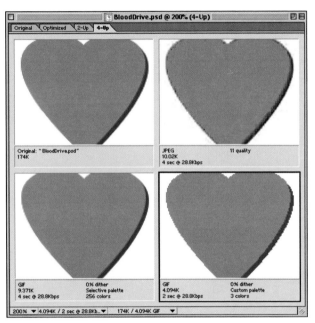

Use ImageReady to view your optimization possibilities.

3 Click the JPEG variation in the upper-right corner and change its settings to those shown in the figure. Use the Colors pop-up menu and select 16. (This has not noticeably affected the image, but it has reduced the size to just over 75% of the 256-color version.)

Using GIF with a Color Table of 256 as a starting point, you can further reduce the image size without sacrificing too much quality. In this case, however, we want to retain the 256-color version as a reference.

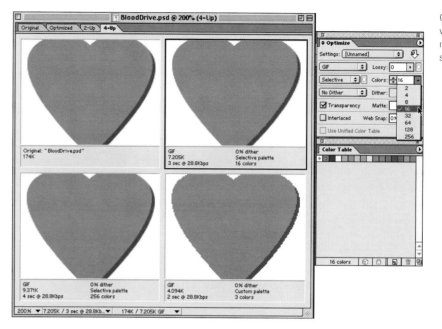

Click on one of the four variations to make adjustments to its optimization settings.

Save for Web and ImageReady offer several GIF presets in the pop-up menu. In addition to the number of colors, you can choose from various dithering styles. Dithering is the use of two colors to represent a gradient blend between the two. In this figure, you can see the differences between the dithering options. Although Diffusion offers a slider to adjust the amount of dithering from 0% to 100%, Pattern and Noise offer no adjustment. This gradient image is used merely as an example of dithering. GIF would not normally be used with a gradated image.

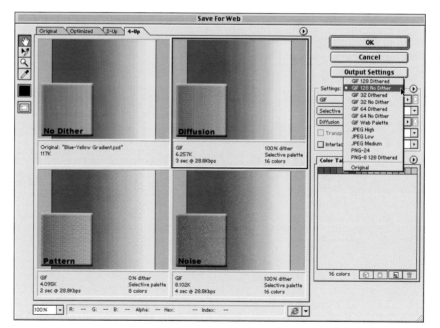

Dither your image to reduce banding where two colors blend. Note that this figure shows the Save for Web interface.

266

UTILIZING THE WEB-SAFE PALETTE

The next step is to ensure that each visitor's Web browser shows the image's colors as close to the original as possible. To do this, we restrict the colors in the image to the 216 that are common to both the Windows and Macintosh system palettes. This is known as using the Web-safe palette.

1 Click in the lower-left pane of the 4-Up window and then click the Optimized tab of the Save for Web window. The 256-color variation is then shown alone.

2 Click on one color in the Color Table and then Shift+click another to select a series of contiguous colors.

Command+clicking (Ctrl+clicking) enables the selection on noncontiguous colors.

3 Select All Non-Web Safe Colors from the palette's pop-up menu. Next, select Web Shift/Un-shift Selected Colors from the pop-up menu.

Notice that the pop-up menu also enables the colors to be sorted in a variety of ways, including by Popularity (the number of pixels in the image of that color).

Because many of the original 256 colors were close to the same members of the Web-safe palette, the total number of colors in the images has dropped to 13. The size of the file has now fallen by approximately one-third.

Note: Shifting each color to its nearest Web-safe equivalent provides more consistency from browser to browser; each visitor sees a similar image. Unshifting, which returns a color to its original appearance, is activated when some of the selected colors have already been shifted.

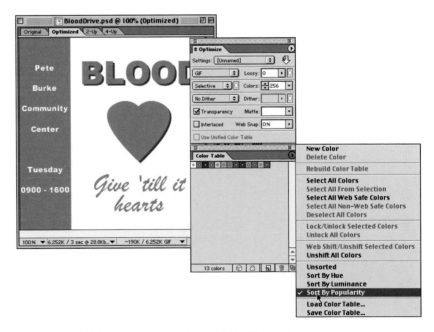

Use the Color Table's pop-up menu to select and Web-shift colors in the image. Both the image and the swatches in the Color Table are adjusted.

4 Check the Interlaced box as shown. This enables the image to download in passes and gives the viewer a visual clue that the image is in fact downloading. With the box unchecked, the image will not appear in the browser windows until completely downloaded.

Note: If the Interlaced option isn't visible, click the Optimize palette's tab to expand it or use the palette's menu command Show Options. The palette's menu can be accessed by clicking the small black triangle in the palette's upper-right corner.

Put a check in the Interlaced box to keep your visitor from waiting too long without visible action. Although it can add slightly to the file size, interlacing actually reduced the file size by an insignificant amount in this particular case.

There are two other ways to reach the same Web-safe color palette with this image. When first opening ImageReady or the Save for Web dialog box, use the pop-up menu to switch from Selective to Web for the Color Table. Another technique is to force the colors to their Web-safe equivalents by using the Web Snap slider.

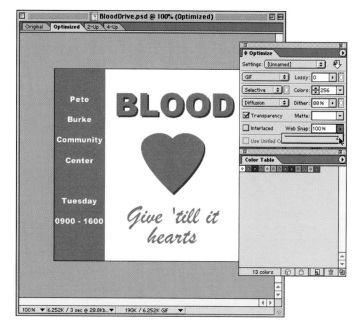

Use the pop-up menu to automatically change to the Web-safe palette or use the slider to dynamically adjust the shift.

With the slider at 100%, all colors in the Color Table will be Web safe. For this particular image, the slider doesn't shift over half of the colors to Web safe until 93%. The progression is shown here:

Web Safe	Total Colors	Web Safe	File Size
0%	256	6	9.37KB
10%	251	9	
25%	221	10	9.22KB
40%	194	11	
50%	180	11	9.03KB
65%	145	12	
75%	98	12	7.16KB
90%	48	13	
100%	13	13	6.25KB

Typically, the colors with higher Popularity (frequency in the image) will be adjusted to Web-safe equivalents before those colors represented by a very few pixels.

Note: The gradated image seen previously can also serve as an example of the importance of your optimization steps. In this figure you can see, in addition to the original image, how color reduction and dithering can interact. In the upper-right, Diffusion dither at 100% was chosen, all the colors in the Color Table were selected, and the Snap to Web Palette button was clicked. The Color Table was reduced to seven colors, and the banding is extreme. In the lower-left image, the two steps were reversed, and the result is a Color Table of six and a marginally better appearance with slightly more dithering. The final image is significantly better. GIF Web Palette was selected from the Settings pop-up menu prior to dithering.

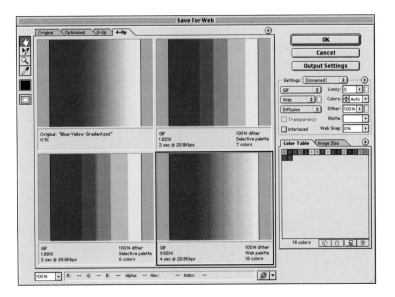

Reverse the order of your optimization steps to see if it's better to dither first or to reduce the color palette.

PNG-8 File Format

Another file format has arrived on the scene to take the place of GIF. PNG (portable network graphics) comes in two varieties: 8-bit color (256 maximum colors, comparable to GIF) and 24-bit color (16.7 million colors, comparable to JPEG). PNG-8 has a couple advantages over GIF, but that might be outweighed by the fact that older Web browsers don't support the format. As more and more Web surfers upgrade to newer versions of Internet Explorer and Netscape Navigator, PNG will become more common.

In addition, PNG typically produces somewhat larger files than GIF. So what's the attraction? PNG is free. Every piece of software that is capable of saving to or reading the GIF file format is licensed. Royalties are paid for the right to use the LZW (Lempel-Ziv-Welch) compression scheme. PNG uses a version that is in the public domain.

1 Taking the same image and using the default PNG-8 settings gives us a decent file size (8.97KB) that appears to be identical to the original. Restrict the image to the Web-safe palette, reducing it to the same 13 colors seen previously and a file size of 7.37KB.

Eliminating the dithering option decreases the file size by an insignificant amount for this image, which contains no gradients.

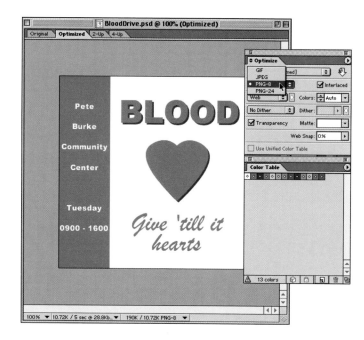

Use the pop-up menu to select PNG-8 as the file format.

270

2   Check the box for Interlacing. The file size balloons to 10.72KB.

This 45% increase in size is typical for an image of this size and composition. Although larger images will see a smaller increase percentage-wise, it's not unusual for a 100KB image to be increased by 20KB when interlaced as PNG-8. Comparable images optimized as GIFs will increase by 5KB to 7KB when interlaced.

Using PNG images on a Web site can lead to frustration for many visitors. Unless they have a browser capable of displaying the file type, they might be greeted with a message asking them to find another way to view the image. Many older browsers will display a broken link symbol.

If you open a PNG-8 file with a browser that doesn't support the format, you might see either a broken link or a warning message.

COMPRESSING CONTINUOUS-TONE IMAGES

Photographs, images that contain gradients, and other images that have subtle shifts in color are referred to as continuous tone. We've seen what GIF's 256-color limit does to gradients. An entirely different file format is required to save and display such images. On the Web, we typically use JPEG. JPEG is not truly a file format; rather, it's the name of the file-compression scheme used by the format. What we refer to as JPEG is actually a format properly known as JFIF (JPEG file interchange format). The file extension is .jpg, no matter what you call it.

JPEG's major advantage over GIF is its ability to handle 24-bit-per-channel color. With three channels (RGB), more than 16.7 million colors are available. Does this mean that all colors can be accurately displayed, regardless of how the visitor's computer is configured? No. Remember that the browser and system limitations that restrict GIF to the 216-color Web-safe palette also apply here. However, maintaining the relationships between colors in a photograph is often more important than showing the exact colors. Keep in mind that the vast majority of Web surfers have not calibrated their monitors. As hard as you try, you cannot be assured that what you're posting is what they are seeing.

COMPARING JPEG AND GIF USING A GRADIENT

Typically, the limited color tables of GIF (256 maximum as 8-bit color) produce banding in images with gradients. Banding is seen as a series of stripes of distinct colors rather than a gradual fade from one color to another. JPEG's 24-bit color allows for a far greater range, producing the subtle shifts in hue required by gradients.

JPEG is a lossy compression system—some information is discarded during compression. The algorithm works on the limitations of the human eye. We are far more capable of seeing a change in brightness than a change in color.

1   Create a simple radial gradient going from pure red (255, 0, 0 in RGB notation) to its color wheel opposite, cyan (RGB 0, 255, 255). This will demonstrate one of the differences between GIF and JPEG.

The original shows a smooth transition between the colors. Next to the original, GIF with the Web palette and no dithering produces an excellent example of banding. With dithering set to Diffusion at 100% (lower-left image), the edges between the various bands of color are blended, helping to soften (somewhat) the transitions. The lower-right image is JPEG at maximum image quality (minimal compression), which provides an image visually identical to the original yet one-quarter the size.

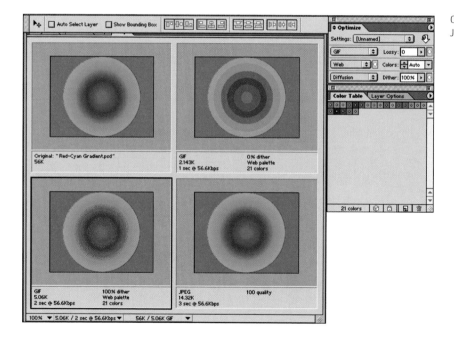

Compress gradients with JPEG to prevent banding.

2   Select the JPEG file format and further reduce the file size by increasing compression. In the upper-right, we can see the start of jaggies around the outside of the circle. By the time JPEG compression is at 25% (lower-left), some blotching has started to appear. As noted previously, it is generally better to view images destined for the Web at 100% zoom.

Notice the trade-off in file size among the three levels of compression. By reducing image quality to 50%, file size is reduced by 75% from the JPEG maximum quality setting. At 25% image quality, the compression has reduced the file to just over 19% of the file size at maximum image quality.

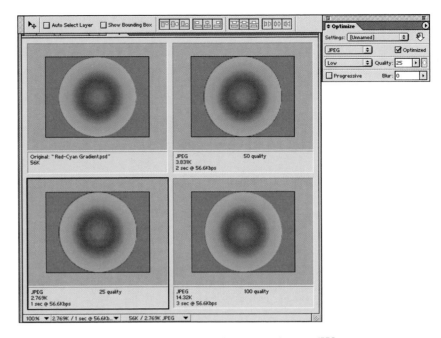

Balance your file size against your image quality when compressing as a JPEG.

3   Zoom in to 300% for illustrative purposes. We can see the difference in image quality among the three levels of compression. Notice that JPEG's lossy compression system has resulted in, at both 50% and 25% image quality, some artifacts in the red background.

Although the background is pure red (RGB 255, 0, 0), a few gray pixels are visible at 50% image quality, and a considerable number have appeared at 25%. Not visible in the figure, such random gray pixels are also visible in the red background a considerable distance from the outer edge of the circle.

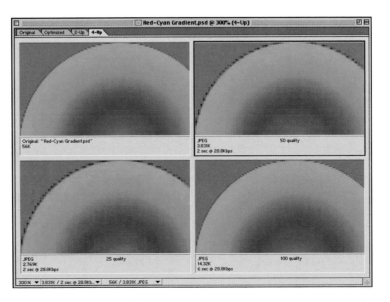

If you compress an image with JPEG's lossy algorithm, you might find randomly colored pixels appearing, even in areas of solid color.

JPEG Compression and Photographic Images

JPEG was designed for photographic images. At the highest image-quality settings, virtually all data is retained or reproduced to near-identical appearance, yet substantial size reduction can be achieved. At the higher compression levels (lower image quality), huge size reductions are possible but at the expense of image quality.

1   Open the file **Alpspitze.psd** from this book's CD-ROM. Experiment with the settings and look at the results in the window. When you're done, choose the settings shown here.

2   Select the 4-Up table and, in the Optimize palette, select JPEG Low.

When compressing to JPEG with ImageReady, several preset values are available. Using JPEG Low gives you an image quality of 10%, Medium raises it to 30%, High is 60%, and Maximum is 80%. You can, of course, go as high as 100% by inputting the value directly into Quality or by using the slider beneath.

Note that the Optimize palette also gives you the options of Optimized and Progressive as well as a slider for Blur. Optimized JPEG creates slightly smaller files, but older Web browsers do not support this variation of the format. Checking the Progressive box will enable the image to appear while downloading, much like GIF's Interlaced option. File size is increased slightly. The Blur slider enables you to add a Gaussian Blur of up to 2 pixels to a JPEG image.

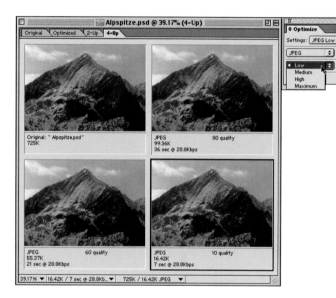

Use the pop-up menu to choose preset JPEG values. (Note that the zoom has been set to Fit to Window, resulting in the fractional value.)

Note: Although the settings in ImageReady and Photoshop's Save for Web refer to JPEG compression "percentages," the figures do not actually relate to the amount of compression or the lossiness of the compression. Different programs use different settings, resulting in different file sizes for the same image at the "same" setting. Even in Photoshop there are differences. One image, measuring 398×554 pixels, was saved using both Save As and Save for Web. Save As with a quality setting of six produced a JPEG file 64KB in size. Using a quality setting of 60% in Save for Web, a more sophisticated tool, yielded a 48KB file.

3 When viewed at 100% zoom, there is very little difference between the 99KB version in the upper-right and the 55KB image in the lower-left, and both are very close in appearance to the 725KB original. The Low Quality version, in the lower-right, is not even 16.5KB in size, less than one-third the size of the High Quality (60%) image.

When compared side by side, there are noticeable differences in quality from Low to High Quality. The clouds appear fluffier and more distinct in the Low Quality version, the ridgeline is a bit blurry, and there are a couple areas of distinct distortion. Notice, for example, the obvious blurring that occurs below the ridgeline to the left of the hand cursor. Also note the pixelization visible below and slightly to the right of the peak. If this image were viewed separately, the degradation would be less obvious but still noticeable.

Looking more closely at the four optimization choices gives us an idea of how JPEG works. Notice the distinct box pattern in the Low Quality version (lower-right). JPEG's compression algorithm works in "blocks" of data, typically 8×8 pixels. (See the sidebar "JPEG: A Simplified Look at How it Works" for more detail.)

It's obvious that the difference between a quality setting of 10 and a setting of 60 is much larger than the difference between 60 and 80. However, the trade-off in file size is also substantial. Refer again to the previous figure that shows the images at 100% zoom. If the image will be the focal point of the Web page, the higher quality is probably in order. If the picture is tangential to the page's content or if the page is image heavy, dropping to a fast-loading file size might be more important than retaining quality.

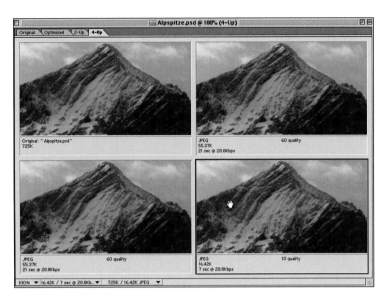

Hold down the spacebar to activate the Hand tool. This enables you to click-and-drag to reposition images larger than the windows. All four versions will shift.

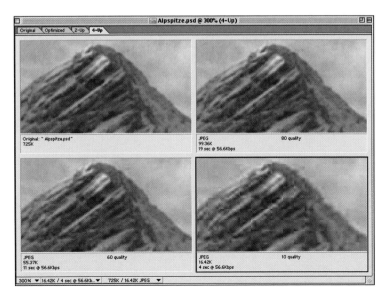

Optimize to lower image quality when file size and download times are more important than exact reproduction of the picture.

PNG-24 FILE FORMAT

As previously discussed, the PNG format is designed to serve as an alternative to GIF and JPEG. PNG-24, which gets its suffix from the 24-bit color it allows, remains limited in capability. It is a lossless compression scheme, unlike JPEG, but is not supported by all browsers. In addition, the losslessness of the compression results in substantially larger files than JPEG, even at extremely high-quality settings.

PNG-24 can reduce a file's size by as much as 50%, but those savings are rather insignificant compared to what we've just seen JPEG do. To the format's credit, however, it does retain all information, allowing an image to be re-created or decompressed to an exact copy of the original, and it also allows for transparency in the form of an alpha channel. Using a channel to convey transparency information allows for up to 256 levels of opacity for each pixel. Remember to select None from the Matte menu when using transparency and keep in mind that not all browsers support the format.

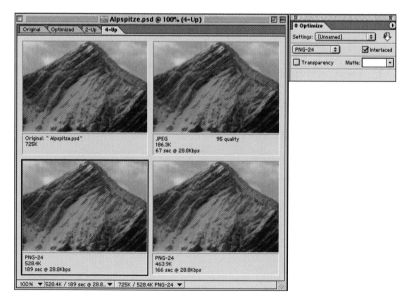

Choose PNG-24 when variable transparency is required and visitors can be expected to have the latest browsers. This file format is also appropriate for archiving images without loss of quality.

Mixed Images

Sometimes a Web graphic has both areas of continuous tone and areas of solid color. Saving it as a GIF would reduce the photographic areas to a maximum of 256 colors, perhaps substantially damaging its appearance. On the other hand, optimizing the file as a JPEG could introduce distracting artifacts into areas of solid color and eliminate anti-aliasing for text. The most effective method of optimization is to combine both GIF and JPEG by using slices.

1   Open the file **Alps-Blood Drive.psd** from the accompanying CD-ROM.

2   Use the Slice tool to drag a box around a portion of an image. In this case, we'll create a slice around the red and white portion of the image.

   This is known as a User Slice. The rest of the image will automatically be divided into the appropriate Auto Slices.

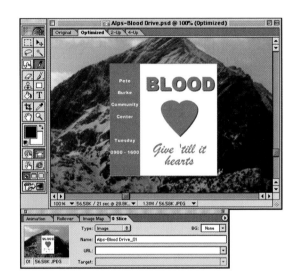

Create a slice with the Slice tool.

3   With the User Slice still selected and active, choose appropriate settings in the Optimization palette. We'll choose GIF with the Web-safe palette, and No Dither.

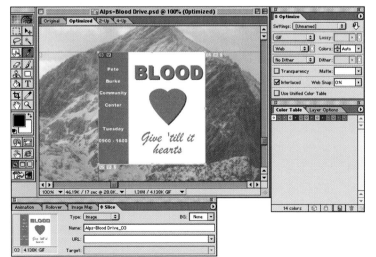

Optimize appropriately for the slice.

4 Use the Slice Select tool to select one of the Auto Slices. When one Auto Slice is selected, changes to optimization settings will be applied to all Auto Slices. We'll use JPEG at High Quality, with Optimized and Progressive checked.

Notice that the file size is slightly smaller than the photo itself compressed as JPEG with the same settings.

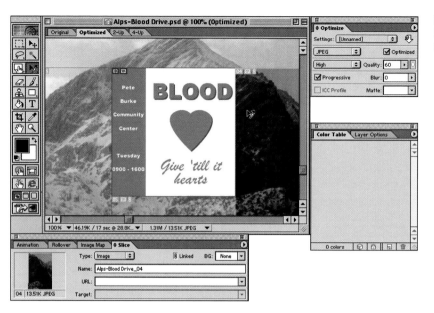

Select one of the Auto Slices and change the optimization settings.

Note: Using this example to explore compression options, we find that both the JPEG (upper-right) and the GIF at 256 colors (lower-left) do adequate jobs of optimization. However, when the GIF image is reduced to the Web-safe palette (lower-right), even dithering doesn't help.

Notice also the file sizes. GIF does a poor job of compressing the continuous tones of the photographic areas of the image. The JPEG image is about 5% larger than the photo alone at the same compression ratio. None of these options, however, compares with the slice-based optimization for both image quality and size.

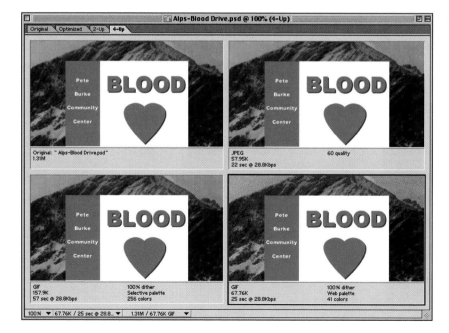

Avoid using GIF with images containing areas of continuous tone.

USING DROPLETS TO AUTOMATE OPTIMIZATION

Droplets are saved optimization settings that can be applied to an image or a batch of images. They also can be inserted into an Action in ImageReady.

1 With an image open in ImageReady, choose the optimization settings that are to be saved. Click the Droplet icon in the upper-right part of the Optimization palette and the standard Save dialog box opens, allowing you to specify a location for the Droplet.

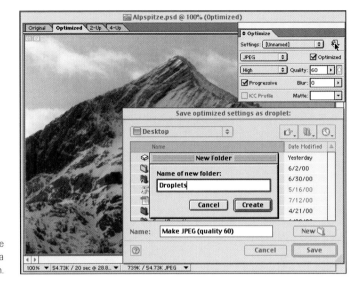

Click the Droplet icon and save your optimization settings in a convenient location.

2 You also can save settings as a Droplet by using the command Create Droplet from the Optimization palette pop-up menu. To apply the settings, simply drag an image's icon or a folder of images onto the Droplet's icon.

Use the Menu command and an identical Save dialog box will appear.

MODIFICATIONS

With the exceptions of slices and droplets, all the optimization techniques discussed in this project can also be utilized through Photoshop's Save for Web feature. Should you need to troubleshoot Save for Web, be aware that it has a separate Preferences file.

THE TOOLS AND PALETTES OF PHOTOSHOP AND IMAGEREADY, FROM A TO Z

"Sometimes it's a little better

to travel than to arrive."

—ROBERT M. PIRSIG

TOOLS AND PALETTES

Photoshop and ImageReady have more than

40 individual tools and 20 different palettes

with which to work. Knowing all the capabilities

of each of them takes years of experience.

Understanding the basics of each tool and

palette is a key to gaining that experience

efficiently.

The Tools and Palettes of Photoshop and ImageReady, from A to Z

by Peter Bauer

Note: Following the presentation of the Toolboxes, each tool and palette is introduced alphabetically with a notation about whether it appears in Photoshop, ImageReady, or both. In addition, Liquify and Extract are shown, although they are menu commands rather than tools or palettes.

PALETTES

Every palette in Photoshop and ImageReady has a pop-out menu that is accessed by clicking on the arrow-in-a-circle icon in the palette's upper-right corner. Several palettes have options, which are accessed through the pop-out menu.

The palettes are "floating palettes." They will remain visible over the document. Palettes can, however, obscure each other. The tabs of the individual palettes can be dragged from one window to another to rearrange them. Palettes can be "docked" by dragging a tab to the bottom of another palette's window. When a thick black line appears at the bottom, release the mouse button to dock palettes. Drag the tab higher in the window, until the thick black line becomes a box, to move the tab into that window.

Palettes can be shown or hidden using the commands under the Window menu. All palettes (including the Options bar and the Toolbox) can be hidden by pressing the Tab key. Pressing Shift+Tab hides all but the Toolbox and Options bar. When palettes are hidden and a Window menu command is used, the command will generally show the default group for the palette selected. The Window menu also contains a command for resetting all palettes to their default locations (this was formerly found in the General Preferences). Most palettes can be enlarged by dragging the lower-right corner.

282

TOOLS

Most tools have options specific to that tool. When the tool is activated by clicking on it or by pressing its keyboard shortcut, the Options bar automatically displays the appropriate options (formerly found in the Options palette). For some tools, the Options bar will change while the tool is in use.

When introduced later, each tool's options will be shown. Numerous tools use the Brushes palette (which has been incorporated into the Options bar), and several have variable Brush Dynamics, which are found at the right end of the Options bar. Generally, the Options bar is shown without the Tab Well. See the section called "The Options Bar (Photoshop/ImageReady)" later in this appendix.

Each tool can be reset to its defaults by clicking once on the tool's icon in the Options bar. This also allows all the tools to be reset at the same time if desired. The General Preferences dialog box also offers the option of resetting all tools.

Many of Photoshop's tools use brushes. The Brushes palette (see Figure A.1) is a drop-down feature of the Options bar when appropriate. Several of the painting tools can also take advantage of Brush Dynamics (see Figure A.2). Brush Dynamics allows the behavior of the brush to be modified to simulate actual application of paint.

Photoshop's painting tools, as well as some others, can generally be constrained to 90° or 45° angles while dragging by depressing the Shift key. Many tools can be forced to a straight line by clicking at one point and Shift+clicking at another.

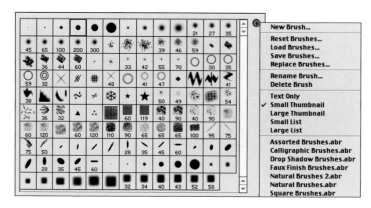

Figure A.1
The Brushes palette can be used to select and modify individual brushes.

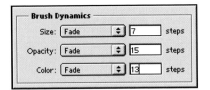

Figure A.2
Brush Dynamics simulates a brush running out of paint during application.

THE PHOTOSHOP TOOLBOX

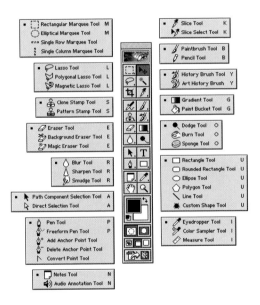

Figure A.3
Photoshop's Toolbox has 15 pop-out menus that show the hidden tools.

Photoshop's Toolbox is the holding area for each of the program's tools. Clicking on a tool makes it active. Holding down the mouse button exposes any hidden tools. (Hidden tools are indicated by a small black triangle in the lower-right corner of an icon in the Toolbox.) Pressing Tab (except when the Type tool is active) will hide the Toolbox and all other palettes.

There have been several changes to the Toolbox for Photoshop 6. New are the Slice, Note, Path Component, and Shape tools. The Pencil, Paint Bucket, and Measure tools all have new homes, and several other tools were rearranged. The Color Sampler tool stands on its own rather than as a function of the Eyedropper tool. The Clone Stamp tool was formerly called the Rubber Stamp tool.

In addition, the Toolbox holds several buttons (see Figure A.3). At the top is a link to Adobe Online, the Internet access for Adobe's Photoshop resources. Below the tools are the color controls. Clicking on the Foreground or Background swatch will open the Color Picker. Clicking on the two-headed arrow to their upper-right will switch the two colors. Clicking on the mini-swatches to the lower-left restores them to the default black (foreground) and white (background).

Below the color controls are two sets of buttons that govern the interface. The top pair is Standard Mode, used for most Photoshop work, and Quick Mask Mode, used to create Alpha channels. Below are three buttons that control how the screen appears (in accordance with their labels). The bottom button opens any active image in ImageReady. The image is automatically saved first. If no file is open, ImageReady starts normally.

THE IMAGEREADY TOOLBOX

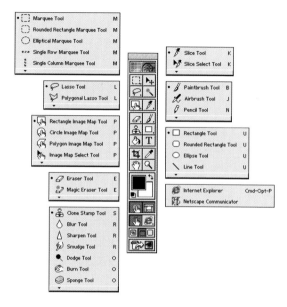

Figure A.4
ImageReady's Toolbox contains many of the same tools as Photoshop's Toolbox, but their locations are often different.

ImageReady's Toolbox looks and functions much the same as Photoshop's. The differences between them deserve mention. One major difference is that the hidden tools in ImageReady are on tear-off palettes. Holding down the mouse button reveals the hidden palettes, and mousing to the triangle at the bottom before releasing the mouse opens a floating palette with those tools.

Several tools are in different locations than in Photoshop. Additionally, there are a couple of changes from earlier versions of ImageReady. ImageReady 3.0's Toolbox holds a pair of newcomers, the Shape and Image Map tools. Both of these are tool sets consisting of several related tools.

The Toolbox also has changes to the buttons below. Show Slices and Hide Slices have been replaced with two toggle buttons to show and hide image maps and

slices. Below them are buttons for previewing rollovers and previewing in a Web browser. Notice that, in Figure A.4, the choice of browsers is limited to Internet Explorer and Netscape Navigator. If alternative browsers are available when ImageReady is installed, they, too, will be listed. Browsers can be added later by putting an alias or shortcut in the Helpers folder within the Photoshop folder.

The button at the bottom of the Toolbox switches from ImageReady to Photoshop.

THE ACTIONS PALETTE (PHOTOSHOP/IMAGEREADY)

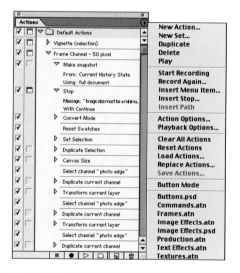

Figure A.5
The Actions palette

The buttons at the bottom of the Actions palette are Stop, Record, Play, New Set (not in ImageReady), New Action, and Delete. The palette can also display Actions in a color-coded Button mode. The left column indicates whether or not a particular step will be played within the Action. The second column shows an icon in which a step within the Action requires user intervention (modal control).

THE AIRBRUSH TOOL (PHOTOSHOP/IMAGEREADY)

Figure A.6
The Airbrush tool is used with the Brushes palette and Brush Dynamics (see Figures A.1 and A.2).

Each time the Airbrush passes over a pixel, color is added until the mouse button is released. Continuing to stroke back and forth across an area with the Airbrush will increase the amount of color until each pixel is completely converted to the foreground color. The Mode pop-up menu offers all of the various blending modes. Pressure controls the amount of color applied by the Airbrush in a single pass.

THE ANIMATION PALETTE (IMAGEREADY)

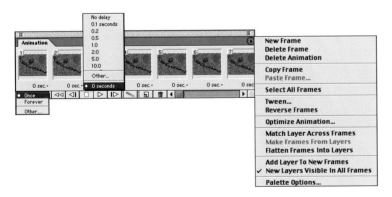

Figure A.7
The Animation palette is frame-based, showing each step of the animation.

The Animation palette is used to control the individual frames of the animation. Below each frame is the timing control, allowing each frame to be shown for a specific period of time. Below that are the palette's buttons: Looping Options, First Frame, Previous Frame, Stop, Play, Next Frame, Last Frame, Tweening, New Frame, and Delete. Frames can be dragged to reorder them. Multiple frames can be selected for dragging or for use with other commands by Shift+clicking to select a series of frames or Cmd+clicking (Ctrl+clicking for Windows) to select noncontiguous frames.

THE ART HISTORY BRUSH (PHOTOSHOP)

Figure A.8
The Art History brush has 10 types of strokes.

Using an earlier state of the image from the History palette (see Figure A.30), the Art History brush allows you to creatively restore portions of an image. Fidelity refers to how closely the paint color will match the original color from the source state. Area determines the radius of the effect. Area is not the same as Brush Size. The size of the brush determines the appearance of the effect; the size of the area determines the placement of the effect. Spacing loosens the pattern of brush strokes applied.

THE AUDIO ANNOTATION TOOL (PHOTOSHOP)

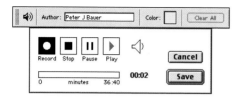

Figure A.9
The Audio Annotation tool's dialog box in Windows lacks the Pause button. This tool is closely related to the Notes tool (see Figure A.44).

The Audio Annotation tool, new with Photoshop 6, leaves visible markers on the image at the point selected. The name of the note's author will be visible at the top. Audio annotations can be saved with both PDF and PSD files. After clicking in the image, a recording box will appear. Windows and Mac users alike can press Record, Stop, and then Save. A microphone must be attached and selected as the audio input device for the Audio Annotation tool to be available. Mac users also have the option of pausing while recording.

THE BACKGROUND ERASER TOOL (PHOTOSHOP)

Figure A.10
The Background Eraser tool can work with noncontiguous areas as well as contiguous.

Used to separate an image from its background, the Background Eraser tool works well when a background is reasonably uniform in color and contrasts starkly with the foreground. When the background and foreground image have many colors in common, the tool must be used with care. Tolerance determines how closely the sampled colors must match the point originally clicked in order to erase them. Designating the foreground color as protected prevents any pixels the color of the Foreground swatch from being erased. Sampling continuously allows the tool to continue to determine what constitutes a background color. Sampling once limits the erasing to that color first clicked on with the tool (within the predetermined Tolerance). The sample is updated every time the mouse is clicked.

THE BLUR TOOL (PHOTOSHOP/IMAGEREADY)

Figure A.11
The Blur tool can take advantage of both the Brushes palette and Brush Dynamics (see Figures A.1 and A.2).

The Blur Tool is used to reduce contrast or oversharpening in an image. (The opposite effect is achieved with the Sharpen tool; see Figure A.60.) The brush size and Blending mode can be adjusted, as can the tool's pressure. Pressure is the amount of blurring on each pass of the cursor.

THE BURN TOOL (PHOTOSHOP/IMAGEREADY)

Figure A.12
The Burn tool uses both the Brushes palette and Brush Dynamics (see Figures A.1 and A.2).

The Burn tool is used to darken selective areas of an image. Use the Options bar to select Shadows, Midtones, or Highlights. Each tonal range of an area must be done separately. Exposure determines the level of effectiveness of the Burn tool.

THE CHANNELS PALETTE (PHOTOSHOP)

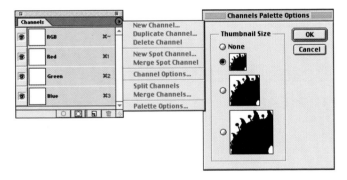

Figure A.13
The Channels palette can shows thumbnails in three sizes.

The Channels palette stores color and masking information. Each color in an image is stored on a separate channel. The palette also shows a composite channel in RGB, CMYK, and Lab color modes. Channels can be selected individually by clicking on them. Shift+clicking allows the selection of multiple channels. Filters, selection tools, painting tools, and other Photoshop editing techniques can be applied to individual channels. Channels can be added to images to contain spot color or other information.

THE CHARACTER PALETTE (PHOTOSHOP/IMAGEREADY)

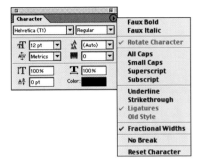

Figure A.14
The Character palette is new with Photoshop 6; it's part of the powerful new typographic capabilities of the program.

The new Character palette gives very fine control over the text in Photoshop documents. In addition to being able to specify fonts, size, and color, Photoshop now adds control over character spacing (kerning and tracking), line spacing (leading), character scaling, and baseline positioning. Color can now be applied on a per-character basis. Attributes can be selected prior to placing the text, or text can be selected with the Type tool and attributes changed. The Type tool is shown in Figure A.68. The Paragraph palette is shown in Figure A.49.

THE CLONE STAMP TOOL (PHOTOSHOP/IMAGEREADY)

Figure A.15
The Clone Stamp tool was formerly known as the Rubber Stamp.

Option+clicking (Alt+clicking for Windows) establishes the source point, the place from which pixels will be copied. The source point maintains the distance and angle from the cursor as it is dragged, thereby copying areas of an image rather than a single point. In Aligned mode, every click of the mouse reestablishes the source point. The distance and angle between the original Opt+click (Alt+click) and the following mouse-button-down will be maintained. In non-Aligned mode, the original source point remains no matter where the mouse is moved for subsequent drags.

THE COLOR PALETTE (PHOTOSHOP/IMAGEREADY)

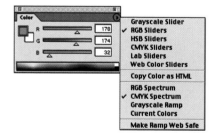

Figure A.16
The Color palette's menu supports two additional commands in ImageReady: Invert and Complement.

The Color palette uses sliders or direct input of numeric values, and the cursor can be clicked on the Color Ramp at the bottom of the palette to select a color.

THE COLOR SAMPLER (PHOTOSHOP)

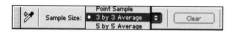

Figure A.17
The Color Sampler was formerly a function of the Eyedropper tool.

The Color Sampler tool places markers in an image that can be used to track color changes. The Info palette displays the values of the pixels under the markers in the document's color mode. The markers will be visible when the Color Sampler tool or the Eyedropper tool is active. They can be relocated within the image by dragging with the Color Sampler tool. They can be deleted by dragging them off the image.

THE COLOR TABLE PALETTE (IMAGEREADY)

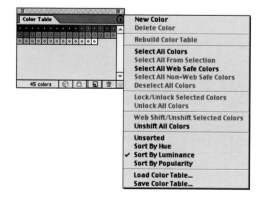

Figure A.18
The Color Table palette is used in ImageReady to prepare images for the Web.

The Color Table palette controls, to a large degree, the number of colors in an 8-bit image. This palette is not used with JPEG or PNG-24 images but rather with GIF and PNG-8 files. Restricting the number of colors can greatly reduce file size. Restricting those colors to the Web-safe palette can help ensure that the image is viewed in the same colors in which it was prepared. (This particularly pertains to older laptops and computers with video boards capable of displaying only 8-bit color.)

THE CROP TOOL (PHOTOSHOP/IMAGEREADY)

Figure A.19
The top image is the Crop tool's default Options bar; the second is available when the tool is in use. The bottom Options bar is from ImageReady's Crop tool.

ImageReady's Crop tool Options bar combines the two Photoshop Options bars but lacks Perspective and Resolution options. Perspective is designed to correct keystoning but has other uses.

THE DIRECT SELECTION TOOL (PHOTOSHOP)

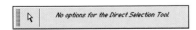

Figure A.20
The Direct Selection tool functions identically under all circumstances.

The Direct Selection tool is used to activate and select path segments or anchor points. Selected segments and points can then be moved or reshaped. The tool can also manipulate anchor point direction lines.

THE DODGE TOOL (PHOTOSHOP/IMAGEREADY)

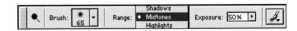

Figure A.21
The Dodge tool is the opposite of the Burn tool.

The Dodge tool is used to selectively lighten areas of an image. Like the Burn tool, it can be used on specific tonal ranges (Shadows, Midtones, Highlights). Exposure represents the effectiveness of the tool. The Brushes palette and Brush Dynamics are shown in Figures A.1 and A.2.

THE ELLIPTICAL MARQUEE TOOL (PHOTOSHOP/IMAGEREADY)

Figure A.22
The Options bar's four left-most buttons allow addition to, subtraction from, or intersection with an existing selection.

Elliptical and circular selections are created with the Elliptical Marquee tool. Holding down the Shift key while dragging constrains the proportions to a circle. Holding down Option (Alt for Windows) creates the selection from the center. When a selection already exists, Shift adds to it and Option (Alt) subtracts from it.

THE ERASER TOOL (PHOTOSHOP/IMAGEREADY)

Figure A.23
The Brushes palette and Brush Dynamics are shown in Figures A.1 and A.2.

The Eraser tool can simulate the Paintbrush, Airbrush, or Pencil tools or can be used as a Block Eraser, which varies in effective size dependent on zoom. In ImageReady, the Eraser cannot erase to a history state, nor can it have wet edges.

THE EXTRACT COMMAND (PHOTOSHOP)

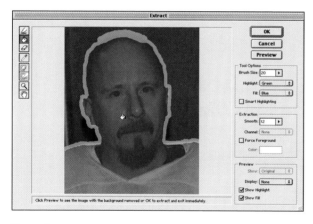

Figure A.24
The dialog box for the Extract command has its own tools.

The Extract command will determine edges and erase a background. The Highlighter tool is used to overlap the edges, identifying background and foreground pixels. The Paint Bucket is then used to identify which side of the line to save.

THE EYEDROPPER TOOL (PHOTOSHOP/IMAGEREADY)

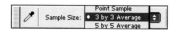

Figure A.25
The Eyedropper tool can sample an individual pixel, a 9-pixel square, or a 25-pixel square.

The Eyedropper tool can be clicked anywhere in an image or on the Color Ramp of the Color palette to select a new foreground color. The tool can be dragged for a dynamic update of the Color palette.

THE FREEFORM PEN TOOL (PHOTOSHOP)

Figure A.26
The Freeform Pen tool can add to, subtract from, or intersect with an existing path. Anchor points on the path can be automatically added or deleted.

The Freeform Pen tool will create a path wherever the cursor is dragged. Curve Fit determines how sharp or rounded corners will be. The Magnetic option allows the tool to follow edges in an image (this replaces the Magnetic Pen tool).

THE GRADIENT TOOL (PHOTOSHOP)

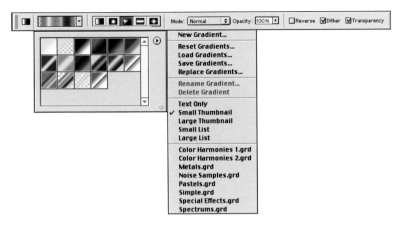

Figure A.27
There are five gradient styles, selected with the buttons to the left of the Mode field.

Gradients are created by dragging the Gradient tool through an image or a selection. The appearance of the gradient is governed by both the gradient (from the Gradient palette shown in Figure A.27) and the gradient's style, which can be linear, radial, angular, or geometric.

THE HAND TOOL (PHOTOSHOP/IMAGEREADY)

Figure A.28
The Hand tool's Options bar contains buttons for the three most common views.

The Hand tool is used to shift the view when an image does not fit in its window. Clicking and dragging in the image repositions it. It is best used in conjunction with Photoshop's Navigator palette (see Figure A.43).

THE HISTORY BRUSH (PHOTOSHOP)

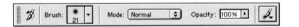

Figure A.29
The History brush is used in conjunction with the History palette (see Figure A.30). It also uses the Brushes palette (see Figure A.1) and Brush Dynamics (see Figure A.2).

The History brush uses a designated state from the History palette to restore the appearance of an image to an earlier condition. It is often used to reduce the effect of a filter in a specific area of an image.

THE HISTORY PALETTE (PHOTOSHOP)

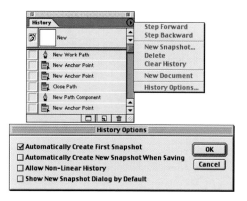

Figure A.30
The History palette is best known as a source of multiple Undos for Photoshop, but that is only part of its power.

In addition to allowing multiple Undos, the History palette can be used in conjunction with the History brush (see Figure A.29) and the Art History brush (see Figure A.8) to selectively restore portions of an image to an earlier state. The number of states stored in the History palette is set in the General Preferences.

THE IMAGE MAP PALETTE (IMAGEREADY)

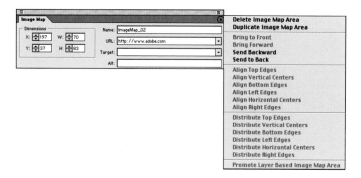

Figure A.31
The Image Map palette is used in conjunction with the Image Map tools (see Figure A.32) to create hyperlinks.

The Image Map palette is used to organize and control various image maps within a document. Image maps are links to World Wide Web resources.

THE IMAGE MAP TOOLS (IMAGEREADY)

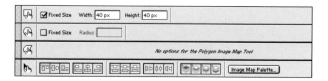

Figure A.32
The Image Map tools each have their own Options bar. Image maps can be rectangular, circular, or polygonal.

The Image Map tools create areas that can be used as hyperlinks. It works in conjunction with the Image Map palette (see Figure A.31).

THE INFO PALETTE (PHOTOSHOP/IMAGEREADY)

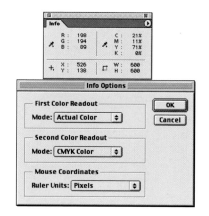

Figure A.33
The Info palette can display two different color readings for the same area. In ImageReady, it displays RGB and Hexadecimal notation rather than CMYK.

The Info palette, in addition to displaying color information for the Eyedropper tool (see Figure A.25) and Color Sampler tool (see Figure A.17), shows cursor location and the dimensions of a selection. It is also used with the Measure tool (see Figure A.41).

THE LASSO TOOL (PHOTOSHOP/IMAGEREADY)

Figure A.34
The Lasso tool can add to, subtract from, or intersect with an existing selection.

The Lasso tool is used to create freeform selections. The edges of the selection can be feathered, and the selection can be anti-aliased. See also the Magnetic Lasso tool (see Figure A.40) and the Polygon Lasso tool (see Figure A.56).

THE LAYER OPTIONS PALETTE (IMAGEREADY)

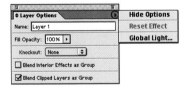

Figure A.35
ImageReady's Layer Options palette fulfills some of the same purposes as the Layers palette and Layer Properties in Photoshop.

In addition to renaming a layer and determining its opacity, ImageReady's Layer Options palette gives additional control over how a layer will interact with those below and above it.

THE LAYERS PALETTE (PHOTOSHOP/IMAGEREADY)

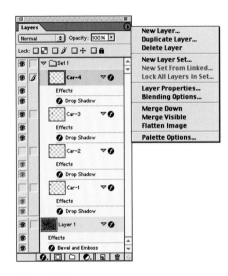

Figure A.36
In ImageReady, the Layers palette also contains two buttons for moving forward and backward in an animation.

The Layers palette has become a bit more sophisticated in Photoshop 6 with the addition of write-protection and move-protection checkboxes, which supplement the preserve transparency and locking capabilities. In addition, it now supports Layer Sets (see Figure A.36) and lists Layer Effects applied. Effects can be dragged between layers to copy them.

THE LIQUIFY COMMAND (PHOTOSHOP)

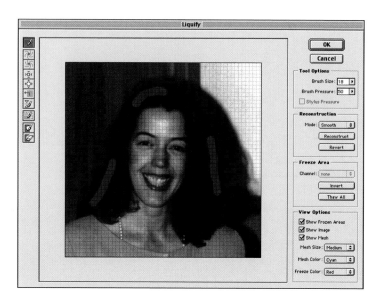

Figure A.37
The Liquify command (under the Edit menu) has an extensive dialog box with its own unique tools. They include Warp, Twirl, Pucker, and Bloat to distort an image and Freeze to protect areas.

In addition to being able to create hideous goo-like special effects, the Liquify command can serve a serious purpose. Using the Freeze tool to stabilize areas from change (the red areas in Figure A.37) and then using the Warp or other distort tools can produce subtle modifications to an image. In this case, the subject's hair is being prepared for the Extract command.

THE MAGIC ERASER TOOL (PHOTOSHOP/IMAGEREADY)

Figure A.38
Unlike the other erasers, the Magic Eraser's options do not include brushes.

A cross between the Magic Wand (see Figure A.39) and the Eraser (see Figure A.23), this tool uses similarities in pixel color to determine which ones to erase. Click once in an area and, depending on the Tolerance setting, pixels within a certain color range of the pixel clicked will be erased.

THE MAGIC WAND TOOL (PHOTOSHOP/IMAGEREADY)

Figure A.39
The four buttons allow the Magic Wand, when a selection already exists, to add to, subtract from, or intersect with the first selection.

The Magic Wand makes selections based on similarity of color. The Tolerance setting determines how closely a color must match the pixel clicked to fall within the selection. The Shift key will add to an existing selection; the Option key (Alt for Windows) subtracts from an existing selection.

THE MAGNETIC LASSO TOOL (PHOTOSHOP)

Figure A.40
The Magnetic Lasso, like the other magnetic tools, uses color differentials to do its job. Its job is to make selections.

Like the other Lasso tools, this one can add to, subtract from, or intersect with an existing selection. It is typically used to follow the outline of an object. It relies on color differences to determine the location of the edge it is following. The Width setting determines the radius from the center of the cursor; Edge Contrast determines the level of difference required for the tool to follow a shape's edge.

THE MEASURE TOOL (PHOTOSHOP)

Figure A.41
The Measure tool's Options bar uses the unit of measure set in the Preferences.

The Measure tool provides the cursor's location and the distance and angle between two points. The distance is measured horizontally (W), vertically (H), and in a straight line (D). Click in one location and drag to another point. Holding down the Option key (Alt for Windows) allows the Measure tool to continue on to a third point, giving the angle and the second distance (D2).

THE MOVE TOOL (PHOTOSHOP/IMAGEREADY)

Figure A.42
The Move tool can now be used with Bounding Boxes to transform selections.

New for Photoshop 6, the Move tool incorporates much of the capability of the Free Transform command. When Bounding Boxes are visible, the Move tool can be used to resize and rotate a selection. In addition, when shapes and a selection are made, the align buttons on the Move tool's Options bar are available.

THE NAVIGATOR PALETTE (PHOTOSHOP)

Figure A.43
The Navigator palette shows what part of an image is currently visible in the document's window with a colored rectangle.

The Navigator palette displays the current view of the document. It is used with the window's scroll bars and the Hand tool (see Figure A.28) to maneuver around the image. Numeric zoom factors can be entered into the box at the lower-left of the palette, and the zoom can be changed using the slider or the smaller and larger icons to either side. This palette can be resized for improved viewing.

THE NOTES TOOL (PHOTOSHOP)

Figure A.44
The Notes tool's annotations can be color-coordinated by author.

The Notes tool, like its relative the Audio Annotation tool (see Figure A.9), is designed to allow reviewers and creators to pass comments to other viewers of the image. The notes are identified by author across the top and appear in the image at small colored markers.

THE OPTIMIZATION PALETTE (IMAGEREADY)

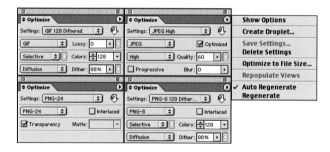

Figure A.45
The Settings pop-up menu contains a group of optimization presets for GIF, JPEG, and PNG. Customized settings can also be created.

Using preset or customized settings, the Optimization palette controls the process of preparing images for the Web. This palette is the heart of ImageReady. The contents of the palette vary according to which file format is selected.

THE OPTIONS BAR (PHOTOSHOP/IMAGEREADY)

Figure A.46
The Options bar varies according to which tool is selected and how it is being used.

One additional feature of the Options bar, the Palette Well, is only available with screen resolutions larger than 800×600 pixels. Pictured here, the Palette Well allows oft-required palettes to be stored out of the way, ready for one-click deployment. The Options bar is hidden with the rest of the palettes and the Toolbar when Tab is pressed (except while the Type tool is active). When Shift+Tab is pressed, the Options bar remains visible with the Toolbox.

THE PAINTBRUSH TOOL (PHOTOSHOP/IMAGEREADY)

Figure A.47
The Paintbrush tool uses both the Brush palette (see Figure A.1) and Brush Dynamics (see Figure A.2)

The Paintbrush tool applies the foreground color to the image. The opacity and blending mode are fully variable.

THE PAINT BUCKET TOOL (PHOTOSHOP/IMAGEREADY)

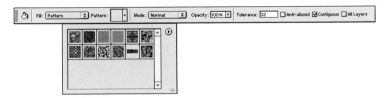

Figure A.48
The Paint Bucket tool can apply either the Foreground color or a pattern (Photoshop only). It is shown here with the Patterns palette open (see Figure A.53).

Now located beneath the Gradient tool, the Paint Bucket tool's Tolerance setting determines whether or not its color or pattern will be applied to neighboring pixels. If the color variation between the pixel clicked and its neighbor is with the set value, the second pixel will also be changed.

THE PARAGRAPH PALETTE (PHOTOSHOP/IMAGEREADY)

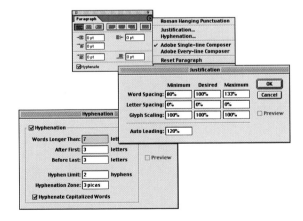

Figure A.49
The Paragraph palette is new to Photoshop 6; it's part of the improved typographic capabilities.

In addition to justification, the new Paragraph palette offers block indent, first-line indent, and spacing before and after paragraphs. The pop-out menu gives access to advanced justification and hyphenation dialog boxes. The Type tool is shown in Figure A.68. The Character palette is shown in Figure A.14.

THE PATH COMPONENT SELECTION TOOL (PHOTOSHOP)

Figure A.50
New to Photoshop, the Path Component Selection tool works with both paths and the new vector shapes created with the Shape tools (see Figure A.59).

This new tool is used to select entire paths. When a Work Path consists of more than one path or when a Shape Layer contains more than one object, this tool can isolate and move an individual path.

THE PATHS PALETTE (PHOTOSHOP/IMAGEREADY)

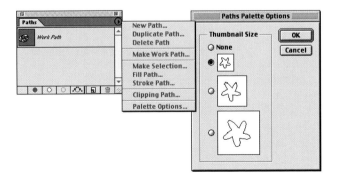

Figure A.51
The Paths palette holds and controls all regular paths, Work Paths, and the clipping paths for the new vector shapes produced by the Shape tools (see Figure A.59).

Double-click a Work Path and rename it to keep it when another path will be drawn. Clipping paths, used primarily for transparency, cannot be created from Work Paths.

THE PATTERN STAMP TOOL (PHOTOSHOP)

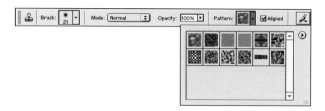

Figure A.52
The Photoshop-only Pattern Stamp tool is hidden under the Clone Stamp tool.

The Pattern Stamp tool uses brushes to apply a pattern to an image. The Brushes palette is shown in Figure A.1; the Patterns palette is shown in Figure A.48.

THE PATTERNS PALETTE (PHOTOSHOP)

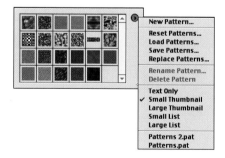

Figure A.53
The Patterns palette is used with several tools including the Paint Bucket and the Pattern Stamp.

Sets of patterns can be loaded using the palette's pop-out menu command Load Patterns. Custom patterns can be created and stored in the Patterns palette, and sets of custom patterns can be saved. Prior to Photoshop 6, a single pattern could be defined but it could not be saved.

THE PEN TOOL (PHOTOSHOP)

Figure A.54
The Pen tool is one of the key components of Photoshop, creating precise lines and curves called paths that can be used for painting, selecting, and clipping.

The Pen tool creates paths, which can then be edited with related tools including the Add Anchor Point and Delete Anchor Point tools. The Pen tool will automatically change to the appropriate related tool when over an existing anchor point or segment. The Convert Anchor Point tool, also found below the Pen tool, changes points on a path between corner and smooth anchors. The Magnetic Pen tool has been dropped in favor of a magnetic capability for the Freeform Pen tool (see Figure A.26).

THE PENCIL TOOL (PHOTOSHOP/IMAGEREADY)

Figure A.55
The Pencil tool is now located with the Paintbrush tool.

The Pencil tool, like the Paintbrush tool, uses brushes to place the Foreground color in the image. By default, however, the Pencil tool does not use hard-edge brushes. The Auto Erase option allows the Pencil to replace one of its lines with the Background color when overdrawn. Shift constrains the tool, while clicking and then Shift-clicking produces a straight line between the points.

THE POLYGON LASSO TOOL (PHOTOSHOP/IMAGEREADY)

Figure A.56
This tool can also add to, subtract from, or create an intersection with an existing path.

Unlike the other Lasso tools, the Polygon Lasso tool is clicked, not dragged. Click each point, and a straight segment will be created between them. Click again on the first point to close the selection.

THE RECTANGULAR MARQUEE TOOL (PHOTOSHOP/IMAGEREADY)

Figure A.57
The Rectangular Marquee tool can also add to, subtract from, or create an intersection with an existing path.

One of the most commonly used tools in Photoshop, the Rectangular Marquee creates selections. Holding the Shift key while dragging makes the selection square; holding down Option (Alt for Windows) draws from the center. In addition to setting a specific size, a proportions ratio can be entered into fields on the Options bar.

THE ROLLOVER PALETTE (IMAGEREADY)

Figure A.58
The Rollover palette includes a Play button at the bottom and several labor-saving commands in its pop-out menu.

This palette is designed to help you create Web page buttons that change appearance when clicked. The various states above the images refer to mouse actions and locations.

THE SHAPE TOOLS (PHOTOSHOP/IMAGEREADY)

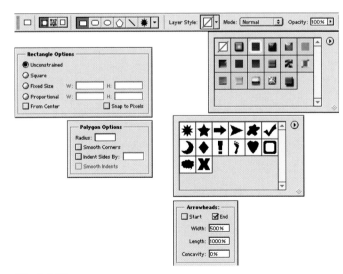

Figure A.59
There are actually six Shape tools including the Custom Shape tool, which can produce a variety of preset and custom objects.

New in Photoshop 6 are the Shape tools, which create clipping paths on colored layers to simulate vector objects. Note that the shape layers can take advantage of the new Layer Effects through a drop-down palette. The former Line tool has been rolled into this collection of tools, now producing a clipping path on a shape layer. Arrowheads are still available. ImageReady did not receive the Polygon or Custom Shape tools.

THE SHARPEN TOOL (PHOTOSHOP/IMAGEREADY)

Figure A.60
The Sharpen tool does the opposite of the Blur tool (see Figure A.11), increasing contrast among adjacent pixels.

The Sharpen tool is used to sharpen selected areas of an image. The Brushes palette (see Figure A.1) and Brush Dynamics (see Figure A.2) help determine the area upon which the tool will work. The Pressure variable determines how much of an effect the tool will have in that area.

THE SINGLE COLUMN/ROW MARQUEE TOOLS (PHOTOSHOP/IMAGEREADY)

Figure A.61
The two Options bars are shown together.

Despite their presence on the Options bar, the grayed out Style, Width, and Height options are never available for these tools. Feathering and anti-aliasing are also ineffective due to the 1-pixel dimension.

THE SLICE TOOL AND PALETTE (PHOTOSHOP/IMAGEREADY)

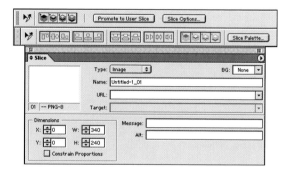

Figure A.62
The Slice tool Option bars differ between the two programs (Photoshop's is shown on top). Also pictured is ImageReady's Slice palette. Contrast this with Figure A.63.

The Slice tool is dragged through an image to divide it into portions for downloading over the World Wide Web. User-defined slices are automatically supplemented by Automatic Slices to ensure that the image is recorded in a series of rectangles.

The Slice Select Tool and Slice Options Palette (Photoshop/ImageReady)

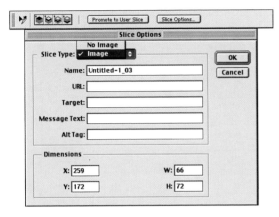

Figure A.63
The Slice Select tool's Options bar differs in ImageReady. Also shown is Photoshop's Slice Options palette. Contrast this with Figure A.62.

The Slice Select tool allows individual slices to be selected for change. The primary methods of change are the Slice palette in ImageReady (see Figure A.62) and Photoshop's Slice Options palette (pictured here).

The Smudge Tool (Photoshop/ImageReady)

Figure A.64
This tool also uses the Brushes palette (see Figure A.1) and Brush Dynamics (see Figure A.2).

The Smudge tool "pushes" colors from one area to another. When Finger Painting is selected, it uses the foreground color.

The Sponge Tool (Photoshop/ImageReady)

Figure A.65
The Sponge tool uses the Brushes palette (see Figure A.1) and Brush Dynamics (see Figure A.2).

The Sponge tool has two modes. In Desaturate mode, it removes color from an area of an image. In Saturate mode, it increases the saturation level of each color. On a grayscale image, the Sponge tool increases or decreases contrast.

The Styles Palette (Photoshop/ImageReady)

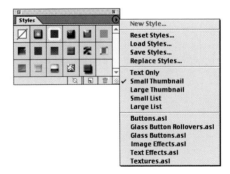

Figure A.66
The preset styles of the palette can be supplemented with additional sets and custom styles.

Photoshop 6's Styles palette holds preset combinations of Layer Effects. The styles can be clicked to apply to the active layer. Custom styles can be added. In ImageReady, the Shapes tools' Option bars have drop-down lists of styles rather than a palette. The ImageReady Styles palette also differs in how it can display the styles, lacking the list and text modes.

THE SWATCHES PALETTE (PHOTOSHOP/IMAGEREADY)

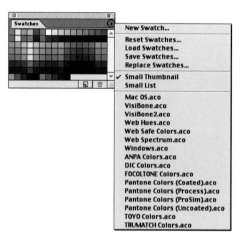

Figure A.67
The ImageReady Swatches palette, due to the Web orientation of the program, does not contain CMYK or spot swatches.

The Swatches palette holds preset colors. They can be clicked to become the Foreground color or Option+clicked (Alt+clicked for Windows) to become the Background color. Additional collections of swatches can be loaded into the palette, and custom swatches can be saved.

THE TYPE TOOL (PHOTOSHOP/IMAGEREADY)

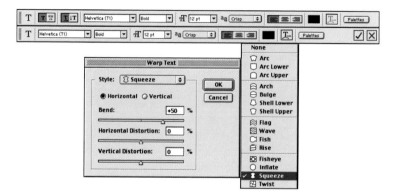

Figure A.68
The top Options bar is the default for the Type tool. When the tool is in use, it changes to the lower bar, complete with the Commit Changes and Cancel Changes buttons on the right. The ImageReady Type tool Options bar lacks the Type Mask option and does not change when the tool is in use.

The improved typographic capabilities of Photoshop 6 include the elimination of the Type dialog box. Text is now entered directly on the image. The Type tool can be used in conjunction with the Character palette (see Figure A.14) and the Paragraph palette (see Figure A.49). Shown in Figure A.68 is the new Warp Text dialog box with the 15 presets.

THE ZOOM TOOL
(PHOTOSHOP/IMAGEREADY)

Figure A.69
The ImageReady Zoom tool Options bar offers only Actual Size, Fit to Screen, and the Resize Windows to Fit checkbox.

The Zoom tool is used to control how much of an image is visible in the document window and at what magnification. When zoomed in, the tool can be used in conjunction with the Navigation palette (see Figure A.43) and the Hand tool (see Figure A.28) to change the view without altering the magnification. The Ignore Palettes checkbox allows the windows to resize underneath the floating palettes.

JAVASCRIPT—
MAKING IT MOVE!

"Few things are harder to put up with

than the annoyance of a good example."

—MARK TWAIN

JavaScript for Rollovers

When you want to make a button do more than just a simple rollover or hot spot, you have to dig into the HTML code that makes it "move"—called JavaScript. Sure, ImageReady can output a truckload of code when you specify for slices to behave as an image map or a table full of rollovers and hot spots, but what is it really doing? Did you know that the script that ImageReady creates isn't compatible with about half of today's popular Web browsers?

This appendix will show you just what ImageReady's script is doing and how you can clean it up so that it can be viewed by any browser.

Appendix B

JavaScript—
Making It Move!

by Jeff Foster

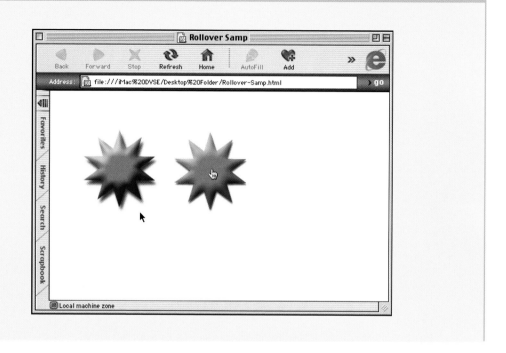

COMPARING CODE

This example is for a simple, one-button rollover. Because we're not going to get into step-by-step JavaScript code instruction in this book, only a visual comparison will be made. The first sidebar shows how a simple 200×200 single rollover image from a slice in ImageReady is turned into HTML code, exactly as the Save Optimized As code was generated.

```html
<HTML>
<HEAD>
<TITLE>Rollover Samp</TITLE>
<META HTTP-EQUIV="Content-Type" CONTENT="text/html; charset=iso-8859-1">
<!-- ImageReady Preload Script (Rollover Samp.psd) -->
<SCRIPT LANGUAGE="JavaScript">
<!--

function newImage(arg) {
        if (document.images) {
                rslt = new Image();
                rslt.src = arg;
                return rslt;
        }
}

function changeImages() {
        if (document.images && (preloadFlag == true)) {
                for (var i=0; i<changeImages.arguments.length; i+=2) {
                        document[changeImages.arguments[i]].src = changeImages.arguments[i+1];
                }
        }
}

var preloadFlag = false;
function preloadImages() {
        if (document.images) {
                Rollover_Samp_03_over = newImage("images/Rollover-Samp_03-over.gif");
                Rollover_Samp_05_Rollover_Samp_03_over = newImage("images/Rollover-Samp_05-Rollover-S.gif");
                preloadFlag = true;
        }
}
```

```
// -->
</SCRIPT>
```

<!-- End Preload Script -->

```
</HEAD>
<BODY BGCOLOR=#FFFFFF ONLOAD="preloadImages();">
```

<!-- ImageReady Slices (Rollover Samp.psd) -->

```
<TABLE WIDTH=200 BORDER=0 CELLPADDING=0 CELLSPACING=0>
        <TR>
                <TD COLSPAN=3>
                        <IMG SRC="images/Rollover-Samp_01.gif" WIDTH=200 HEIGHT=38></TD>
        </TR>
        <TR>
                <TD ROWSPAN=2>
                        <IMG SRC="images/Rollover-Samp_02.gif" WIDTH=37 HEIGHT=162></TD>
                <TD>
                        <A HREF="#"
                                ONMOUSEOVER="changeImages('Rollover_Samp_03', 'images/Rollover-Samp_03-over.gif',
➡'Rollover_Samp_05', 'images/Rollover-Samp_05-Rollover-S.gif'); return true;"
                                ONMOUSEOUT="changeImages('Rollover_Samp_03', 'images/Rollover-Samp_03.gif', 'Rollover_Samp_05',
➡'images/Rollover-Samp_05.gif'); return true;">
                                <IMG NAME="Rollover_Samp_03" SRC="images/Rollover-Samp_03.gif" WIDTH=125 HEIGHT=129
➡BORDER=0></A></TD>
                <TD ROWSPAN=2>
                        <IMG SRC="images/Rollover-Samp_04.gif" WIDTH=38 HEIGHT=162></TD>
        </TR>
        <TR>
                <TD>
                        <IMG NAME="Rollover_Samp_05" SRC="images/Rollover-Samp_05.gif" WIDTH=125 HEIGHT=33></TD>
        </TR>
</TABLE>
```

<!-- End ImageReady Slices -->

```
</BODY>
</HTML>
```

The next sidebar shows the exact same rollover images,
table, and document sizes, only with a straightforward
JavaScript code. Notice how simple the code appears to be
in comparison. This makes for easier modification for use
in other applications and Web page designs. Remember
that these two scripts do exactly the same thing.

```
<HTML>
<HEAD>
   <TITLE>Rollover Samp</TITLE>
<SCRIPT LANGUAGE = "JavaScript">if (document.images)
{
img1on = new Image(); img1on.src = "images/Rollover-Samp_03-over.gif";

img1off = new Image(); img1off.src = "images/Rollover-Samp_03.gif";
}

function imgOn(imgName) { if (document.images) { document[imgName].src = eval(imgName + "on.src"); } } function imgOff(imgName)
➡{ if (document.images) { document[imgName].src = eval(imgName + "off.src");
}
}
</SCRIPT>
</HEAD>
<BODY BGCOLOR="#FFFFFF">
<TABLE WIDTH=200 BORDER=0 CELLPADDING=0 CELLSPACING=0>
      <TR>
              <TD COLSPAN=3>
                      <IMG SRC="images/Rollover-Samp_01.gif" WIDTH=200 HEIGHT=38></TD>
      </TR>
      <TR>
              <TD ROWSPAN=2>
                      <IMG SRC="images/Rollover-Samp_02.gif" WIDTH=37 HEIGHT=162></TD>
              <TD>
                      <A HREF="#" onmouseover="imgOn('img1')" onmouseout="imgOff('img1')"><IMG SRC="images/Rollover-Samp_03.gif" WIDTH=125
➡HEIGHT=129 BORDER=0 ALIGN=middle name=img1></A>
      </TD>
```

```
            <TD ROWSPAN=2>
                    <IMG SRC="images/Rollover-Samp_04.gif" WIDTH=38 HEIGHT=162></TD>
        </TR>
        <TR>
            <TD>
                    <IMG NAME="Rollover_Samp_05" SRC="images/Rollover-Samp_05.gif" WIDTH=125 HEIGHT=33></TD>
        </TR>
</TABLE>
</BODY>
</HTML>
```

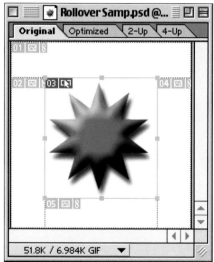

It's amazing how a little task, such as making this simple rollover, gets to be such a huge HTML file!

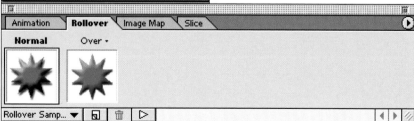

A Custom Fade In and Out Rollover

This example uses multiple images that are preloaded when the page is loaded in the browser. Then, when the mouse is rolled over the button area, the shape slowly appears from beneath the surface. How it really works is that the initial "off" state is static, and the rest of the images in the animation sequence are faded in according to their numbered order at the rate set by the **var_fadespeed** command. When the mouse is no longer over the area, the sequence is reversed at the same rate.

You will find the Photoshop master file, HTML source code, and the JPG images on the enclosed CD-ROM in the JavaScript folder.

Simply replace the **BOLD TEXT** areas of the script to make changes to accept your image sequence. Keep in mind that this script only contains the code necessary for the fade in rollover effect, not a complete Web page design template.

```
<!— Paste this code into the HEAD of your HTML document  —>
<!— Make changes to the BOLD TEXT areas to reflect your images and preferences —>

<HEAD>
<SCRIPT LANGUAGE="JavaScript">

var maximages = 6;          // how many fade images do you have?
var fadespeed = 25;         // fade frame time in milliseconds;  125 = 125 ms

var fadeintimer;
var fadeouttimer;
var fadeincount = 0;
var fadeoutcount = maximages-1;
var fadearray = new Array(maximages);       // enter all the fade images here

// the first item should be 0, then numbered through 1 less than your maximages
```

```
fadearray[0] = "fish00.jpg";
fadearray[1] = "fish01.jpg";
fadearray[2] = "fish02.jpg";
fadearray[3] = "fish03.jpg";
fadearray[4] = "fish04.jpg";
fadearray[5] = "fish05.jpg";

for (var i = 0; i < maximages; i++) {
eval('pic' + i + ' = new Image();');
eval('pic' + i + '.src = fadearray[i];');     // preloads fade images
}
function fade_in() {
clearTimeout(fadeouttimer);
document.images['fade-pic'].src = fadearray[fadeincount];
if (fadeincount != maximages-1) {
fadeincount++;
fadeintimer = setTimeout('fade_in()', fadespeed);
}
else {
clearTimeout(fadeintimer);
fadeincount = 0;
    }
}
function fade_out() {
clearTimeout(fadeintimer);
document.images['fade-pic'].src = fadearray[fadeoutcount];
if (fadeoutcount != 0) {
fadeoutcount—;
fadeouttimer = setTimeout('fade_out()', fadespeed);
}
else {
clearTimeout(fadeouttimer);
fadeoutcount = maximages-1;
    }
}
</SCRIPT>
```

```
</HEAD>

<!-- Copy this code into the BODY of your HTML document  -->
<!-- Make changes to the BOLD TEXT areas to reflect your images and preferences -->

<BODY>

<center>

<a href="http://www.photoshopwebmagic.com" onmouseover="fade_in()" onmouseout="fade_out()">

<img name="fade-pic" height=82 width=202 border=0 src="fish00.jpg"></a>

</center>
```

It pays to learn a bit about hard coding your HTML code instead of merely letting ImageReady do it all for you. You can use any other WYSIWYG application to generate your code as well, using just the table and images that ImageReady will save out. Learn more about JavaScripts and customizing them on the enclosed CD-ROM in the JavaScripts folder, as well as on our Web site at **www.photoshopwebmagic.com**.

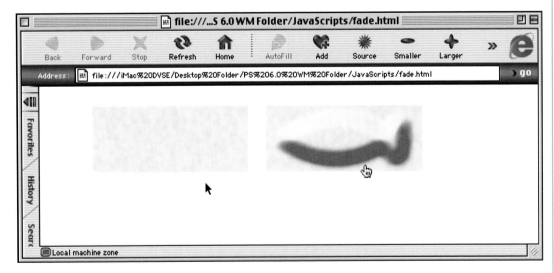

Rolling on and off the button area will create a fade in and out effect.

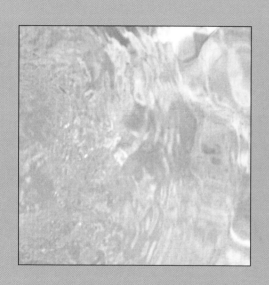

WHAT'S ON THE CD-ROM

"C is for cookie, it's good enough for me;

oh cookie cookie cookie starts with C."

—COOKIE MONSTER